## ACC 303

# INTERMEDIATE ACCOUNTING PROBLEM SOLVING SURVIVAL GUIDE

## Chapters 1-7

2010 Custom Edition

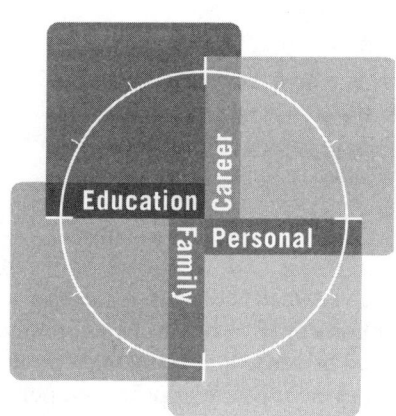

ACC 303: INTERMEDIATE ACCOUNTING
PROBLEM SOLVING SURVIVAL GUIDE
2010 Custom Edition

To order books or for customer service, please call 1(800)-CALL-WILEY (225-5945).

Printed in the United States of America.

ISBN 978-0-470-57571-0
Printed and bound by Victor Graphics Inc.

10 9 8 7 6 5 4 3 2 1

# CONTENTS

Chapter 1:     Financial Accounting and Accounting Standards

Chapter 2:     Conceptual Framework Underlying Financial Accounting

Chapter 3:     The Accounting Information System

Chapter 4:     Income Statement and Related Information

Chapter 5:     Balance Sheet and Statement of Cash Flows

Chapter 6:     Accounting and the Time Value of Money

Chapter 7:     Cash and Receivables

# Problem Solving Survival Guide
VOLUME I: CHAPTERS 1-14

...................................................................................................

# INTERMEDIATE ACCOUNTING
## Thirteenth Edition

...................................................................................................

**Marilyn F. Hunt,** M.A., C.P.A.

**Donald E. Kieso,** Ph.D., C.P.A.
KPMG Peat Marwick Emeritus Professor of Accounting
Northern Illinois University
DeKalb, Illinois

**Jerry J. Weygandt,** Ph.D., C.P.A.
Arthur Andersen Alumni Professor of Accounting
University of Wisconsin
Madison, Wisconsin

**Terry D. Warfield,** Ph.D.
Associate Professor
Director, Andersen Center for Financial Reporting and Control
University of Wisconsin
Madison, Wisconsin

**WILEY**
**JOHN WILEY & SONS, INC.**

COVER PHOTO: Jon Arnold Images/Superstock, Inc.

To order books or for customer service call 1-800-CALL-WILEY (225-5945).

ISBN-13  9780470380574
ISBN-10  0470380578

Printed in the United States of America

10 9 8 7 6 5 4 3 2 1

Printed and bound by Courier Kendallville, Inc.

# CHAPTER 1

# FINANCIAL ACCOUNTING AND ACCOUNTING STANDARDS

## OVERVIEW

Accounting is the language of business. As such, accountants collect and communicate economic information about business enterprises or other entities to a wide variety of persons. To be useful, financial statements must be clearly understandable and comparable so that users may compare the performance of one business with the performance of the same business for a prior period or with the performance of another similar business. Therefore, all general purpose financial statements should be prepared in accordance with the same uniform guidelines. In this chapter, we will examine the history and sources of current financial accounting standards (generally accepted accounting principles).

## SUMMARY OF LEARNING OBJECTIVES

1.  **Identify the major financial statements and other means of financial reporting.** Companies most frequently provide (1) the balance sheet, (2) the income statement, (3) the statement of cash flows, and (4) the statement of owners' or stockholders' equity. Financial reporting other than financial statements may take various forms. Examples include the president's letter and supplementary schedules in the corporate annual report, prospectuses, reports filed with government agencies, news releases, management's forecasts, and descriptions of an enterprise's social or environmental impact.

2.  **Explain how accounting assists in the efficient use of scarce resources.** Accounting provides reliable, relevant, and timely information to managers, investors, and creditors so that resources are allocated to the most efficient enterprises. Accounting also provides measurements of efficiency (profitability) and financial soundness.

3.  **Identify some of the challenges facing accounting.** Financial reports fail to provide (1) some key performance measures widely used by management, (2) forward-looking information needed by investors and creditors, (3) sufficient information about a company's soft assets (intangibles) and (4) real-time financial information.

4.  **Identify the objectives of financial reporting.** The objectives of financial reporting are to provide (1) information that is useful in investment and credit decisions, (2) information that is useful in assessing cash flow prospects, and (3) information about enterprise resources, claims to those resources, and changes in the resources and claims to resources.

5.    **Explain the need for accounting standards.** The accounting profession has attempted to develop a set of standards that is generally accepted and universally practiced. Without this set of standards, each company would have to develop its own standards. Readers of financial statements would have to familiarize themselves with every company's peculiar accounting and reporting practices. As a result, it would be almost impossible to prepare statements that could be compared with the statements of other companies.

6.    **Identify the major policy-setting bodies and their role in the standard-setting process.** The **Securities and Exchange Commission (SEC)** is an agency of the federal government that has the broad powers to prescribe, in whatever detail it desires, the accounting standards to be employed by companies that fall within its jurisdiction. The **American Institute of Certified Public Accountants (AICPA)** issued standards through its Committee on Accounting Procedure and Accounting Principles Board (APB). The **Financial Accounting Standards Board (FASB)** establishes and improves standards of financial accounting and reporting for the guidance and education of the public, which includes issuers, auditors, and users of financial information.

7.    **Explain the meaning of generally accepted accounting principles.** Generally accepted accounting principles (GAAP) are those principles that have substantial authoritative support, such as FASB Standards, Interpretations and Staff Positions, APB Opinions and Interpretations, AICPA Accounting Research Bulletins, and other authoritative pronouncements. All these documents and others are now classified in one document referred to as the Codification. The purpose of the Codification is to simplify user access to all authoritative U.S. GAAP. The codification changes the way GAAP is documented, presented, and updated.

8.    **Describe the impact of user groups on the standard-setting process.** User groups may want particular economic events accounted for or reported in a particular way, and they fight hard to get what they want. They especially target the FASB to influence changes in the existing standards and the development of new ones. Because of the accelerated rate of change and the increased complexity of our economy, these pressures have been multiplying. Accounting standards are as much a product of political action as they are of careful logic or empirical findings. The International Accounting Standards Board (IASB) is working with U.S. standard setters toward international convergence of standards.

9.    **Understand issues related to ethics and financial accounting.** Financial accountants are called on for moral discernment and ethical decision making. Decisions sometimes are more difficult because a public consensus has not emerged to formulate a comprehensive ethical system that provides guidelines in making ethical judgments.

## TIPS ON CHAPTER TOPICS

**TIP:**    Because most business owners (stockholders of corporations) are not involved with the operation of the business, the **stewardship function**—measuring and reporting data to absentee owners—has emerged as a critical role for accounting. This situation greatly increases the need for accounting standards.

**TIP:**    The financial statements most frequently provided by an entity (often called the **basic financial statements** or **general purpose financial statements**) are: (1) the income statement, (2) the statement of owners' equity (or statement of stockholders' equity), (3) the balance sheet, and (4) the statement of cash flows. In addition, note disclosures are an integral part of the financial statements.

**TIP:**    The primary focus of this textbook concerns the development of two types of financial information which are governed by generally accepted accounting principles: (1) the basic financial statements and (2) the related note disclosures.

| TIP: | An effective process of capital allocation is critical to a healthy economy. It promotes productivity, encourages innovation, and provides an efficient and liquid market for buying and selling securities and obtaining and granting credit. Reliable and relevant information is needed for the securities market to operate effectively. |
| --- | --- |
| TIP: | Most companies publish their annual reports in several formats on the world wide web. Many format their financial reports using extensible business reporting language (XBRL) which permits quicker and lower cost access to companies' financial information. Some companies offer sections of their reports in a format that the user can import into an Excel spreadsheet. |
| TIP: | The terms **principles** and **standards** are used interchangeably in practice and throughout this book. |
| TIP: | The **accrual basis of accounting** is used in preparing the basic financial statements. The accrual basis provides for (1) reporting revenues in the period they are earned (which may not be the same period in which the related cash is received), and (2) reporting expenses in the period they are incurred (which may not be the same period in which the related cash is paid). Information based on accrual accounting better indicates a company's present and continuing ability to generate favorable cash flows than does information limited to the financial effects of cash receipts and cash payments for a recent time period. |
| TIP: | Presently, there are two sets of standards accepted for international use – U.S. GAAP and the International Financial Reporting Standards (IFRS), also known as iGAAP, issued by the London-based International Accounting Standards Board (IASB). There are many similarities between U.S. and IASB standards. The IASB and the FASB are working hard to accomplish an ambitious goal which is to converge their concepts and standards. |
| TIP: | The **Governmental Accounting Standards Board (GASB)** establishes and improves standards of financial accounting for state and local governments. |

## CASE 1-1

**Purpose:**   (L.O.6) This case will identify the organizations responsible for various accounting documents.

### Instructions
Presented below are a number of accounting organizations and the type of documents they have issued. Match the appropriate document to the organization involved. Note that more than one document may be issued by the same organization.

**Organization**

1. _____   Accounting Principles Board (APB)

2. _____   AICPA Committee on Accounting Procedure

3. _____   Financial Accounting Standards Board (FASB)

4. _____   International Accounting Standards Board (IASB)

5. _____   Accounting Standards Executive Committee of the AICPA

**Document**

(a)   Practice Bulletins
(b)   Accounting Research Bulletins
(c)   Opinions
(d)   Staff Positions
(e)   International Financial Reporting Standards
(f)   Statements of Financial Accounting Standards
(g)   Technical Bulletins
(h)   Statements of Position (SOP)
(i)   Interpretations
(j)   Industry Audit and Accounting Guides
(k)   Statements of Financial Accounting Concepts

## Solution to Case 1-1

| 1. | c, i | 3. | d, f, g, i, k | 5. | a, h, j |
|----|------|----|--------------|----|---------|
| 2. | b    | 4. | e            |    |         |

## CASE 1-2

**Purpose:**    (L.O.7) This case will review the meaning of generally accepted accounting principles and their significance.

All publicly-held companies must have their annual financial statements audited by an independent CPA. In accordance with generally accepted auditing standards (which you will study in an auditing class), the auditor expresses an opinion regarding the fairness of the financial statements which are to be in conformity with generally accepted accounting principles.

## Instructions

(a)    Define generally accepted accounting principles.
(b)    Identify at least six types of documents that comprise GAAP.
(c)    Explain the significance of GAAP to an auditor of financial statements.
(d)    Describe the "Codification" of GAAP and explain why it was initiated.
(e)    Describe the Codification Research System.

## Solution to Case 1-2

(a)    The accounting profession has adopted a common set of standards and procedures called **generally accepted accounting principles** (often referred to as GAAP). The word "principles" refers to methods or procedures or standards. The phrase "generally accepted" means having "substantial authoritative support." A method can be considered to have substantial authoritative support if it has been approved by a rule-making body or if it has gained acceptance over time because of its universal application.

(b)    GAAP is composed of a mixture of over 2,000 documents that have developed over the last 60 years or so. The major sources of GAAP have come from the Financial Accounting Standards Board (FASB), Accounting Principles Board (APB), and Committee on Accounting Procedure (CAP). The many types of documents that comprise GAAP include the following:
a. FASB Standards, Interpretations, and Staff Bulletins
b. APB Opinions
c. AICPA Accounting Research Bulletins
d. FASB Technical Bulletins
e. AICPA Industry Audit and Accounting Guides
f. AICPA Statements of Position
g. FASB Emerging Issues Task Force Consensus Positions
h. AICPA AcSEC Practice Bulletins
i. AICPA Accounting Interpretations
j. FASB Implementation Guides (Q and A)

(c)     An enterprise shall not represent that its financial statements are presented in accordance with GAAP if its selection of accounting principles departs from GAAP and that departure has a material impact on its financial statements. Furthermore, the AICPA's Code of Professional Conduct requires that members prepare financial statements in accordance with generally accepted accounting principles. Specifically, Rule 203 of this Code prohibits a member from expressing an opinion (upon the completion of an audit) that financial statements conform with GAAP if those statements contain a material departure from a generally accepted accounting principle.

(d)     As might be expected, the documents that comprise GAAP vary in format, completeness, and structure. In some cases, these documents are inconsistent and difficult to interpret. As a result, financial statement preparers sometimes are not sure whether they have the right GAAP; determining what is authoritative and what is not becomes difficult.

In response to these concerns, the FASB developed the **Financial Accounting Standards Board Accounting Standards Codification** (or more simply, "the Codification"). The FASB's primary goal in developing the Codification is to provide in one place all the authoritative literature related to a particular topic. This will simplify user access to all authoritative U.S. generally accepted accounting principles. The Codification changes the way GAAP is documented, presented, and updated. It explains what GAAP is and eliminates nonessential information such as redundant document summaries, basis for conclusions sections, and historical content. In short, the Codification is a major restructuring of accounting and reporting standards. Its purpose is to integrate and synthesize existing GAAP—not to create new GAAP. It creates one level of GAAP; all of the material included is considered authoritative. All other accounting literature is considered to be nonauthoritative (such as FASB Concepts Statements and textbooks). (Prior to Codification, there was a "hierarchy of GAAP" which deemed certain authoritative documents to be more authoritative then others which led to various levels of GAAP). Now there is only one level of authoritative GAAP.

The Codification includes the "essential content" of all of the documents listed in the Solution to part (b) above and relevant portions of authoritative content issued by the Securities and Exchange Commission (SEC) such as Regulation S-X and Financial Reporting Releases (FRR)/Accounting Series Releases (ASR).

**TIP:**     In the event that there is an accounting issue that is not addressed in the Codification, the accountant should seek support from other accounting literature. Examples of other accounting literature that is not in the Codification and therefore not authoritative include FASB Concepts Statements; AICPA Issues Papers; International Financial Reporting Standards (IFRSs) of the International Accounting Standards Board (IASB); pronouncements of other professional associations or regulatory agencies; and accounting textbooks, handbooks, and articles. (The FASB Concepts Statements would normally be more influential than other sources in this category.)

(e)    To provide easy access to the Codification, the FASB also developed the Financial Accounting Standards Board Codification Research System (CRS). CRS is an online real-time database that provides easy access to the Codification. The Codification and the related CRS provide a topically organized structure, subdivided into topics, subtopics, sections, and paragraphs, using a numerical index system.

For purposes of referencing authoritative GAAP material in your textbook, the authors will use the Codification framework. Here is an example of how the Codification framework is cited, using Intangibles as the example. The purpose of the search shown below is to determine GAAP for accounting for intangible assets other than goodwill subsequent to initial measurement.

| | |
|---|---|
| **Topic** | Go to FASB ASC 350 to access Intangibles topic. |
| **Subtopics** | Go to FASB ASC 350-30 to access the General Intangibles Other Than Goodwill Subtopic of the Topic 350. |
| **Sections** | Go to FASB ASC 350-30-35 to access the Subsequent Measurement Section of the Subtopic 350-30. |
| **Paragraph** | Go to FASB ASC 350-30-35-6 to access the Intangible Assets Subject to Amortization paragraph of Section 350-30-35. |

The following shows the Codification framework graphically.

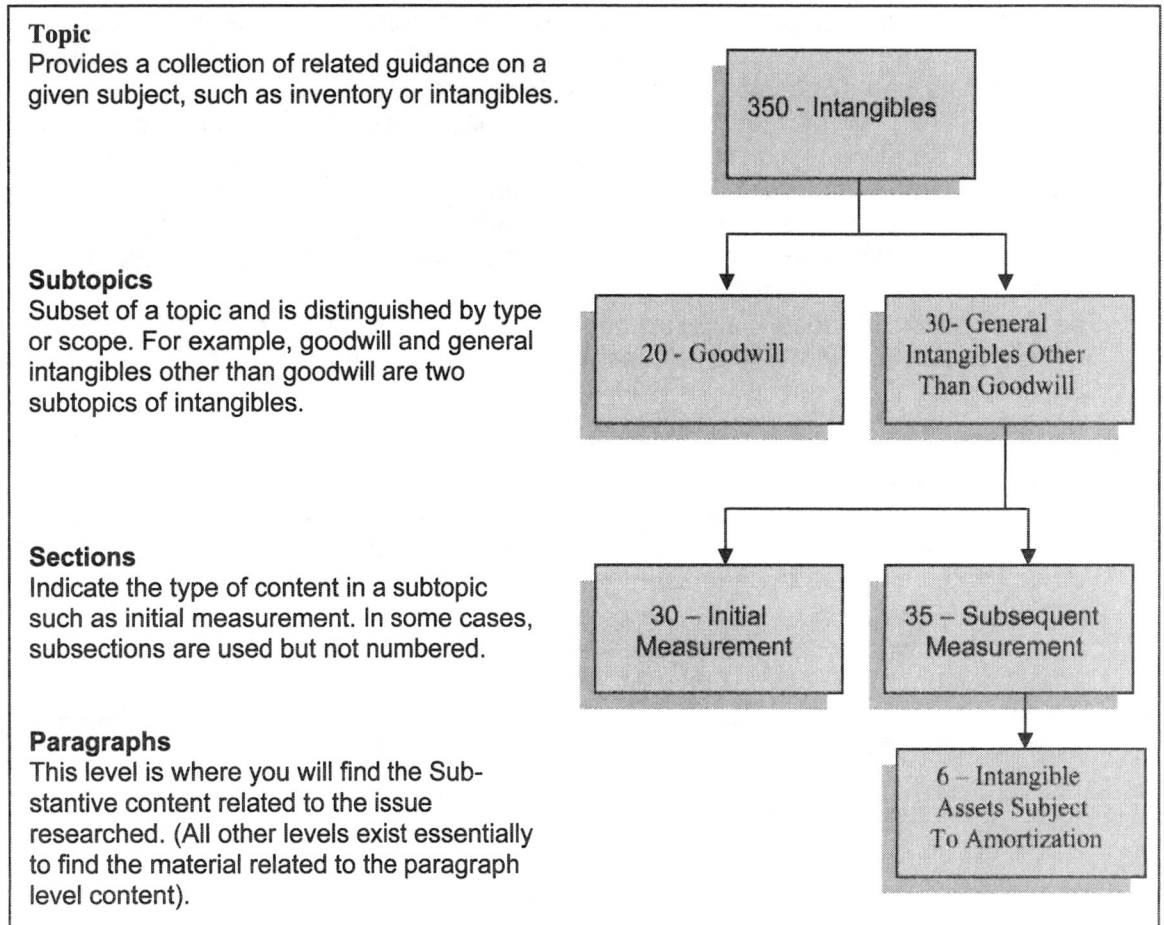

## CASE 1-3

**Purpose:** (L.O.8) This case looks at the key provisions of the Sarbanes-Oxley Act.

In 2002, Congress enacted the Sarbanes-Oxley Act in response to what then were recent accounting scandals at large companies including Enron, Cendant, Sunbeam, Rite-Aid, Xerox, and WorldCom. The new law increases the resources for the SEC to combat fraud and poor reporting practices.

**Instructions**
Describe six of the key provisions of the Sarbanes-Oxley legislation.

## Solution to Case 1-3

Some of the key provisions of the Sarbanes-Oxley Act are that it:

1. Establishes an oversight board [the **Public Company Accounting Oversight Board (PCAOB)**] for accounting practices. The PCAOB has oversight and enforcement authority and establishes auditing, quality control, and independence standards and rules for auditors of public companies.

2. Implements stronger independence rules for auditors of public companies. For example, audit partners are required to rotate off clients every five years so that different partners can take responsibility for the audit. Also, the accounting firm that performs auditing services for a particular client is prohibited from offering certain types of consulting services to that same corporate client.

3. Requires CEOs, (Chief Executive Officers) and CFOs (Chief Financial Officers) of public companies to personally certify that financial statements and disclosures are accurate and complete; also requires CEOs and CFOs to forfeit bonuses and profits when there is an accounting restatement.

4. Requires audit committees of public companies to be comprised of independent members and members with financial expertise.

5. Requires codes of ethics for senior financial officers of public companies.

6. Requires public companies to attest to the effectiveness of their internal controls over financial reporting.

| | |
|---|---|
| **TIP:** | Internal controls are a system of checks and balances designed to prevent and detect fraud and errors. |
| **TIP:** | The changes required by the Sarbanes-Oxley Act are hopefully going to help in closing the **expectations gap** – which is the gap between what the public thinks accountants **should** do and what accountants think they **can** do – but they come with a cost to society. |

# ANALYSIS OF MULTIPLE-CHOICE TYPE QUESTIONS

**QUESTION**

1.  (L.O. 1) The process of identifying, measuring, analyzing, and communicating financial information needed by management to plan, evaluate, and control an organization's operations is called
    a.  financial accounting.
    b.  managerial accounting.
    c.  tax accounting.
    d.  auditing.

**Approach and Explanation:** Define each answer selection. Select the answer item for which your definition matches the stem of the question. **Financial accounting** is the process that culminates in the preparation of financial reports on the enterprise as a whole for use by parties both internal and external to the enterprise. (Users of these financial reports include investors, creditors, managers, unions, and government agencies.) **Managerial accounting** is the process of identifying, measuring, analyzing, and communicating financial information needed by management to plan, evaluate, and control an organization's operations. (These reports are only for the use of parties internal to the enterprise.) **Tax accounting** usually refers to tax planning, advising on tax matters, and/or preparing tax returns. **Auditing** refers to the examination of financial statements by a certified public accountant in order to express an opinion on their fairness. An auditor attests to the fairness of financial statements and their conformity to generally accepted accounting principles. (Solution = b.)

**QUESTION**

2.  (L.O. 4) One objective of financial reporting is to provide:
    a.  information about the investors in the business entity.
    b.  information about the liquidation values of the resources held by the enterprise.
    c.  information that is useful in assessing cash flow prospects.
    d.  information that will attract new investors.

**Approach and Explanation:** Before you read the possible answers, mentally list the objectives of financial reporting or write down the key words of each objective. Then carefully read the suggested answers. As you read an answer choice, note whether it is a match to an item in your list or not. The objectives of financial reporting are to provide (1) information that is useful in investment and credit decisions, (2) information that is useful in assessing the amounts, timing, and uncertainty of prospective cash receipts, and (3) information about enterprise resources, claims to those resources, and changes in the resources and claims to resources. (Solution = c.)

**QUESTION**

3.  (L.O. 6) The most significant current source of generally accepted accounting principles is the:
    a.  NYSE.
    b.  IRS.
    c.  APB.
    d.  FASB.

**Explanation:** The mission of the Financial Accounting Standards Board (FASB) is to establish and improve standards of financial accounting and reporting. The Accounting Principles Board (APB) was the predecessor of the FASB. The New York Stock Exchange (NYSE) has nothing to do with the development of generally accepted accounting principles. The IRS (Internal Revenue Service) oversees compliance with the income tax code for the U.S. Department of the Treasury. (Solution = d.)

**QUESTION**
4.   (L.O. 6) Members of the Financial Accounting Standards Board are:
   a.   employed by the American Institute of Certified Public Accountants (AICPA).
   b.   part-time employees.
   c.   required to hold a CPA certificate.
   d.   independent of any other organization.

**Explanation:** The members of the FASB are well-paid, full-time members. The FASB is not affiliated with the AICPA; it is not associated with any single professional organization. The FASB is answerable only to the Financial Accounting Foundation. It is not necessary to be a CPA or a member of the AICPA to be a member of the FASB. FASB members must sever all ties with CPA firms, companies, or institutions. (Solution = d.)

**QUESTION**
5.   (L.O. 6) Which of the following pronouncements were issued by the Accounting Principles Board?
   a.   Accounting Research Bulletins
   b.   Opinions
   c.   Statements of Position
   d.   Statements of Financial Accounting Concepts

**Explanation:** The Accounting Principles Board issued 31 APB Opinions between the years 1962-1973. Accounting Research Bulletins (51 of them) were issued by the Committee on Accounting Procedure between 1939 and 1959. Statements of Position are issued by the AICPA (but not the APB). The FASB issues Statements on Financial Accounting Concepts (there are 7 of these to date and six of them relate to financial reporting for business enterprises). (Solution = b.)

**QUESTION**
6.   (L.O. 6) The body charged with the mission of establishing and improving standards of financial accounting and reporting for business enterprises is the:
   a.   Financial Accounting Foundation (FAF).
   b.   Financial Accounting Standards Board (FASB).
   c.   Financial Accounting Standards Advisory Council (FASAC).
   d.   Governmental Accounting Standards Board (GASB).

**Explanation:** The FASB is responsible for establishing and improving GAAP. The FAF selects the members of the FASB, and the FASAC funds their activities and generally oversees the FASB's activities (from an operational rather than from a technical standpoint). Generally, the SEC has relied on the AICPA and FASB to regulate the accounting profession and develop and enforce accounting standards. The GASB deals only with standards pertaining to state and local government reporting. (Solution = b.)

**QUESTION**
7.   (L.O. 6) The demise of the APB and the creation of the FAF, FASB, and FASAC are largely and most directly attributed to the:
   a.   IRS.
   b.   Great Depression.
   c.   Securities Exchange Act.
   d.   recommendations of the Wheat Committee.

**Explanation:** The Great Depression of the 1930s resulted in the Securities Exchange Act of 1934 which led to the formation of the Securities and Exchange Commission (SEC). These developments prompted the formation of the Committee on Accounting Procedure (CAP) which was replaced by the Accounting Principles Board (APB). When the APB needed an overhaul, it was the recommendations of the Wheat

Committee that resulted in the demise of the APB and the creation of the new standard-setting structure composed of three organizations—the Financial Accounting Foundation (FAF), the Financial Accounting Standards Board (FASB), and the Financial Accounting Standards Advisory Council (FASAC). (Solution = d.)

## QUESTION

8.  (L.O. 6) The American Institute of Certified Public Accountants (AICPA) continues to be the sole entity responsible for
    a.  developing financial accounting standards.
    b.  developing auditing standards.
    c.  developing and enforcing professional ethics.
    d.  developing and grading the Certified Public Accountant (CPA) examination.

**Explanation:** Recently, the role of the AICPA in standard-setting has diminished. However, the AICPA continues to develop and grade the CPA examination, which is administered in all 50 states. (Solution = d.)

## QUESTION

9.  (L.O. 6) The following are part of the "due process" system used by the FASB in the evolution of a typical FASB Statement of Financial Accounting Standards:
    1.  Exposure Draft
    2.  Statement of Financial Accounting Standards
    3.  Public Hearing

The chronological order in which these items are released is as follows:
    a.  1, 2, 3.
    b.  1, 3, 2.
    c.  2, 3, 1.
    d.  3, 1, 2.

**Explanation:** The following steps are taken in the evolution of a typical FASB Statement of Financial Accounting Standards:
1.  A topic or project is identified and placed on the Board's agenda.
2.  Research and analysis are conducted by the FASB technical staff and preliminary views of pros and cons are issued.
3.  A public hearing is held on the proposed standard.
4.  The Board analyzes and evaluates the public response; The Board deliberates on the issues and prepares an **exposure draft** for release.
5.  After a 30-day (minimum) exposure period for public comment, the Board evaluates all of the responses received. A committee studies the exposure draft in relation to the public responses, reevaluates its position, and revises the draft if necessary. The full Board gives the revised draft final consideration and votes on issuance of a **Standards Statement**. The passage of a new FASB Standards Statement requires the support of three of the five Board members. (Solution = d.)

**QUESTION**
10.  (L.O. 6) All of the following organizations are directly involved in the development of financial accounting standards (GAAP) in the United States, **except** the:
     a.    Internal Revenue Service (IRS).
     b.    Financial Accounting Standards Board (FASB).
     c.    American Institute of Certified Public Accountants (AICPA).
     d.    Securities and Exchange Commission (SEC).

**Explanation:** The Internal Revenue Service (IRS) is responsible for federal income tax rules and administration. Although the IRS and its Internal Revenue Code are influences on accounting practice, they are not directly involved in the development of accounting standards (for financial statements) as are the other organizations listed. (Solution = a.)

**QUESTION**
11.  (L.O. 8) A Brazilian corporation listed on a U.S. exchange
     a.    is permitted to use iGAAP.
     b.    must follow the accounting standards set forth by the government of Brazil.
     c.    must use U.S. GAAP.

**Explanation:** Presently, there are two sets of standards accepted for international use—U.S. GAAP and the International Financial Reporting Standards (IFRS), also known as iGAAP, issued by the London-based International Accounting Standards Board (IASB). U.S. companies that list overseas are still permitted to use U.S. GAAP, and foreign companies listed on U.S. exchanges are permitted to use iGAAP. There are many similarities between U.S. and IASB standards. Already over 100 countries use iGAAP, and the European Union now requires all listed companies in Europe (over 7,000 companies) to use it. It is now highly probable that the United States will adopt IFRS in the new future because the FASB recognizes the need for one set of high-quality global accounting standards. To achieve this goal, the FASB and the IASB are now working hard to find common ground related to existing and proposed standards. Both parties recognize the global markets will best be served if only one set of GAAP is used. For example, the FASB and the IASB formalized their commitment to the convergence of U.S. GAAP and iGAAP by issuing a memorandum of understanding (often referred to as the Norwalk agreement). (Solution = a).

# CHAPTER 2

# CONCEPTUAL FRAMEWORK
# UNDERLYING FINANCIAL ACCOUNTING

## OVERVIEW

Financial statements are needed for decision making. In order to make informed decisions, a financial statement user must understand both the financial information conveyed and how it is derived. To be useful, financial statements must be clearly understandable and comparable so that users may compare the performance of one business with the performance of the same business for a prior period or with the performance of another similar business. Therefore, all general purpose financial statements should be prepared in accordance with the same uniform guidelines. In this chapter, we will examine basic accounting principles.

## SUMMARY OF LEARNING OBJECTIVES

1.  **Describe the usefulness of a conceptual framework.** The accounting profession needs a conceptual framework to: (1) build on and relate to an established body of concepts and objectives, (2) provide a framework for solving new and emerging practical problems, (3) increase financial statement users' understanding of and confidence in financial reporting, and (4) enhance comparability among companies' financial statements.

2.  **Describe the FASB's efforts to construct a conceptual framework.** The FASB has issued six Statements of Financial Accounting Concepts that relate to financial reporting for business enterprises. These concepts statements provide the basis for the conceptual framework and include objectives, qualitative characteristics, and elements. In addition, measurement and recognition concepts are developed.

3.  **Understand the objectives of financial reporting.** Financial reporting should provide information that is (1) useful to those making investment and credit decisions who have a reasonable understanding of business activities; (2) helpful to present and potential investors, creditors, and other users in assessing future cash flows; and (3) about economic resources and the claims to those resources and changes in them.

4.  **Identify the qualitative characteristics of accounting information.** The over-riding criterion by which accounting choices can be judged is decision usefulness--that is, providing information that is most useful for decision making. Relevance and reliability are the two primary qualities and comparability and consistency are the secondary qualities that make accounting information useful for decision making.

5.  **Define the basic elements of financial statements.** The basic elements of financial statements are (1) assets, (2) liabilities, (3) equity, (4) investments by owners, (5) distributions to owners, (6) comprehensive income, (7) revenues, (8) expenses, (9) gains, and (10) losses. These ten elements are defined in **Illustration 2-3**.

6.  **Describe the basic assumptions of accounting.** Four basic assumptions underlying the financial accounting structure are (1) **Economic entity:** the assumption that the activity of a business enterprise can be kept separate and distinct from its owners and any other business unit. (2) **Going concern:** the assumption that the business enterprise will have a long life. (3) **Monetary unit:** the assumption that money is the common denominator by which economic activity is conducted, and that the monetary unit provides an appropriate basis for measurement and analysis. (4) **Periodicity:** the assumption that the economic activities of an enterprise can be divided into artificial time periods.

7.  **Explain the application of the basic principles of accounting.** (1) **Measurement principle:** Existing GAAP permits the use of historical cost, fair value, and other valuation bases. Although the historical cost principle (measurement based on acquisition price) continues to be an important basis for valuation, recording and reporting of fair value information is increasing. (2) **Revenue recognition:** As a general rule, a company recognizes revenue when (a) realized or realizable and (b) earned. (3) **Expense recognition principle:** A company generally recognizes expenses when the work (service) or the product actually makes its contribution to revenue (commonly referred to as **matching.**) (4) **Full disclosure principle:** Companies generally provide information that is of sufficient importance to influence the judgment and decisions of an informed user.

8.  **Describe the impact that constraints have on reporting accounting information.** The constraints and their impact are: (1) **Cost-benefit relationship:** The costs of providing the information must be weighed against the benefits that can be derived from using the information. (2) **Materiality:** Sound and acceptable standards should be followed if the amount involved is significant when compared with the other revenues and expenses, assets and liabilities, or net income of the company. (3) **Industry practices:** Follow the general practices in the company's industry, which sometimes requires departure from basic theory. (4) **Conservatism:** When in doubt, choose the solution that will be least likely to overstate net assets and net income.

## TIPS ON CHAPTER TOPICS

**TIP:**  Although it can sometimes be confusing, accountants often use the terms **assumptions, concepts, principles, conventions, constraints,** and **standards** interchangeably. Regardless of the particular term used, they are all a part of GAAP (generally accepted accounting principles).

**TIP:**  The revenue recognition principle is applied before the matching principle is applied. The revenue recognition principle gives guidance in determining what revenues to recognize in a given period. The matching principle then gives guidance as to what expenses to recognize during the period. According to the **revenue recognition principle,** revenues are to be recognized in the period earned. Per the **expense recognition principle** (or **matching principle**), expenses are to be recognized in the same period as the revenues they helped generate.

**TIP:**  The term **recognition** refers to the process of formally recording or incorporating an item in the accounts and thus into the body of the financial statements of an entity.

| | |
|---|---|
| **TIP:** | You should study **Illustration 2-2** on the hierarchy of accounting qualities until you can close your eyes and visualize that diagram. Frequently, exam questions (including CPA Examination questions) over *SFAC No. 2* can be answered by describing what is on that diagram. |
| **TIP:** | Accounting assumptions underlie the more detailed accounting principles or standards. These assumptions include the economic entity assumption, the going concern assumption, the monetary unit assumption, and the periodicity assumption. They are the foundation for the basic principles which include the historical cost principle, the revenue recognition principle, the matching principle, and the full disclosure principle. For example, the historical cost principle and the matching principle would not be appropriate if it were not for the going concern assumption. If an entity is not expected to continue in business, then plant assets would be reported on the balance sheet at their liquidation or net realizable value (estimated selling price less estimated cost of disposal) rather than at their cost, and depreciation of these assets would not be appropriate. |
| **TIP:** | There are three common bases of expense recognition: (1) cause and effect, (2) systematic and rational allocation, and (3) immediate recognition. You should be able to explain and give examples for each of these. (See **Case 2-3**.) |
| **TIP:** | GAAP requires that companies account for and report many assets and liabilities on the balance sheet on the basis of acquisition price; this is an application of the **historical cost principle**. Cost is a reliable valuation; it is usually established by an exchange transaction between parties with conflicting interests (that is, a buyer wants to buy at the lowest price possible and a seller wants to sell at the highest price possible). However, **fair value information** may be more useful for the balance sheet for certain types of assets and liabilities and in certain industries. For example, companies report financial instruments, including derivatives, at fair value (more on this topic will be discussed in **Chapter 17**). Certain industries, such as brokerage houses and mutual funds, prepare their basic financial statements on a fair value basis. |
| **TIP:** | When an asset or liability is initially recorded by a company, the historical cost for that item equals the fair value of that item. In subsequent periods, as market and economic conditions change, historical cost and fair value often diverge. As a result, fair value measures or estimates often provide more relevant information about the expected future cash flows related to the asset or liability. For example, when long-lived assets decline in value, a fair value measure determines any impairment loss (see **Chapters 11 and 12** for discussions of this topic). We presently have a "mixed attribute" system that permits the use of historical cost, fair value, and other valuation bases. Although historical cost continues to be the primary basis for valuation (due to the historical cost principle), reporting of fair value information is increasing. As you progress through the chapters of this book, watch for items and situations that call for a departure from the historical cost principle. |

# ILLUSTRATION 2-1
# A CONCEPTUAL FRAMEWORK FOR FINANCIAL REPORTING
# (L.O. 2 THRU 8)

---

| Recognition and Measurement Concepts |
|---|

**ASSUMPTIONS**
1. Economic entity
2. Going concern
3. Monetary unit
4. Periodicity

**PRINCIPLES**
1. Historical cost
2. Revenue recognition
3. Matching
4. Full disclosure

**CONSTRAINTS**
1. Cost-benefit
2. Materiality
3. Industry practices
4. Conservatism

Third Level:
"The how"
implementation

**QUALITATIVE CHARACTERISTICS**
1. Primary qualities
   A. Relevance
      (1) Predictive value
      (2) Feedback value
      (3) Timeliness
   B. Reliability
      (1) Verifiability
      (2) Neutrality
      (3) Representational faithfulness
2. Secondary qualities
   A. Comparability
   B. Consistency

**ELEMENTS**
1. Assets
2. Liabilities
3. Equity
4. Investment by owners
5. Distribution to owners
6. Comprehensive income
7. Revenues
8. Expenses
9. Gains
10. Losses

Second Level:
Bridge between first and third levels.

**OBJECTIVES**
Provide information:
1. Useful in investment and credit decisions
2. Useful in assessing future cash flows
3. About enterprise resources, claims to resources, and changes in them.

First Level:
"The Why"—
goals and purposes of accounting.

---

This illustration provides an overview of the FASB's conceptual framework.[1] At the first level, the **objectives** identify the goals and purposes of financial accounting and are the building blocks for the conceptual framework. At the second level are the **qualitative characteristics** that make financial accounting information useful and the **elements** of financial statements (assets, liabilities, and so on). At the final, or third level, are the measurement and recognition concepts that accountants use in establishing and applying financial accounting standards. These concepts include assumptions, principles, and constraints that describe the present reporting environment.

---

[1]Adapted from William C. Norby, *The Financial Analysts Journal* (March-April, 1982), p. 22.

# ILLUSTRATION 2-2
# A HIERARCHY OF ACCOUNTING QUALITIES (L.O. 4)

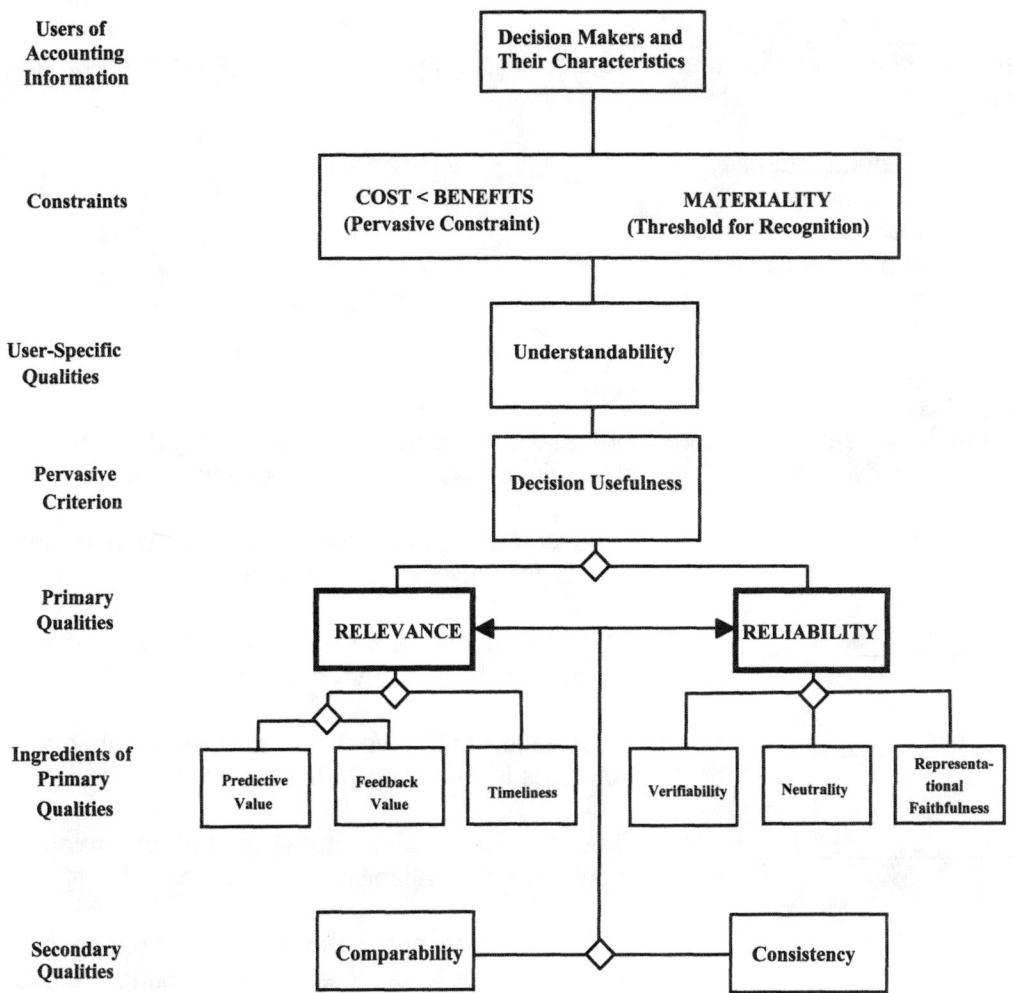

**SOURCE:** FASB, *Statement of Financial Accounting Concepts No. 2*, "Qualitative Characteristics of Accounting Information."

## CASE 2-1

**Purpose:**    (L.O.4) This exercise is designed to review the qualitative characteristics that make accounting information useful for decision making purposes (per *SFAC No. 2*).

The qualitative characteristics that make accounting information useful for decision making are as follows:

| | |
|---|---|
| Understandability | Verifiability |
| Relevance | Neutrality |
| Reliability | Representational faithfulness |
| Predictive value | Comparability |
| Feedback value | Consistency |
| Timeliness | |

## Instructions
Fill in the blank to identify the appropriate qualitative characteristic(s) being described in each of the statements below. A qualitative characteristic may be used more than once.

_____ 1. Two primary qualities that make accounting information useful for decision-making purposes.

_____ 2. Information that is capable of making a difference in a decision is said to have this primary quality.

_____ 3. Information that is verifiable and reasonably free of error and bias is said to have this primary quality.

_____ 4. Two qualitative characteristics that are related to both relevance and reliability.

_____ 5. An entity is to apply the same accounting methods to similar events for successive accounting periods; that is, when an entity selects one method from a list of alternative acceptable methods, that same method is used period after period.

_____ 6. Information is measured and reported in a similar manner for different enterprises.

_____ 7. Neutrality is an ingredient of this primary quality of accounting information.

_____ 8. Requires that information cannot be selected to favor one set of interested parties over another.

_____   9.   Predictive value is an ingredient of this primary quality of information.

_____  10.   When information provides a basis for forecasting annual earnings for future periods, it is said to have this ingredient of a primary quality of accounting information.

_____  11.   Quality of information that confirms or corrects users' prior expectations.

_____  12.   Information must be available to decision makers before it loses its capacity to influence their decisions.

_____  13.   Imperative for providing comparisons of a single firm from period to period.

_____  14.   Qualitative characteristic being employed when companies in the same industry are using the same accounting principles.

_____  15.   A company cannot suppress information just because such disclosure is embarrassing or damaging to the entity.

_____  16.   The amounts and descriptions in financial statements agree with the elements or events that these amounts and descriptions purport to represent.

_____  17.   Independent measurers, using the same measurement methods, obtain similar results.

_____  18.   The numbers and descriptions in financial statements represent what really existed or happened.

_____  19.   Requires information to be free of personal bias.

_____  20.   Requires a high degree of consensus among individuals on a given measurement.

_____  21.   Financial information is a tool and, like most tools, cannot be much direct help to those who are unable or unwilling to use it or who misuse it.

## Solution to Case 2-1

1. Relevance and reliability
2. Relevance
3. Reliability
4. Comparability and consistency
5. Consistency
6. Comparability
7. Reliability
8. Neutrality
9. Relevance
10. Predictive value
11. Feedback value
12. Timeliness
13. Consistency
14. Comparability
15. Neutrality
16. Representational faithfulness
17. Verifiability
18. Representational faithfulness
19. Neutrality
20. Verifiability
21. Understandability

**Approach:** Before beginning to fill in the twenty-one blanks required, visualize the diagram for the hierarchy of accounting qualities (**Illustration 2-2**). Also, take a few minutes to individually consider the eleven characteristics listed and think of the key phrases involved in describing those items. Such as:

**Understandability:** information provided by financial reporting should be comprehensible to those who have a reasonable understanding of business and economic activities and are willing to study the information with reasonable diligence.

**Relevance:** capable of making a difference in a decision.

**Reliability:** users can depend on information to be verifiable, reasonably free of error and bias, and to represent what it purports to represent.

**Predictive value:** helps users make predictions about the outcome of past, present, and future events.

**Feedback value:** helps to confirm or correct prior expectations.

**Timeliness:** information must be available to decision makers before it loses its capacity to influence their decisions.

**Verifiability:** is demonstrated when a high degree of consensus can be secured among independent measurers using the same measurement methods.

**Neutrality:** information is not to be selected to favor one set of interested parties over another and is to be free from bias towards a predetermined result.

**Representational faithfulness:** correspondence or agreement between the accounting numbers and descriptions and the resources or events that these numbers and descriptions purport to represent.

**Comparability:** information that has been measured and reported in a similar manner for different enterprises is considered comparable.

**Consistency:** a company is to apply the same methods to similar accountable events from period to period.

## ILLUSTRATION 2-3
## ELEMENTS OF FINANCIAL STATEMENTS (L.O. 5)

**Assets:** Probable future economic benefits obtained or controlled by a particular entity as a result of past transactions or events.

**Liabilities:** Probable future sacrifices of economic benefits arising from present obligations of a particular entity to transfer assets or provide services to other entities in the future as a result of past transactions or events.

**Equity:** Residual interest in the assets of an entity that remains after deducting its liabilities. In a business enterprise, the equity is the ownership interest.

**Investments by owners:** Increases in net assets of a particular enterprise resulting from transfers to it from other entities of something of value to obtain or increase ownership interests (or equity) in it. Assets are most commonly received as investments by owners, but that which is received may also include services or satisfaction or conversion of liabilities of the enterprise.

**Distributions to owners:** Decreases in net assets of a particular enterprise resulting from transferring assets, rendering services, or incurring liabilities by the enterprise to owners. Distributions to owners decrease ownership interests (or equity) in an enterprise.

**Comprehensive income:** Change in equity (net assets) of an entity during a period from transactions and other events and circumstances from nonowner sources. It includes all changes in equity during a period except those resulting from investments by owners and distributions to owners.

**Revenues:** Inflows or other enhancements of assets of an entity or settlement of its liabilities (or a combination of both) during a period from delivering or producing goods, rendering services, or other activities that constitute the entity's ongoing major or central operations.

**Expenses:** Outflows or other using up of assets or incurrences of liabilities (or a combination of both) during a period from delivering or producing goods, rendering services, or carrying out other activities that constitute the entity's ongoing major or central operations.

**Gains:** Increases in equity (net assets) from peripheral or incidental transactions of an entity and from all other transactions and other events and circumstances affecting the entity during a period except those that result from revenues or investments by owners.

**Losses:** Decreases in equity (net assets) from peripheral or incidental transactions of an entity and from all other transactions and other events and circumstances affecting the entity during a period except those that result from expenses or distributions to owners.

## ILLUSTRATION 2-4
## BASIC ACCOUNTING ASSUMPTIONS, PRINCIPLES, AND CONSTRAINTS (L.O. 6, 7, and 8)

**Economic entity assumption:** States that economic events can be identified with a particular unit of accountability. The activities of an accounting entity can be and should be kept separate and distinct from its owners and all other accounting entities. The entity concept does not necessarily refer to a legal entity.

**Going concern assumption:** Assumes that the enterprise will continue in operation long enough to carry out its existing objectives and commitments. Sometimes called the **continuity assumption**, it assumes the entity will continue in operation long enough to recover the cost of its assets. This assumption serves as a basis for basic principles such as the historical cost principle. Because of this assumption, liquidation values of assets are not relevant.

**Monetary unit assumption:** States that only transaction data capable of being expressed in terms of money should be included in the accounting records of the economic entity. All transactions and events can be measured in terms of a common denominator—units of money. A corollary is the added assumption that the unit of measure remains constant from one period to the next (some people call the corollary the "stable dollar assumption").

**Periodicity assumption:** Assumes that the economic life of a business can be divided into artificial time periods. Although some companies choose to subdivide the business life into months or quarters, others report financial statements only for an annual period.

**Historical cost principle:** States that many assets should initially be recorded and subsequently accounted for at acquisition cost. The principle also states that cost is measured by the fair market value (cash equivalent value) of the consideration given or the fair market value (cash equivalent value) of the consideration received, whichever is the more objectively determinable. In addition, the cost of an asset includes all costs necessary to acquire the item and get it in the place and condition for its intended use.

**Revenue recognition principle:** Dictates that revenue should be recognized when (1) **realized** or **realizable** and (2) **earned**. Revenues are **realized** when products (goods or services, merchandise, or other assets) are exchanged for cash or claims to cash. Revenues are **realizable** when assets received or held are readily convertible into cash or claims to cash. Assets are readily convertible when they are salable or interchangeable in an active market at readily determinable prices without significant additional cost. Revenues are considered **earned** when the entity has substantially accomplished what it must do to be entitled to the benefits represented by the revenues. The revenue generating process for most entities includes a number of steps. As a result, revenue is **earned** when the "critical point" in the earnings process is reached. This critical point is different for different circumstances as the following examples illustrate. Examples are: (1) when a sale is involved, the point of sale is the critical event, (2) when long-term construction contracts are involved, progress toward completion is the critical event, (3) when products are salable in an active market at readily determinable prices without significant additional cost, the completion of production is the critical event, and (4) when uncertainty about the collection of receivables exists for credit

## ILLUSTRATION 2-4 (Continued)

sales of goods and services, the receipt of cash is the critical event. In example (1), the sales basis is used for revenue recognition. In example (2), the percentage-of-completion method is appropriate for revenue recognition. In example (3), recognition of revenue at the end of production is justified. In example (4), the installment method is used.

**Expense Recognition (or Matching principle):** Dictates that expenses be matched with revenues whenever it is reasonable and practical to do so. Expenses (efforts) are recognized in the same period as the related revenue (accomplishment) is recognized. Thus, a factory worker's wages are not recognized as an expense when cash is paid or when the work is performed, or when the product is produced; they are recognized as an expense when the labor (service) or the product actually makes its contribution to the revenue generating process (which is when the related product is sold).

**Full disclosure principle:** Dictates that circumstances and events that make a difference to financial statement users be disclosed. An entity is to disclose through the data contained in the financial statements and the information in the notes that accompany the statements all information necessary to make the statements not misleading. To be recognized in the main body of the financial statements, an item should meet the definition of one of the basic elements, be measurable with sufficient certainty, and be relevant and reliable. The notes to financial statements generally amplify or explain the items presented in the body of the statements. Information in the notes does not have to be quantifiable, nor does it need to qualify as an element.

**Cost-benefit relationship:** States that the costs of providing the information must be weighed against the benefits that can be derived from using the information. In order to justify requiring a particular measurement or disclosure, the benefits perceived to be derived from it must exceed the costs perceived to be associated with the measurement or disclosure. When the perceived costs exceed the perceived benefits, a measurement or disclosure may be foregone based on its lack of practicality.

**Materiality constraint:** Dictates that an immaterial item need not be given strict accounting treatment; it can be given expedient treatment. An immaterial item or amount is one that does not make a difference in the decisions that are being made based on an analysis of the financial statements. The point involved here is one of relative size and importance. If the amount involved is significant when compared with other revenues and expenses, assets and liabilities, or net income of the entity, it is a material item and generally acceptable standards should be followed. If the amount is so small that it is quite unimportant when compared with other items, strict treatment is of less importance. The nature of an item may also affect the judgment of its materiality. A misclassification affecting cash has a lower threshold of materiality than the same dollar amount of a misclassification affecting plant assets.

## ILLUSTRATION 2-4 (Continued)

**Industry practices constraint:** States that the peculiar nature of some industries and business concerns sometimes requires departure from what would normally be considered good accounting practice. For example, current assets usually appear first on a balance sheet; however, for a public utility, it is an acceptable industry practice to report plant assets (noncurrent items) first on the balance sheet to highlight the entity's capital-intensive nature.

**Conservatism constraint:** Dictates that in matters of doubt and uncertainty, the accountant should choose the solution that will be least likely to overstate assets and net income. The axiom "anticipate no gains but provide for all losses" comes from this constraint. There is no virtue, however, in being overconservative. If the accountant is overconservative, other accounting principles such as historical cost, revenue recognition, and matching will be violated.

> **TIP:** Accounting constraints are justifications for departure from the basic accounting principles in certain situations. They are sometimes referred to as "exception principles." For example, the cost of an item that will benefit operations for five years should be initially recorded as an asset and amortized (expensed) over the related five-year period as dictated by the matching principle. However, if the item is a recycling container that cost $20, the amount is deemed to be insignificant and the whole amount is handled with expedience—that is, it is expensed in the period the container is acquired. This departure from the matching principle is justified by the materiality constraint. For another example, if the market value (replacement value) of inventory is below the cost of inventory, the inventory is to be reported at the market value (the lower value). Thus, there is a departure from the historical cost principle with the justification being the conservatism constraint.

## CASE 2-2

**Purpose:**    (L.O.6, 7, 8) This exercise will test your comprehension of the essence and significance of basic accounting assumptions, principles, and constraints.

### Instructions
For each of the following statements, identify (by letter) the basic accounting assumption, principle or constraint that is **most directly** related to the given phrase. Each code letter may be used more than once.

## Assumptions, Principles, and Constraints

a. Economic entity assumption
b. Going concern assumption
c. Monetary unit assumption
d. Periodicity assumption
e. Historical cost principle
f. Revenue recognition principle

g. Expense recognition (or Matching) principle
h. Full disclosure principle
i. Cost-benefit relationship
j. Materiality constraint
k. Industry practices constraint
l. Conservatism constraint

> **TIP:** Before you begin to read and answer the items listed, it would be helpful to briefly think about what you know about each of the assumptions, principles, and constraints. An explanation of each appears in **Illustration 2-4**.

## Statements

_____ 1. Revenue should be recognized when it is earned, which is usually at the point of sale.

_____ 2. All information necessary to ensure that the financial statements are **not** misleading should be reported.

_____ 3. This concept eliminates the "liquidation concept" in viewing business affairs.

_____ 4. Measurement of the standing and progress of entities should be made at regular intervals rather than at the end of the business's life.

_____ 5. Although an item such as a wastebasket may be of service for eight years, the total cost of the item may be expensed when it is purchased, because the amount is too insignificant to warrant the strict treatment of depreciation over the eight years.

_____ 6. The lower-of-cost-or-market rule for inventories is an application of this concept.

_____ 7. The recorded amount of an acquired item should be the fair market value of what was given or the fair market value of what was received in the exchange, whichever can be more objectively determined.

_____ 8. There must be complete and understandable reporting on financial statements.

_____ 9. The president of a business should **not** loan his spouse the company's credit card for personal gasoline purchases.

_____ 10. In matters of doubt or uncertainty, select the accounting treatment that will result in the lowest figure for net income, assets, and owners' equity.

_____ 11. Expenses should be recognized in the same period that the related revenues are recognized.

_____ 12. This concept is often exemplified by numerous notes to the financial statements.

_____ 13. If revenue is deferred to a future period, the related costs of generating that revenue should be deferred to the same future period.

_____ 14. This concept includes a set of rules concerning when to recognize revenue and how to measure its amount.

_____ 15. All transactions and events are expressed in terms of a common denominator.

_____ 16. Avoid overstatement of net income, assets, and owners' equity, but do not intentionally understate them.

_____ 17. It is assumed that an organization will remain in business long enough to recover the cost of its assets.

_____ 18. Changes in the purchasing power of the dollar are so small from one period to the next that they are ignored in preparing the basic financial statements.

_____ 19. Items whose amounts are very small relative to other amounts on the financial statements may be accounted for in the most expedient manner, rather than requiring strict accounting treatment under GAAP.

_____ 20. The cost of an item should be measured by the amount of the resources expended to acquire it.

_____ 21. Accruals and deferrals are often necessary in order to report expenses in the proper time periods.

_____ 22. Each accounting unit is considered separate and distinct from all other accounting units.

_____ 23. An accountant assumes that a business will continue indefinitely.

_____ 24. Assets which have appreciated in value are **not** reported at their current worth subsequent to acquisition because of this principle.

_____ 25. Depreciation of a long-term tangible asset is based on the asset's original acquisition cost rather than the asset's current market value.

_____ 26. If an item will not affect any business decisions, it need **not** be separately reported in the financial statements.

_____ 27. In order to justify requiring a particular measurement or disclosure, the benefits perceived to be derived from it must exceed the costs expected to be associated with it.

_____ 28. Externally acquired intangible assets are capitalized and amortized over the periods benefited.

_____ 29. Repair tools are expensed when purchased even though they may be of use for more than one period.

_____ 30. Brokerage firms use market value for purposes of valuation of all marketable securities. Changes in those market values are recognized in the income statement in the periods the changes occur.

_____ 31. All significant postbalance sheet events are reported in the notes to the financial statements.

_____ 32. Revenue for a retail establishment is recorded at the point of sale.

_____ 33. All important aspects of bond indentures (contracts) are presented in the financial statements.

_____ 34. Reporting must be done at defined time intervals. The time intervals are of equal length.

_____ 35. An allowance for doubtful (uncollectible) accounts is established.

_____ 36. All payments out of petty cash are charged to Miscellaneous Expense, even though some expenditures will benefit the following period. (Do not use conservatism.)

_____ 37. No profits are anticipated but all possible losses are recognized.

_____ 38. A company charges its sales commission costs to expense in the same period that the sale is made.

_____ 39. When the liquidation of an enterprise looks imminent, this assumption is inapplicable and thus, the historical cost principle does not apply. Rather, assets are reported at their net realizable values.

_____ 40. The initial note to financial statements is usually a summary of significant accounting policies.

## Solution to Case 2-2

| | | | | | | | | |
|---|---|---|---|---|---|---|---|---|
| 1. f | 11. g | 21. g | 31. h | |
| 2. h | 12. h | 22. a | 32. f | |
| 3. b | 13. g | 23. b | 33. h | |
| 4. d | 14. f | 24. e | 34. d | |
| 5. j | 15. c | 25. e* | 35. g | *An argument could be |
| 6. l | 16. l | 26. j | 36. j | made for answer "g." |
| 7. e | 17. b | 27. i | 37. l | |
| 8. h | 18. c | 28. g | 38. g | |
| 9. a | 19. j | 29. j | 39. b | |
| 10. l | 20. e | 30. k | 40. h | |

## CASE 2-3

**Purpose:**    (L.O.7) This case is designed to review three methods of matching expenses with revenues and examples of each.

An unexpired cost represents probable future benefits and hence is accounted for as an asset. An expired cost represents an expiration of benefits and hence is accounted for as an expense or a loss. There are three common bases of expense recognition (that is, guides for determining the timing of recording an expense): (1) cause and effect, (2) systematic and rational allocation, and (3) immediate recognition.

## Instructions

Describe each of the three bases of expense recognition and give a few examples of each for a retail establishment.

## Solution to Case 2-3

1.    **Cause and effect:** When there is a direct association between the expiration of a cost and a particular revenue transaction, the expense recognition should accompany the revenue recognition; that is, the cost is expensed in the same time period that the related specific revenue is recognized.

    *Examples:*    Cost of goods sold, sale commissions, transportation-out.

2.    **Systematic and rational allocation:** This basis is used when, although a cost benefits the revenue generating process of two or more accounting periods, the cost cannot be related to particular revenue transactions. Even though a close cause-and-effect relationship between revenue and cost cannot be determined, this relationship is assumed to exist. The cost is thus initially accounted for as an asset and then allocated to the periods benefited (as an expense) in a systematic and rational manner. The allocation method used should appear reasonable to an unbiased observer and should be consistently applied from period to period.

*Examples:*   Depreciation of plant assets, amortization of intangibles, allocation (amortization) of prepaids (such as rent and insurance).

3.    **Immediate recognition:** This basis is used when a company cannot determine a direct relationship between costs and revenue. These costs may fall in the following categories:

(a)    Their incurrence during the period provides no discernible future benefits.

(b)    They must be incurred each accounting period, and no build-up of expected future benefits occurs.

(c)    By their nature, they relate to current revenues even though they cannot be directly associated with any specific revenues.

(d)    The amount of cost to be deferred can be measured only in an arbitrary manner or great uncertainty exists regarding the realization of future benefits.

(e)    Uncertainty exists regarding whether allocating them to current and future periods will serve any useful purpose.

(f)    They are measures of asset costs recorded in prior periods from which no future benefits are now discernible.

*Examples:*   Sales salaries, office salaries, utilities, repairs, advertising, accounting and legal, research and development, postage, write-off of worthless patent.

> **TIP:**   Costs incurred by a manufacturing company are often classified into two groups: product costs and period costs. **Product costs** such as material, labor, and manufacturing overhead attach to the product and are carried into future periods (as a balance in inventory) if the product remains unsold at the end of the current period, and, therefore, the revenue recognition is deferred to the period of sale. Product costs are expensed in the period of sale in accordance with the cause and effect basis of expense recognition. **Period costs** such as officers' salaries and other administrative expenses are charged off immediately, even though benefits associated with these costs may occur in the future, because no direct relationship between cost and revenue can be determined and it is highly uncertain what, if any, benefits relate to the future.

> **TIP:**   For a manufacturing company, depreciation of the office building is determined and expensed based on a systematic and rational allocation. On the other hand, depreciation of factory machinery is a component of manufacturing overhead; thus, it is an element of product cost. The amount of depreciation that pertains to the products produced during a period is first determined by use of the selected depreciation method. The amount of depreciation that ends up being reflected as an expense on the income statement for the same period depends on the number of products sold (not produced) during the period; it is included as a part of cost of goods sold expense.

## ILLUSTRATION 2-5
## FAIR VALUE BASIS (MEASUREMENT) (L.O. 7)

We presently have a "mixed-attribute" system that permits the use of various measurement bases. The most commonly used measurements are based on historical cost and fair value. Fair value may be more useful for certain types of assets and liabilities.

For example, companies report many financial instruments, including derivatives, at fair value. Also, companies in certain financial industries, such as brokerage houses and mutual funds, prepare their basic financial statements on a fair value basis. At initial acquisition, historical costs equals fair value. In subsequent periods, as market and economic conditions change, historical cost and fair value often diverge. As a result, fair value measures or estimates often provide more relevant information about the expected future cash flows related to the asset or liability. For example, when long-lived assets decline in value, a fair value measure determines any impairment loss. To increase consistency and comparability in fair value measures, the FASB established the following fair value hierarchy that provides insight into the priority of valuation techniques to use to determine fair value.

| | |
|---|---|
| Level 1: Observable inputs that reflect quoted prices for identical assets or liabilities in active markets. | Most Reliable |
| Level 2: Inputs other than quoted prices included in Level 1 that are observable for the asset or liability either directly or through corroboration with observable data. | |
| Level 3: Unobservable inputs (for example, a company's own data or assumptions). | Least Reliable |

Level 1 is the most reliable because it is based on quoted prices, like a closing stock price in the *Wall Street Journal*. Level 2 is the next most reliable and would rely on evaluating similar assets or liabilities in active markets. At the least-reliable level, Level 3, much judgment is needed based on the best information available, to arrive at a relevant and reliable fair value measurement.

It is easy to arrive at fair values when markets are liquid with many traders, but fair value answers are not readily available in other situations. A great deal of expertise and sound judgment will be needed to arrive at appropriate answers. GAAP also provides guidance on estimating fair values when market-related data is not available. In general, these valuation issues relate to Level 3 fair value measurements. These measurements may be developed using expected cash flow and present value techniques discussed in **Chapter 6.**

Recently the Board has taken the additional step of giving companies the option to use fair value as the basis for measurement of financial assets and liabilities in the financial statements. The Board believes that fair value measurement for financial instruments provides more relevant and understandable information than historical cost. It considers fair value to be more relevant because it reflects the current cash equivalent value of financial instruments. As a result, companies now have the option to record fair value in their accounts for most financial instruments, including such items as receivables, investments, and debt securities.

# ANALYSIS OF MULTIPLE-CHOICE TYPE QUESTIONS

**QUESTION**
1.   (L.O.3) The objectives of financial reporting include all of the following **except** to provide information that:
a.   is useful to the Internal Revenue Service in allocating the tax burden to the business community.
b.   is useful to those making investment and credit decisions.
c.   is helpful in assessing future cash flows.
d.   identifies the economic resources (assets), the claims to those resources (liabilities), and the changes in those resources and claims.

**Explanation:** Financial reporting is for the use of investors, potential investors, management, and other interested parties. It is not for the IRS. The information required to be reported to the IRS is provided by the reporting entity on tax forms and is referred to as income tax accounting as opposed to financial reporting. (Solution = a)

**QUESTION**
2.   (L.O.4) According to *Statement of Financial Accounting Concepts No. 2*, timeliness is an ingredient of:

|     | Relevance | Reliability |
| --- | --- | --- |
| a. | Yes | Yes |
| b. | Yes | No |
| c. | No | No |
| d. | No | Yes |

**Approach and Explanation:** In answering this question, read the stem and answer "Yes" (true) or "No" (false) when completing the statement with the word **relevance**. Then reread the stem and answer "Yes" or "No" when completing the statement with the word **reliability**. Then look for the corresponding combination of "Yes" and "No" to select your answer. In the diagram of the hierarchy of accounting qualities, timeliness is linked to relevance and not reliability. Therefore, we want to respond "Yes" to the relevance column and "No" to the reliability column. (Solution = b.)

**QUESTION**
3.   (L.O.4) According to *Statement of Financial Accounting Concepts No. 2*, which of the following is considered a pervasive constraint?
a.   Representational faithfulness
b.   Verifiability
c.   Comparability
d.   Costs < Benefits

**Approach and Explanation:** In visualizing the diagram for a hierarchy of accounting qualities (**Illustration 2-2**), it is an easy task to identify why "costs < benefits" is the pervasive constraint in question and why the other selections can be eliminated in selecting the correct response. Selection "d" is correct because *SFAC No. 2* states that "in order to justify requiring a particular measurement or disclosure, the benefits perceived to be derived from it must exceed the costs perceived to be associated with it." Selections "a" and "b" are incorrect because representational faithfulness and verifiability are both ingredients of primary qualities of accounting information. Selection "c" is incorrect because comparability is a secondary quality of accounting information. (Solution = d.)

**QUESTION**
4.  (L.O.4) According to *Statement of Financial Accounting Concepts No. 2*, neutrality is an ingredient of the primary quality of:

| | Relevance | Reliability |
|---|---|---|
| a. | Yes | Yes |
| b. | Yes | No |
| c. | No | No |
| d. | No | Yes |

**Approach and Explanation:** In answering this question, read the stem and answer "Yes" (true) or "No" (false) when completing the statement with the word **relevance**. Then reread the stem and answer "Yes" or "No" when completing the statement with the word **reliability.** Then look for the corresponding combination of "Yes" and "No" to select your answer. In the diagram of the hierarchy of accounting qualities, neutrality is linked to reliability and not relevance. Therefore, we want to respond "No" to the relevance column and "Yes" to the reliability column. (Solution = d.)

**QUESTION**
5.  (L.O.4) If the LIFO inventory method was used last period, it should be used for the current and following periods because of:
    a.  materiality.
    b.  verifiability.
    c.  timeliness.
    d.  consistency.

**Approach and Explanation:** In reading the stem of the question, cover up the answer selections. Anticipate the correct answer by attempting to complete the statement given. This process should yield the answer of "consistency." If you cannot think of the word to complete the statement, then take each answer selection and write down what each means. You should then be able to match up the question with answer selection "d."

Selection "d" is correct because consistency is a secondary quality of accounting information. To be useful, financial statements should reflect consistent application of generally accepted accounting principles. This means that a company should apply the same methods to similar accountable events from period to period. Selection "a" is incorrect because materiality refers to a constraint whereby an item is to be given strict accounting treatment unless it is insignificant. Selection "b" is incorrect because verifiability refers to an ingredient of reliability (it is demonstrated when a high degree of consensus can be secured among independent measurers using the same measurement methods). Selection "c" is incorrect because timeliness is an ingredient of relevance which indicates that for information to be relevant, it must be prepared on a timely basis. (Solution = d.)

**QUESTION**

6.   (L.O.5) The term "articulation" refers to the:
   a.   expression of dollar amounts in terms of a foreign currency.
   b.   correction of amounts previously reported on the financial statements.
   c.   interaction of the elements of financial statements.
   d.   degree of preciseness of financial reports.

**Approach and Explanation:** Define or explain articulation before you read the answer selections. Select the answer that best fits your description.  The FASB classifies the elements of financial statements into two distinct groups. The first group of three elements—assets, liabilities, and equity—describes amounts of resources and claims to resources at a **moment in time**. The other seven elements (comprehensive income and its components—revenues, expenses, gains, and losses—as well as investments by owners and distributions to owners) describe transactions, events, and circumstances that affect an enterprise during a **period of time**. The first class—assets, liabilities, and equity—is changed by elements of the second class and at any time is the cumulative result of all changes. This interaction is referred to as "articulation." That is, key figures in one statement (e.g. balance sheet) correspond to or are influenced by amounts reported in another statement (e.g. income statement). (Solution = c.)

**QUESTION**

7.   (L.O. 5) The calculation of comprehensive income includes which of the following?

|     | Operating Income | Distributions to Owners |
| --- | --- | --- |
| a.  | Yes | Yes |
| b.  | Yes | No |
| c.  | No | Yes |
| d.  | No | No |

**Approach and Explanation:** Define comprehensive income before reading the answer selections. Then answer "Yes" or "No" for the inclusion of each of the items in question (Operating Income and Distributions to Owners). Then look for the corresponding combination of "Yes" and "No" to select your answer. **Comprehensive income** is a change in equity (net assets) of an entity during a period from transactions and other events and circumstances from nonowner sources. It includes all changes in equity during a period except those resulting from investments by owners and distributions to owners. Thus it includes net income and all of its components (such as revenues, expenses, gains, and losses) and subtotals of various components of net income (such as gross profit and operating income). (Solution = b.)

**QUESTION**

8.   (L.O. 5) Which of the following is **false** with regard to the element "comprehensive income"?
   a.   It is more inclusive than the traditional notion of net income.
   b.   It includes net income and all other changes in equity exclusive of owners' investments and distributions to owners.
   c.   This concept is not yet being applied in practice.
   d.   It excludes prior period adjustments (transactions that relate to previous periods, such as corrections of errors).

**Explanation:** Comprehensive income includes all changes in equity during a period except those resulting from investments by owners and distributions to owners. Prior period adjustments (such as corrections of errors) are included under comprehensive income; they are excluded from the concept of net income (as it is currently applied in practice). (Solution = d.)

**QUESTION**

9.   (L.O. 6) The assumption that an enterprise will remain in business indefinitely and will **not** liquidate in the near future is called the:
 a.   economic entity assumption.
 b.   going concern assumption.
 c.   monetary unit assumption.
 d.   periodicity assumption.

**Approach and Explanation:** Read the stem (while covering up the answer selections) and attempt to complete the statement. Compare your attempt with the selections. Hopefully, you anticipated the correct answer. If your attempt does not match any of the selections given, take each selection and write down the key words in the definitions of the term. This process should lead you to the correct response.

Answer selection "b" is correct because the going concern assumption implies that an enterprise will continue in business and will not liquidate within the foreseeable future. Selection "a" is incorrect because the economic entity assumption indicates that the activities of an accounting entity should be kept separate and distinct from all other accounting entities. Selection "c" is incorrect because the monetary unit assumption indicates that all transactions and events can be measured in terms of a common denominator—units of money. Selection "d" is incorrect because the periodicity assumption indicates that the economic activities of an enterprise can be divided into equally spaced artificial time periods. (Solution = b.)

**QUESTION**

10. ′ (L.O. 7) Pluto Magazine Company sells space to advertisers. The company requires an advertiser to pay for services one month before publication. Advertising revenue should be recognized when:
 a.   an advertiser places an order.
 b.   a bill is sent to an advertiser.
 c.   the related cash is received.
 d.   the related ad is published.

**Approach and Explanation:** Read the last sentence of the stem. We want to know the point at which revenue should be recognized. Write down what you know from the revenue recognition principle. Revenue is generally recognized when (1) realized or realizable, and (2) earned. Read the stem and think of how to apply the revenue recognition principle to the facts given. At the points when an order is placed and a bill is sent to an advertiser, revenue has neither been realized nor earned. At the point when the cash is received in advance of the publication, the revenue is realized but not earned. The revenue is earned when the related ad is published and, thus, should be recognized then. (Solution = d.)

**QUESTION**

11.   (L.O. 7) The historical cost principle provides that:
 a.   items whose costs are insignificant compared to other amounts on the financial statements may be accounted for in the most expedient manner.
 b.   assets and equities be expressed in terms of a common denominator.
 c.   the recorded amount of an acquired item should be the fair market value of what is given or the fair market value of what is received in the exchange, whichever is more objectively determinable.
 d.   the expenses of generating revenue should be recognized in the same period that the related revenue is recognized.

**Approach and Explanation:** Briefly define the historical cost principle before you read the answer selections. See **Illustration 2-4**. Answer selection "a" describes the materiality constraint. Selection "b" describes the monetary unit assumption. Selection "d" relates to the matching principle. (Solution = c.)

**QUESTION**

12.   (L.O. 7) If revenue is received in the current period, but it is **not** earned until a future period, the related expenses of generating the revenue should **not** be recognized until that future period. This guideline is an application of the:
   a.   revenue recognition principle.
   b.   full disclosure principle.
   c.   matching principle.
   d.   conservatism constraint.

**Explanation:** The revenue recognition principle dictates that revenue be recognized (recorded and reported) in the period it is realized (or realizable) and earned. The matching principle dictates that expenses be recognized in the same period as the revenue which they helped to generate is recognized. Thus, if revenue is deferred, the related expenses should also be deferred. (Solution = c.)

**QUESTION**

13.   (L.O. 7) The process of reporting an item in the financial statements of an enterprise is:
   a.   recognition
   b.   realization.
   c.   allocation.
   d.   incorporation.

**Explanation:** The term recognition refers to the process of formally recording or incorporating an item in the accounts and financial statements of an entity. An item that gets recorded in the accounts eventually gets reported in the financial statements of the enterprise. Realization is the process of converting noncash resources and rights into money and is most precisely used in accounting and financial reporting to refer to sales of assets for cash or claims to cash. The term allocation refers to the process or result of allocating (assigning costs or systematically spreading costs). The term incorporation refers to the process of establishing a business in the corporate form of organization. (Solution = a.)

**QUESTION**

14.   (L.O. 7) Revenue is to be recognized when it is realized (or realizable) and earned. This statement refers to the:
   a.   revenue recognition principle.
   b.   matching principle.
   c.   going concern assumption.
   d.   consistency concept.

**Approach and Explanation:** Briefly define each of the answer selections. Choose the item for which your definition most closely agrees with the stem of the question. **See Illustration 2-4**. The revenue recognition principle dictates that revenue be recognized (recorded and reported) in the period it is realized (or realizable) and earned. The matching principle dictates that expenses be recognized in the same period as the revenue which they helped to generate is recognized. The going concern assumption implies that an enterprise will continue in business indefinitely. The consistency concept or characteristic dictates that for financial information to be useful, an entity is to apply the same accounting methods to similar events for successive accounting periods. (Solution = a.)

**QUESTION**

15.  (L.O. 8) In matters of doubt and great uncertainty, accounting issues should be resolved by choosing the alternative that has the least favorable effect on net income, assets, and owners' equity. This guidance comes from the:
   a.    materiality constraint.
   b.    industry practices constraint.
   c.    conservatism constraint.
   d.    full disclosure principle.

**Approach and Explanation:** Briefly define each of the answer selections. Choose the item for which your definition most closely agrees with the stem of the question. See **Illustration 2-4**. In matters of doubt and uncertainty, the accountant is conservative and chooses the accounting alternative that is the least likely to cause an overstatement of net income, assets, and owners' equity. (Solution = c.)

**QUESTION**

16.  (L.O. 8) When an entity charges the entire cost of an electric pencil sharpener to expense in the period when it was purchased even though the appliance has an estimated life of five years, we have an application of the:
   a.    matching principle.
   b.    materiality constraint.
   c.    historical cost principle.
   d.    conservatism constraint.

**Explanation:** When an item benefits operations of more than one period, the matching principle will dictate the cost of the item be allocated (spread) systematically over the periods benefited. However, the materiality constraint dictates that an immaterial item need not be given strict accounting treatment; it can be given expedient treatment. The cost of a pencil sharpener would obviously be small and thus immaterial. Consequently, the materiality constraint is justification for departure from the matching principle in accounting for the cost of the pencil sharpener. (Solution = b.)

# CHAPTER 3

# THE ACCOUNTING INFORMATION SYSTEM

## OVERVIEW

Accounting information must be accumulated and summarized before it can be communicated and analyzed. In this chapter, we will discuss the steps involved in the accounting cycle. We will emphasize the subject of adjusting entries. Throughout an accounting period, cash receipts and cash disbursements are recorded. At the end of the accounting period, adjusting entries are required so that revenues and expenses are reflected on the accrual basis of accounting. Adjusting entries are simply entries required to bring account balances up to date. The failure to record proper adjustments will cause errors on both the income statement and the balance sheet.

## SUMMARY OF LEARNING OBJECTIVES

1.   **Understand basic accounting terminology.** It is important to understand the following eleven terms: (1) Event, (2) Transaction, (3) Account, (4) Real and Nominal accounts, (5) Ledger, (6) Journal, (7) Posting, (8) Trial Balances, (9) Adjusting entries, (10) Financial statements, and (11) Closing entries.

2.   **Explain double-entry rules.** The left side of an account is the debit side; the right side is the credit side. All asset and expense accounts are increased on the left or debit side and decreased on the right or credit side. Conversely, all liability and revenue accounts are increased on the right or credit side and decreased on the left or debit side. Stockholders' equity accounts, Common Stock and Retained Earnings, are increased on the credit side. The Dividends account is increased on the debit side.

3.   **Identify steps in the accounting cycle.** The basic steps in the accounting cycle are (1) identifying and measuring of transactions and other events, (2) journalizing (3) posting, (4) preparing an unadjusted trial balance, (5) making adjusting entries, (6) preparing an adjusted trial balance, (7) preparing financial statements, and (8) closing.

4.   **Record transactions in journals, post to ledger accounts, and prepare a trial balance.** The simplest journal form chronologically lists transactions and events expressed in terms of debits and credits to particular accounts. The items entered in a general journal must be transferred to the general ledger; this procedure is called posting. Companies should prepare an unadjusted trial balance at the end of a given period after the entries have been recorded in the journal and posted to the ledger. A trial balance is a list of all open accounts in the general ledger and their balances; it proves the equality of debits and credits after the recording and posting processes.

5.   **Explain the reasons for preparing adjusting entries.** Adjustments to achieve a proper matching of revenues and expenses, so as to determine net income for the current period and to achieve an accurate statement of end-of-the period balances in assets, liabilities, and owners' equity accounts.

6.  **Prepare financial statements from the adjusted trial balance.** Companies can prepare financial statements directly from the adjusted trial balance. The income statement is prepared from the revenue and expense account balances. The statement of retained earnings is prepared from the retained earnings account balance, dividends amount, and the net income (or net loss) amount. The balance sheet is prepared from the asset, liability, and equity accounts.

7.  **Prepare closing entries.** In the closing process, the company transfers all of the revenue and expense account balances (income statement items) to a clearing account called Income Summary, which is used only at the end of the fiscal year. Revenues and expenses are matched in the Income Summary account and the net result of this matching represents the net income or net loss for the period. The net income or net loss amount is then transferred to an owners' equity account (Retained Earnings for a corporation and capital accounts for proprietorships and partnerships.)

*8.  **Differentiate the cash basis of accounting from the accrual basis of accounting.** The cash basis of accounting records revenues when cash is received and expenses when cash is paid. The accrual basis recognizes revenue when earned and expenses in the period incurred, without regard to the time of the receipt or payment of cash. Accrual-basis accounting is theoretically preferable because it provides information about future cash inflows and outflows associated with earnings activities as soon as a company can estimate these cash flows with an acceptable degree of certainty. Cash-basis accounting is not in conformity with GAAP.
     *This material is covered in Appendix 3A in the text.

**9.  **Identify adjusting entries that may be reversed.** Reversing entries are most often used to reverse two types of adjusting entries: accrued revenues and accrued expenses. Adjusting entries for deferrals (prepaid expenses and unearned revenues) may also be reversed if the initial entry to record the related cash transaction is made to an expense or revenue account.
     **This material is covered in Appendix 3B in the text.

***10.  **Prepare a 10-column work sheet.** The 10-column work sheet provides columns for the first (unadjusted) trial balance, adjustments, adjusted trial balance, income statement, and balance sheet. The work sheet does not replace the financial statements. Instead, it is the accountant's informal device for accumulating and sorting information needed for the financial statements. Completing the work sheet provides considerable assurance that all of the details related to the end-of-period accounting procedures and preparation of the financial statements have been properly brought together.
     ***This material is covered in Appendix 3C in the text.

## TIPS ON CHAPTER TOPICS

**TIP:** This chapter is an extremely important one. A good understanding of this chapter and an ability to think and work quickly with the concepts incorporated herein are necessary for comprehending subsequent chapters. Although adjusting entries were introduced in your principles course, you are likely to discover new dimensions to this subject in your intermediate accounting course. Pay close attention when studying this chapter!

**TIP:** When you encounter a transaction, always analyze it in terms of its effects on the elements of the basic **accounting equation** (or **balance sheet equation**). For your analysis to be complete, it must maintain balance in the basic accounting equation. The **basic accounting equation** is as follows:

$$\text{ASSETS} = \text{LIABILITIES} + \text{OWNERS' EQUITY}$$
$$\text{or}$$
$$A = L + OE$$

Assets are economic resources. Liabilities and owners' equity are sources of resources; liabilities are creditor sources, and owners' equity represents owner sources (owner investments and undistributed profits). The basic accounting equation simply states that the total assets (resources) at a point in time equal the total liabilities plus total owners' equity (sources of resources) at the same point in time.

**TIP:** **An understanding of the following eleven terms is important.** (1) **Event:** a happening of consequence. An event generally is the source or cause of changes in assets, liabilities, and equity. Events may be external or internal. (2) **Transaction:** an external event involving a transfer or exchange between two or more entities. (3) **Account:** a systematic arrangement that shows the effect of transactions and other events on a specific financial item. A separate account is kept for each type of asset, liability, revenue, and expense, and for capital (owners' equity). (4) **Real and nominal accounts:** real (permanent) accounts are asset, liability, and equity accounts. They appear on the balance sheet. Nominal (temporary) accounts are revenue, expense, and dividend accounts. Except for dividends, they contain information that appears on the income statement. Nominal accounts are periodically closed; real accounts are not closed. (5) **Ledger:** the book (or computer system) containing the accounts. (6) **Journal:** the book of original entry where transactions and selected other events are initially recorded. (7) **Posting:** the process of transferring the essential facts and figures from the book of original entry to the ledger accounts. (8) **Trial balance:** a list of all open accounts in the ledger and their balances. (9) **Adjusting entries:** entries made at the end of an accounting period to bring all accounts up to date on an accrual accounting basis so that correct financial statements can be prepared. (10) **Financial statements:** statements that reflect the collection, tabulation, and final summarization of the accounting data. (11) **Closing entries:** the formal process by which all nominal accounts are reduced to zero, and the net income or net loss is determined and transferred to the appropriate owners' equity account.

**TIP:** **Transactions** are the economic events of an entity recorded by accountants. Some events (happenings of consequence to an entity) are not measurable in terms of money and do not get recorded in the accounting records. Hiring employees, placing an order for supplies, greeting a customer and quoting prices for products are examples of activities that do not by themselves constitute transactions.

**TIP:** In accordance with the **revenue recognition principle**, revenue is to be recognized (reported) in the period in which it is realized (or realizable) and earned. In accordance with the **matching principle**, the expenses incurred in generating revenues should be recognized in the same period as the revenues they helped to generate. First, the revenue recognition principle is applied to determine in what period(s) to recognize revenue. Then, the matching principle is applied to determine in what period(s) to recognize expense.

With the **cash basis of accounting,** a revenue item is reported in the time period when the related cash is received from the customer and an expense is recorded in the time period in which the related cash is paid. Cash basis financial statements are **not** in conformity with generally accepted accounting principles. Most companies use the **accrual basis of accounting,** whereby a revenue item is reported in the time period in which it is earned and an expense item is reported in the time period in which it is incurred.

**TIP:** Adjusting entries are often required so that revenues and expenses are reflected on an accrual basis of accounting (revenues recognized when earned and expenses recognized when incurred) rather than on a cash basis of accounting. Therefore, adjusting entries reflect the **accruals** and **deferrals of revenues and expenses** and also **estimated expenses. Adjusting entries** are simply entries required to bring account balances up to date before financial statements can be prepared. The failure to record proper adjustments will cause errors in both the income statement and the balance sheet.

**TIP:** **Deferrals** result from **cash** flows that occur **before** expense or revenue recognition. That is, cash is paid for expenses that apply to more than one accounting period or cash is received for revenue that applies to more than one accounting period. The portion of the expense that applies to future periods is deferred by reporting a prepaid expense (asset) or the portion of the revenue that applies to future periods is deferred by reporting unearned revenue (liability) on the balance sheet.

**Accruals** result from **cash** flows that occur **after** expense or revenue recognition. That is, cash is to be paid or received in a future accounting period for an expense incurred or a revenue earned in the current period.

**TIP:** Notice that **none** of the adjusting entries discussed in Chapter 3 involves the **Cash** account. Therefore, if you are instructed to record **adjusting entries,** double check your work when it is completed. If you have used the Cash account in any adjusting entry, it is very likely in error. (The only time Cash belongs in an adjusting entry is when a bank reconciliation discloses a need to adjust the Cash account—this will be explained in **Chapter 7**—or when an error has been made that involves the Cash account, in which case a correcting entry is required.) There are, however, situations in homework assignments in which errors involving the Cash account must be corrected; in such a case, the Cash account will be involved in your **correcting** entry.

**TIP:** Notice that each adjusting entry discussed in this chapter involves a balance sheet account **and** an income statement account.

**TIP:** When preparing homework assignments, working through *The Problem Solving Survival Guide,* and answering exam questions, pay careful attention to whether a prepayment situation relates to a **cash inflow** or **cash outflow** for the entity in question. Be sure you then use the proper related account for recording the cash receipt or disbursement and correct terminology in explaining the scenario. If cash is **received** in a rental situation, the amount will be recorded (by a credit) in either an earned rent revenue account or an unearned rent revenue account, **not** in an expense or a prepaid expense account. If cash is **paid** in a rental situation, the amount will be recorded (by a debit) in either an expense or a prepaid expense account.

**TIP:** In an adjusting entry for an accrual (accrued revenue or accrued expense), the word "accrued" is **not** needed in either account title. If you choose to use the word "accrued" in an account title, it is appropriate to do so **only** in the balance sheet account title. For example, the entry to record accrued salaries of $1,000 is as follows:

| | | |
|---|---|---|
| Salaries Expense | 1,000 | |
| Salaries Payable | | 1,000 |

The word "accrued" is not needed in either account title, but it could be used in the liability account title if desired (the account title would then be Accrued Salaries Payable). It would be wrong to insert the word "accrued" in the expense account title. Some people simply call the credit account "Accrued Salaries" (rather than "Salaries Payable") but we advise that you include the key word "Payable" and omit the unnecessary word "Accrued."

**TIP:** The cost of most long-lived tangible assets is allocated to expense in a systematic and rational manner. The entry to record the expiration of cost due to the consumption of benefits yielded by the asset is a debit to Depreciation Expense and a credit to Accumulated Depreciation. The amortization of intangibles is similar to depreciation.

**TIP:** A reduction in the net realizable value of accounts receivable or inventories is recorded in an adjusting entry by a charge to expense and a credit to a contra asset account.

**TIP:** An unadjusted trial balance is referred to as either "unadjusted trial balance" or simply "trial balance." An adjusted trial balance is referred to as either "adjusted trial balance" or the "adjusted trial."

**TIP:** Closing entries are necessary at the end of an accounting period to prepare the nominal accounts (revenues, expenses, gains, and losses) for the recording of transactions for the next accounting period. Closing entries are prepared after the nominal account balances have been used to prepare the income statement. Only nominal accounts are closed. Real accounts are never closed; their balances continue into the next accounting period. **Nominal** accounts are often called **temporary** accounts; **real** accounts are often called **permanent** accounts.

**TIP:** A nominal account with a credit balance is closed by a debit to that account and a credit to Income Summary. A nominal account with a debit balance is closed by a credit to that account and a debit to Income Summary. The Income Summary account is closed to an owners' equity account (Retained Earnings for a corporation) and is often called the Revenue and Expense Summary.

**TIP:** If a separate account is used to record owner withdrawals or owner distributions (such as Dividends or Dividends Declared for a corporation or Owner's Drawings for a proprietorship or partnership), this account is also closed at the end of the accounting period, but it is **not** closed to the Income Summary account because it is **not** a component of the net income computation. Rather, it is closed directly to Retained Earnings (for a corporation) or to Owner's Capital (for a proprietorship or partnership).

**TIP:** A **post-closing trial balance** contains only real accounts because the nominal accounts all have a zero balance after the closing process. A post-closing trial balance is prepared to check on the equality of debits and credits after the closing process.

**\*\*\*TIP:** In preparing a 10-column work sheet, the debit and credit columns for every column pair must be equal before you can proceed to the next column pair. (This pertains to the first three column pairs). All five pairs of columns must balance for a work sheet to be complete.

# ILLUSTRATION 3-1
# DOUBLE-ENTRY (DEBIT AND CREDIT)
# ACCOUNTING SYSTEM (L.O. 2)

The debit and credit rules are summarized below:

| Asset Accounts | |
|---|---|
| Debit | Credit |
| Increase | Decrease |
| + | - |

| Liability Accounts | |
|---|---|
| Debit | Credit |
| Decrease | Increase |
| - | + |

| Dividends Account | |
|---|---|
| Debit | Credit |
| Increase | Decrease |
| + | - |

| Stockholders' Equity Accounts | |
|---|---|
| Debit | Credit |
| Decrease | Increase |
| - | + |

| Expense Accounts | |
|---|---|
| Debit | Credit |
| Increase | Decrease |
| + | - |

↑
**Normal
Balance**

| Revenue Accounts | |
|---|---|
| Debit | Credit |
| Decrease | Increase |
| - | + |

↑
**Normal
Balance**

Notice that the accounts above are arranged in such a way that all of the increases ("+" signs) are on the outside and all of the decreases ("-" signs) are on the inside of this diagram.

**TIP:** An **account** is an individual accounting record of increases and decreases in a specific asset, liability, or stockholders' equity item. In its simplest form, an account consists of three parts: (1) the title of the account, (2) a left or debit side, and (3) a right or credit side. Because the alignment of these parts of an account resembles the letter T, it is often referred to as a **T-account.**

**TIP:** "Credit" does **not** always mean favorable or unfavorable. In accounting, "debit and "credit" simply mean left and right, respectively. "Debit" is a term that refers to the left side of any account. Thus, the debit side of an account is always the left side. "Credit" is a word that simply refers to the right side of an account. Thus, the credit side of an account is always the right side of the account. The phrase "to debit an account" means to enter an amount on the debit (left) side of an account. Debit can be abbreviated as "Dr." and credit is abbreviated as "Cr."

**TIP:** A "+" indicates an increase and a "-" indicates a decrease. Therefore, a transaction which causes an increase in an asset is recorded by a debit to the related asset account; a transaction which causes a decrease in the same asset is recorded by a credit to the same account.

**TIP:** The normal balance of an account is the side where increases are recorded. Therefore, the normal balance of an asset account is a debit balance; the normal balance of a liability account is a credit balance.

## ILLUSTRATION 3-1 (Continued)

TIP:    A company's **ledger** is the book (or computer system) containing the company's accounts. Each account usually has a separate page. The **general ledger** is a collection of all the asset, liability, owners' equity, revenue, expense, and dividends accounts. A separate account should exist in the general ledger for each item that will appear on the financial statements. A **subsidiary ledger** contains the detail related to a given general ledger account.

TIP:    At this stage of your study of accounting, you should be able to quickly and correctly identify the debit and credit rules for any given account. If you are slow at this process, drill on the rules until you improve. If you memorize the rules for an asset account, you can figure out the rules for all other types of accounts by knowing which rules are the opposite of the rules for assets and which are the same. Increases in assets are recorded by debits. Because liabilities and owners' equity are on the other side of the equals sign in the basic accounting equation, they must have debit and credit rules opposite of the rules for assets. Therefore, a liability or an owners' equity account is increased by a credit entry. Revenues earned increase owners' equity (retained earnings for a corporate form of organization) so the rules to record increases in revenue are the same as the rules to record increases in an owners' equity account (increases are recorded by credits). Because expenses and owners' withdrawals reduce owners' equity, they have debit/credit rules which are opposite of the rules for an owners' equity account.

TIP:    In the double-entry system of accounting, for every debit there must be a credit(s) of equal amount, and vice versa.

## EXERCISE 3-1

**Purpose:**    (L.O. 2) This exercise will test your understanding of the debit and credit rules.

### Instructions

For each account listed below, put a check mark (√) in the appropriate column to indicate if it is increased by an entry in the debit (left) side of the account or by an entry in the credit (right) side of the account. The first one is done for you.

| | | Debit | Credit |
|---|---|---|---|
| 1. | Cash | √ | |
| 2. | Sales Revenue | | |
| 3. | Commissions Expense | | |
| 4. | Advertising Expense | | |
| 5. | Salaries Payable | | |
| 6. | Prepaid Insurance | | |
| 7. | Property Taxes Payable | | |
| 8. | Property Tax Expense | | |
| 9. | Dividends Declared | | |
| 10. | Interest Revenue | | |
| 11. | Salaries Expense | | |
| 12. | Commissions Revenue | | |
| 13. | Unearned Rent Revenue | | |
| 14. | Equipment | | |
| 15. | Note Payable | | |
| 16. | Building | | |
| 17. | Accounts Payable | | |
| 18. | Supplies on Hand | | |
| 19. | Accounts Receivable | | |
| 20. | Common Stock | | |
| 21. | Retained Earnings | | |
| 22. | Mortgage Payable | | |
| 23. | Loan Receivable | | |
| 24. | Bank Loan Payable | | |
| 25. | Audit Fees Incurred | | |
| 26. | Dividend Income | | |
| 27. | Fees Incurred | | |
| 28. | Fees Earned | | |
| 29. | Utilities Expense | | |
| 30. | Utilities Payable | | |

**TIP:**    In essence, you are being asked to identify the normal balance of each of the accounts listed. The **normal balance** of an account is the side where increases are recorded.

## Solution to Exercise 3-1

**Approach:** Determine the classification of the account (asset, liability, owners' equity, revenue or expense). Think about the debit and credit rules for that classification. Refer to **Illustration 3-1** and the related **TIPS** for those rules. In determining the classification of an account, look for the key words, if any, in each individual item. For example: (1) the words Revenue, Earned, or Income are often associated with a revenue account, (2) the words Expense, Incurred, or Expired are often associated with an expense account, (3) the words Receivable, Prepaid or Deferred Expense refer to types of asset accounts, and (4) the words Payable, Unearned Revenue, or Deferred Revenue refer to types of liabilities.

| | | Debit | Credit | Classification |
|---|---|:---:|:---:|---|
| 1. | Cash | √ | | Asset |
| 2. | Sales Revenue | | √ | Revenue |
| 3. | Commissions Expense | √ | | Expense |
| 4. | Advertising Expense | √ | | Expense |
| 5. | Salaries Payable | | √ | Liability |
| 6. | Prepaid Insurance | √ | | Asset |
| 7. | Property Taxes Payable | | √ | Liability |
| 8. | Property Tax Expense | √ | | Expense |
| 9. | Dividends Declared | √ | | Owners' Equity (Owners' Withdrawals) |
| 10. | Interest Revenue | | √ | Revenue |
| 11. | Salaries Expense | √ | | Expense |
| 12. | Commissions Revenue | | √ | Revenue |
| 13. | Unearned Rent Revenue | | √ | Liability |
| 14. | Equipment | √ | | Asset |
| 15. | Note Payable | | √ | Liability |
| 16. | Building | √ | | Asset |
| 17. | Accounts Payable | | √ | Liability |
| 18. | Supplies on Hand | √ | | Asset |
| 19. | Accounts Receivable | √ | | Asset |
| 20. | Common Stock | | √ | Owners' Equity (Owners' Investments) |
| 21. | Retained Earnings | | √ | Owners' Equity (Earned Capital) |
| 22. | Mortgage Payable | | √ | Liability |
| 23. | Loan Receivable | √ | | Asset |
| 24. | Bank Loan Payable | | √ | Liability |
| 25. | Audit Fees Incurred | √ | | Expense |
| 26. | Dividend Income | | √ | Revenue |
| 27. | Fees Incurred | √ | | Expense |
| 28. | Fees Earned | | √ | Revenue |
| 29. | Utilities Expense | √ | | Expense |
| 30. | Utilities Payable | | √ | Liability |

## EXERCISE 3-2

**Purpose:** (L.O. 4) This exercise will review how to record transactions in the general journal.

Transactions for the Smooth Sailing Repair Shop, Inc. for August 2010 are listed below.

1. August 1 Joan and Phillip began the business by each depositing $2,500 of personal funds in the business bank account in exchange for common stock of the newly formed corporation.
2. August 2 Joan rented space for the shop behind a strip mall and paid August rent of $800 out of the business bank account.
3. August 3 The shop purchased supplies for cash, $3,000.
4. August 4 The shop paid Cupboard News, a local newspaper, $300 for an ad appearing in the Sunday edition.
5. August 5 The shop repaired a boat for a customer. The customer paid cash of $1,300 for services rendered.
6. August 13 The shop purchased supplies for $900 by paying cash of $200 and charging the rest on account.
7. August 14 The shop repaired a boat for Zonie Kinkennon for $3,600. Phillip collected $1,000 in cash and put the rest on Zonie's account.
8. August 24 The shop collected cash of $400 from Zonie Kinkennon.
9. August 28 The shop paid $200 to Mini Maid for cleaning services for the month of August.
10. August 31 The board of directors of the corporation declared and paid a dividend of $400 in cash to its stockholders.

### Instructions
(a) Explain the impact of each transaction on the elements of the basic accounting equation and translate that into debit and credit terms.
(b) Journalize the transactions listed above. Include a brief explanation with each journal entry.

## SOLUTION TO EXERCISE 3-2

(a)  1.  Increase in Cash.
         Increase in Common Stock.

         Debit Cash
         Credit Common Stock

     2.  Increase in Rent Expense.
         Decrease in Cash.

         Debit Rent Expense
         Credit Cash

     3.  Increase in Supplies on Hand.
         Decrease in Cash.

         Debit Supplies on Hand
         Credit Cash

     4.  Increase in Advertising Expense.
         Decrease in Cash.

         Debit Advertising Expense
         Credit Cash

| | | |
|---|---|---|
| 5. | Increase in Cash.<br>Increase in Service Revenue. | Debit Cash<br>Credit Service Revenue |
| 6. | Increase in Supplies on Hand.<br>Decrease in Cash.<br>Increase in Accounts Payable. | Debit Supplies on Hand<br>Credit Cash<br>Credit Accounts Payable |
| 7. | Increase in Cash.<br>Increase in Accounts Receivable.<br>Increase in Service Revenue | Debit Cash<br>Debit Accounts Receivable<br>Credit Service Revenue |
| 8. | Increase in Cash.<br>Decrease in Accounts Receivable. | Debit Cash<br>Credit Accounts Receivable |
| 9. | Increase in Cleaning Expense.<br>Decrease in Cash. | Debit Cleaning Expense<br>Credit Cash |
| 10. | Decrease in Retained Earnings.<br>Decrease in Cash. | Debit Retained Earnings<br>Credit Cash |

**Approach:** Write down the effects of each transaction on the basic accounting equation. Think about the individual asset, liability, or stockholders' equity accounts involved. Apply the debit and credit rules to translate the effects into a journal entry. Refer to **Illustration 3-1** for the debit and credit rules for each type of account.

## GENERAL JOURNAL                                                        J1

| | Date | Account Titles and Explanations | Ref. | Debit | Credit |
|---|---|---|---|---|---|
| (b) | | | | | |
| | 2010 | | | | |
| 1. | Aug. 1 | Cash | | 5,000 | |
| | | Common Stock | | | 5,000 |
| | | (Issued shares of stock for cash) | | | |
| 2. | 2 | Rent Expense | | 800 | |
| | | Cash | | | 800 |
| | | (Paid August rent) | | | |
| 3. | 3 | Supplies on Hand | | 3,000 | |
| | | Cash | | | 3,000 |
| | | (Purchased supplies for cash) | | | |
| 4. | 4 | Advertising Expense | | 300 | |
| | | Cash | | | 300 |
| | | (Paid Cupboard News for advertising) | | | |
| 5. | 5 | Cash | | 1,300 | |
| | | Service Revenue | | | 1,300 |
| | | (Received cash for service fees earned) | | | |
| 6. | 13 | Supplies on Hand | | 900 | |
| | | Cash | | | 200 |
| | | Accounts Payable | | | 700 |
| | | (Purchased supplies for cash and on credit) | | | |
| 7. | 14 | Cash | | 1,000 | |
| | | Accounts Receivable | | 2,600 | |
| | | Service Revenue | | | 3,600 |
| | | (Performed services for customer for cash and on credit) | | | |
| 8. | 24 | Cash | | 400 | |
| | | Accounts Receivable | | | 400 |
| | | (Received cash from Zonie Kinkennon on account) | | | |
| 9. | 28 | Cleaning Expense | | 200 | |
| | | Cash | | | 200 |
| 10. | 31 | Retained Earnings (or Dividends Declared) | | 400 | |
| | | Cash | | | 400 |

## EXERCISE 3-3

**Purpose:**    (L.O. 5) This exercise will provide you with examples of adjusting entries for the accrual of expenses and revenues.

The following information relates to the Yuppy Clothing Sales Company at the end of 2010. The accounting period is the calendar year. This is the company's first year of operations.

1.   Employees are paid every Friday for the five-day work week ending on that day. Salaries amount to $2,400 per week. The accounting period ends on a Wednesday.
2.   On October 1, 2010, Yuppy borrowed $8,000 cash by signing a note payable due in one year at 8% interest. Interest is due when the principal is paid.
3.   A note for $2,000 was received from a customer in a sales transaction on May 1, 2010. The note matures in one year and bears 12% interest per annum. Interest is due when the principal is due.
4.   A portion of Yuppy's parking lot is used by executives of a neighboring company. A person pays $6 per day for each day's use, and the parking fees are due by the fifth business day following the month of use. The fees for December 31, 2010 amount to $1,260.

### Instructions

Using the information given above, prepare the necessary adjusting entries at December 31, 2010.

### Solution to Exercise 3-3

1.   Salaries Expense ............................................................... 1,440
        Salaries Payable ...........................................................         1,440
            ($2,400 ÷ 5 = $480); ($480 x 3 = $1,440
            accrued salaries)

2.   Interest Expense ............................................................... 160
        Interest Payable ...........................................................         160
            ($8,000 x 8% x 3/12 = $160 accrued interest)

3.   Interest Receivable ........................................................... 160
        Interest Revenue ..........................................................         160
            ($2,000 x 12% x 8/12 = $160 accrued interest)

4.   Parking Fees Receivable .................................................... 1,260
        Parking Fees Revenue .................................................         1,260

**Approach and Explanation:** Write down the definitions for accrued expense and accrued revenue. Think about what is to be accomplished by each of the adjustments required in this exercise. An **accrued expense** is an expense that has been incurred but not paid. The "incurred" part results in an increase in Expense (debit) and the "not paid" part results in an increase in Payable (credit). An **accrued revenue** is a revenue that has been earned but not received. The "earned" part results in an increase in Revenue (credit) and the "not received" part results in an increase in Receivable (debit).

| TIP: | In an adjusting entry to record accrued salaries expenses (expense incurred, but not paid) the debit is to an expense account and the credit is to a liability account. The expense account is usually titled Salaries Expense. Possible names for the liability account include Salaries Payable and Accrued Salaries Payable. |
|---|---|
| TIP: | In an adjusting entry to record accrued interest revenue (revenue earned but not received), the debit is to an asset account and the credit is to a revenue account. Possible names for that asset account are Interest Receivable and Accrued Interest Receivable. Possible names for the revenue account include Interest Revenue, Interest Income, and Interest Earned. |

## EXERCISE 3-4

**Purpose:** (L.O. 5) This exercise will provide you with examples of adjusting entries for prepaid expenses and unearned revenues (that is, for the deferral of expenses and revenues).

The following information relates to the Brittany Spears Magazine Company at the end of 2010. The accounting period is the calendar year.

1.  An insurance premium of $8,000 was paid on April 1, 2010, and was charged to Prepaid Insurance. The premium covers a 24-month period beginning April 1, 2010.

2.  The Office Supplies on Hand account showed a balance of $3,500 at the beginning of 2010. Supplies costing $12,000 were purchased during 2010 and debited to the asset account. Supplies of $2,200 were on hand at December 31, 2010.

3.  On July 1, 2010, cash of $48,000 was received from subscribers (customers) for a 36-month subscription period beginning on that date. The receipt was recorded by a debit to Cash and a credit to Unearned Subscription Revenue.

4.  At the beginning of 2010, the Unearned Advertising Revenue account had a balance of $75,000. During 2010, collections from advertisers of $800,000 were recorded by credits to Unearned Advertising Revenue. At the end of 2010, revenues received but not earned are computed to be $51,000.

## Instructions

Using the information given above, prepare the necessary adjusting entries at December 31, 2010.

## SOLUTION TO EXERCISE 3-4

| | | | |
|---|---|---|---|
| 1. | Insurance Expense ............................................ | 3,000 | |
| | Prepaid Insurance ............................................. | | 3,000 |
| | ($8,000 X 9/24 = $3,000 expired cost) | | |

| | | | |
|---|---|---|---|
| 2. | Supplies Expense .............................................. | 13,300 | |
| | Office Supplies on Hand..................................... | | 13,300 |
| | ($3,500 + $12,000 - $2,200 = $13,300 supplies consumed) | | |

| | | | |
|---|---|---|---|
| 3. | Unearned Subscription Revenue .................................... | 8,000 | |
| | Subscription Revenue ......................................... | | 8,000 |
| | ($48,000 X 6/36 = $8,000 earned revenue) | | |

| | | | |
|---|---|---|---|
| 4. | Unearned Advertising Revenue ...................................... | 824,000 | |
| | Advertising Revenue ........................................... | | 824,000 |
| | ($75,000 + $800,000 - $51,000 = $824,000 earned revenue) | | |

**Approach and Explanation:** Write down the definitions for prepaid expense and unearned revenue. Think about what is to be accomplished by each of the adjustments required in this exercise. A **prepaid expense** is an expense that has been paid but not incurred. In a case where the prepayment was recorded as an increase in an asset account (such as Prepaid Expense or Supplies on Hand), the adjusting entry will record the increase in Expense (debit) and a decrease in the recorded Asset (credit) due to the consumption of the benefits yielded by the earlier prepayment. An **unearned revenue** is a revenue that has been received but not earned. In a case where the cash receipt was recorded as an increase in a liability account (such as Unearned Revenue or Deferred Revenue), the adjusting entry will record a decrease in the recorded liability Unearned Revenue (debit) and an increase in Earned Revenue (credit) due to the earning of all or a portion of the revenue represented by the earlier cash receipt.

It is helpful to sketch a T-account for the related asset or liability account. Enter the amounts reflected in that account before adjustment, enter the desired ending balance, and notice how the required adjustment is then obvious from facts reflected in your T-account. The T-accounts would appear as follows:

1.

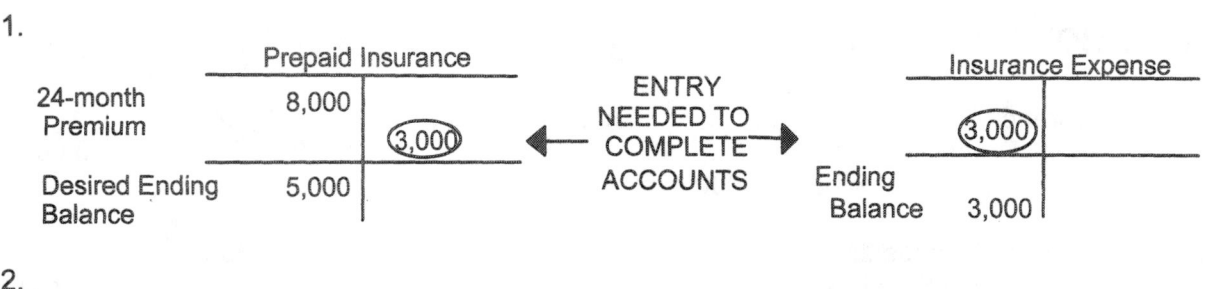

2.

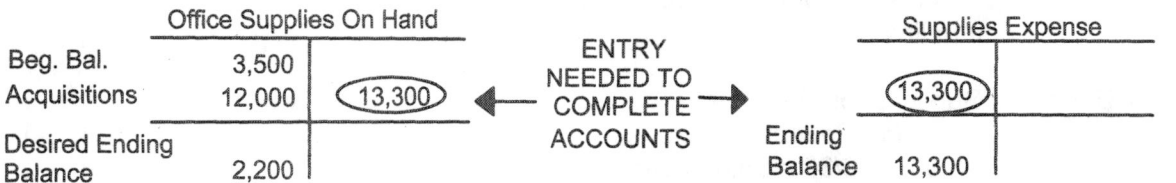

3.

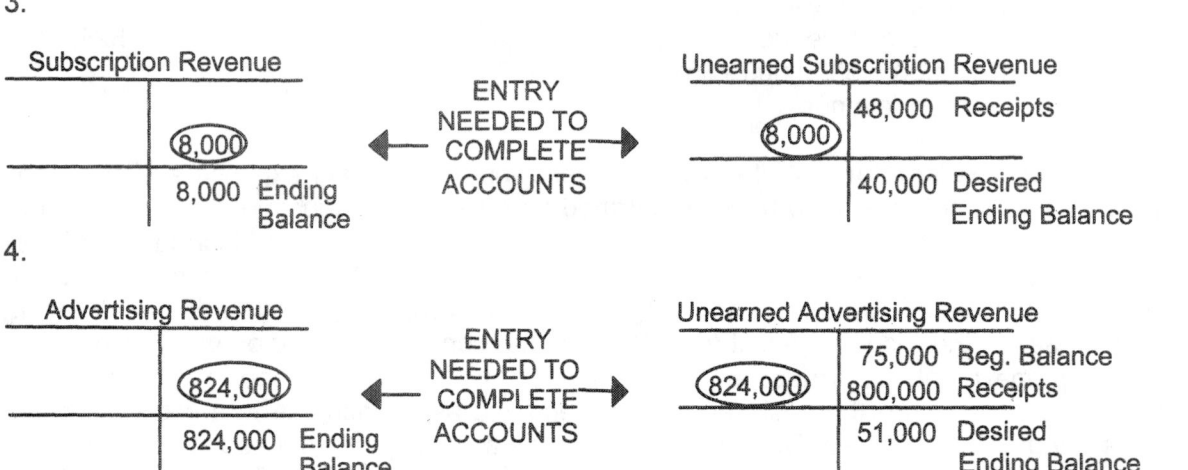

4.

| Advertising Revenue | | Unearned Advertising Revenue | |
|---|---|---|---|
| (824,000) | ENTRY NEEDED TO COMPLETE ACCOUNTS | (824,000) | 75,000 Beg. Balance |
| | | | 800,000 Receipts |
| 824,000 Ending Balance | | | 51,000 Desired Ending Balance |

---

**TIP:** A **prepaid expense** may be called a **deferred expense**. A deferred expense is so named because the recognition of expense is being deferred (put-off) to a future period; thus, a debit is carried on the balance sheet now and will be released to the income statement in a future period when the related benefits are consumed (i.e., when the expense is incurred).

**TIP:** An **unearned revenue** is often called a **deferred revenue** because the recognition of revenue is being deferred to a future period; thus, a credit is carried on the balance sheet now and will be released to the income statement in a future period when the related revenue is earned.

**TIP:** An adjusting entry for prepaid insurance expense (expense paid but not incurred) involves an expense account and an asset account. The expense account is often called Insurance Expense or Expired Insurance. Possible titles for the asset account include Prepaid Insurance, Deferred Insurance Expense, Prepaid Insurance Expense, Deferred Insurance, and Unexpired Insurance.

**TIP:** An adjusting entry for **deferred** rent revenue (revenue collected but not earned) involves a liability account and a revenue account. Possible titles for the liability account include Unearned Rent Revenue, Unearned Rent, Deferred Rent Revenue, Rent Revenue Received in Advance, and Rental Income Collected in Advance. The use of Prepaid Rent Revenue as an account title is not appropriate because the term prepaid usually refers to the payment of cash in advance, not the receipt of cash in advance. The revenue account is often called Rent Revenue or Rental Income or Rent Earned.

## EXERCISE 3-5

**Purpose:**  (L.O. 4, 5, 7) This exercise is designed to test your knowledge of what information is reflected on a trial balance, an adjusted trial balance, and a post-closing trial balance.

The following selected list of accounts are only a few taken from the trial balance at December 31, 2010 for Yasmin's Card Haven Corporation:

| Account | Trial Balance Dec. 31, 2010 | Adjusted Trial Balance Dec. 31, 2010 | Post-Closing Trial Balance Dec. 31, 2010 |
|---|---|---|---|
| Cash | $ 40,000 | | |
| Land | 250,000 | | |
| Prepaid Insurance | 36,000 | | |
| Insurance Expense | -0- | | |
| Interest Expense | 5,900 | | |
| Interest Payable | -0- | | |
| Note Payable | 50,000 | | |
| Rent Revenue | -0- | | |
| Unearned Rent Revenue | 24,000 | | |
| Common Stock | 310,000 | | |
| Retained Earnings | 79,000 | | |

## Instructions
(a)  In the Adjusted Trial Balance column, for each account, indicate if the balance of the account on the Adjusted Trial Balance is most likely to be the **SAME** amount as on the Trial Balance or a **DIFFERENT** amount. Explain the reasoning for your answers.

(b)  In the Post-closing Trial Balance column, for each account, indicate if the balance of the account on the Post-Closing Trial Balance is most likely to be the **SAME** amount as on the Adjusted Trial Balance or a **DIFFERENT** amount. Explain the reasoning for your answers.

**TIP:** The list of all open accounts in the general ledger and their balances is called the **trial balance**. A company may prepare a trial balance at any time. A trial balance is always prepared at the end of an accounting period as an initial step in the process of preparing financial statements. It verifies that the equality of debits and credits has been maintained during the recording and posting of transactions throughout the accounting period. The trial balance taken after all adjusting entries have been made and posted is called an **adjusted trial balance**. A trial balance taken immediately after closing entries have been made and posted is called a **post-closing** or **after-closing trial balance.**

## SOLUTION TO EXERCISE 3-5

| Account | Trial Balance Dec. 31, 2010 | Adjusted Trial Balance Dec. 31, 2010 | Post-Closing Trial Balance Dec. 31, 2010 |
|---|---|---|---|
| Cash | $ 40,000 | SAME | SAME |
| Land | 250,000 | SAME | SAME |
| Prepaid Insurance | 36,000 | DIFFERENT | SAME |
| Insurance Expense | -0- | DIFFERENT | DIFFERENT |
| Interest Expense | 5,900 | DIFFERENT | DIFFERENT |
| Interest Payable | -0- | DIFFERENT | SAME |
| Note Payable | 50,000 | SAME | SAME |
| Rent Revenue | -0- | DIFFERENT | DIFFERENT |
| Unearned Rent Revenue | 24,000 | DIFFERENT | SAME |
| Common Stock | 310,000 | SAME | SAME |
| Retained Earnings | 79,000 | SAME | DIFFERENT |

**Approach:** Think about the types of accounts that are involved in adjusting entries. These include:

(1) Prepaid Expenses (such as Prepaid Insurance, Prepaid Rent, Supplies on Hand, and Unexpired Advertising).

(2) Unearned Revenues (such as Rent Received in Advance, Unearned Subscription Revenue, and Unearned Fees).

(3) Accrued Receivables (such as Interest Receivable, Fees Receivable, and Commission Receivable).

(4)  Accrued Payables (such as Interest Payable, Taxes Payable, and Utilities Payable).

(5)  Revenue and Expense accounts related to the foregoing four items (such as Insurance Expense, Rent Expense, Supplies Expense, Advertising Expense, Rent Revenue, Subscription Revenue, Fees Earned, Interest Revenue, Fees Revenue, Commissions Earned, Interest Expense, Taxes Expense and Utilities Expense).

(6)  Depreciation and amortization expense (such as Depreciation Expense and Amortization of Patent Expense) and the related real accounts (Accumulated Depreciation and Patents).

An account involved in an adjusting entry will have its balance changed by that entry so its balance on the Adjusted Trial will be **DIFFERENT** than its balance on the first (unadjusted) Trial Balance.

Accounts unaffected by adjusting entries will have the **SAME** balance on both the Adjusted Trial Balance and the Trial Balance.

Only accounts that are closed (temporary accounts — revenue, expense, and dividends accounts) will have a **DIFFERENT** balance on the Post-closing Trial Balance when compared with the Adjusted Trial Balance.

**Explanation:** Balance sheet accounts such as Cash, Land, Investments, Note Payable, Bonds Payable, and Common Stock are rarely affected by an adjusting entry [except when an error is discovered, which requires a correcting entry, or when there is an impairment loss such as discussed in **Chapter 5** or when a bank reconciliation discloses that some minor adjustments are needed to Cash (see **Chapter 7**)].

Balance Sheet accounts such as Prepaid Insurance Expense, Interest Payable, and Unearned Rent Revenue are real accounts involved in adjusting entries; but being real accounts, they are **never** closed.

Income Statement accounts such as Insurance Expense and Rent Revenue are accounts involved in adjusting entries and are temporary so they are closed at the end of an accounting period.

## EXERCISE 3-6

**Purpose:** (L.O. 5) This exercise will illustrate the preparation of adjusting entries from an unadjusted trial balance and additional data.

Opey's Equipment Rentals, Inc. began business in 2006. The following list of accounts and their balances represents the unadjusted trial balance of Opey's Equipment Rentals, Inc. at December 31, 2010, the end of the annual accounting period.

**OPEY'S EQUIPMENT RENTALS, INC.**
**Trial Balance**
**December 31, 2010**

|  | Debit | Credit |
|---|---|---|
| Cash | $ 16,500 | |
| Prepaid Insurance | 4,320 | |
| Supplies | 13,200 | |
| Land | 62,000 | |
| Building | 50,000 | |
| Equipment | 130,000 | |
| Accumulated Depreciation    Building | | $ 10,000 |
| Accumulated Depreciation    Equipment | | 52,000 |
| Note Payable | | 50,000 |
| Accounts Payable | | 9,310 |
| Unearned Rent Revenue | | 10,200 |
| Common Stock | | 30,000 |
| Retained Earnings | | 60,660 |
| Dividends | 31,000 | |
| Rent Revenue | | 161,960 |
| Salaries Expense | 70,600 | |
| Interest Expense | 3,500 | |
| Miscellaneous Expense | 3,010 | |
| | $384,130 | $384,130 |

**Additional data:**

1. On November 1, 2010, Opey received $10,200 rent from a lessee for a 12-month equipment lease beginning on that date and credited Unearned Rent Revenue for the entire collection.
2. Per a physical observation at December 31, 2010, Opey determines that supplies costing $2,200 were on hand at the balance sheet date. The cost of supplies is debited to an asset account when purchased.
3. Prepaid Insurance contains the premium cost of a policy that is for a 3-year term and was taken out on May 1, 2010.
4. The cost of the building is being depreciated at a rate of 5% per year.
5. The cost of the equipment is being depreciated at a rate of 10% per year.
6. The note payable bears interest at 12% per year. Interest is payable each August 1. The $50,000 principal is due in full on August 1, 2015.
7. At December 31, 2010, Opey has some equipment in the hands of renters who have used the equipment but have not yet been billed. They will make payment of $1,400 on January 2, 2011.
8. Employees are paid total salaries of $6,400 every other Friday for a two-week period ending on that payday. December 31, 2010 falls on a Monday. The last payday of the year is the last Friday in the year. The work week is Monday through Friday.

**Instructions**

(a) Prepare the year-end adjusting entries in general journal form using the information above.

(b) Prepare an adjusted trial balance at December 31, 2010.

## SOLUTION TO EXERCISE 3-6

(a) 1. Unearned Rent Revenue ....................................................... 1,700
     Rent Revenue .............................................................    1,700
       (To record rent revenue earned: $10,200 X 2/12 = $1,700)

  2. Supplies Expense ................................................................ 11,000
     Supplies........................................................................    11,000
       (To record supplies used: $13,200 - $2,200 = $11,000)

  3. Insurance Expense .............................................................. 960
     Prepaid Insurance .......................................................    960
       (To record insurance expired: $4,320 X 8/36 = $960)

  4. Depreciation Expense   Building ........................................... 2,500
     Accumulated Depreciation   Building ..............................    2,500
       (To record annual depreciation on building:
       $50,000 X  5% = $2,500)

  5. Depreciation Expense   Equipment....................................... 13,000
     Accumulated Depreciation   Equipment...........................    13,000
       (To record annual depreciation on equipment:
       $130,000 X 10% = $13,000)

  6. Interest Expense................................................................. 2,500
     Interest Payable ...........................................................    2,500
       (To record interest accrued on note:
       $50,000 X 12% X 5/12 = $2,500)

  7. Accounts Receivable (or Rent Receivable) ........................... 1,400
     Rent Revenue ..............................................................    1,400
       (To record accrued revenue)

  8. Salaries Expense................................................................ 640
     Salaries Payable ..........................................................    640
       (To record accrued salaries: $6,400 X 1/10 = $640)

**Approach and Explanation:** Identify each item as involving: (1) a prepaid expense, (2) an unearned revenue, (3) an accrued revenue, or (4) an accrued expense. From the facts, determine the existing account balances. Read the facts carefully to determine the desired account balances for financial statements in accordance with generally accepted accounting principles (cost principle, revenue recognition principle, matching principle, etc.). Determine the adjusting entries necessary to bring existing account balances to the appropriate account balances.

1. On November 1, 2010, cash was received and recorded as follows:

   Cash ......................................................................... 10,200

     Unearned Rent Revenue.......................................... 10,200

   This situation involves unearned revenue. At December 31, 2010, before adjustment, there is an Unearned Rent Revenue account with a balance of $10,200. The amount unearned at that date is $10,200 X 10/12 = $8,500. Therefore, an adjusting entry is necessary to transfer the $1,700 earned from the Unearned Rent Revenue account to an earned revenue account.

2. This situation involves a prepaid expense. All supplies are charged to an asset account, Supplies, when purchased. Therefore, Supplies has an unadjusted balance of $13,200, which reflects the balance at the beginning of the year plus the cost of all supplies acquired during the year. Supplies on hand of $2,200 are to appear on the balance sheet. Thus, $11,000 of consumed supplies must be transferred from the asset account to an expense account in an adjusting entry.

3. This item involves a prepaid expense. The Prepaid Insurance account reflects a $4,320 balance which represents the cost of a three-year premium. That three-year period began on May 1, 2010. Therefore, eight of the total 36 months have gone by and the cost of the eight month's coverage ($960) has expired. The expired portion must be transferred from the asset account to an expense account. This will leave 28 months of coverage ($4,320 X 28/36 = $3,360 or $4,320 - $960 = $3,360) in the asset account, Prepaid Insurance, to be charged to expense in future periods.

4. This item involves a long-term prepaid expense. A long-lived tangible item such as building or equipment represents a bundle of benefits when it is acquired. These benefits are to be used up (consumed) over the course of the asset's estimated service life.

   **Depreciation** is a term that refers to the process of allocating the cost of a long-lived tangible asset to the periods benefited from its use. The process of depreciation is necessary to comply with the matching principle. The building or equipment is used to generate revenue during the period. Consequently, a portion of the bundle of benefits represented by the asset is consumed. There is a cost associated with those consumed benefits. This cost is to be matched with the revenues it helped generate. Thus, an expense is recorded (Depreciation Expense), and an asset is reduced. It is customary, however, to make use of a contra asset account, Accumulated Depreciation, rather than to credit the asset account itself.

5. See the explanation for 4. above. Notice that a credit to Accumulated Depreciation has the same impact as a credit to the account being depreciated (Equipment, for example). Thus, total assets are reduced by the journal entry to record depreciation.

6. This situation involves an accrued expense. Interest is a function of debt balance, interest rate, and time. Interest is due and payable at the end of an interest period. The last interest payment date was August 1, 2010. Thus, interest incurred and not yet paid or payable amounts to five months worth or $2,500 ($50,000 X 12% X 5/12 = $2,500). The accrued interest is recorded by an increase to the Interest Expense account and a credit to a liability account, Interest Payable. (Note the balance before adjustment in the Interest Expense account represents seven months of interest. On August 1, 2010, an interest payment of $6,000 was made and $3,500 of that represented the interest from January 1, 2010 through July 31, 2010. The other $2,500 paid for interest would have been accrued earlier at the end of 2009.)

7. This situation involves an accrual of revenue. Revenue has been earned but has not yet been billed or recorded or received. The "earned" part is recorded in the adjusting entry by a credit to Rent Revenue. The "not received" part is recorded by a debit to Accounts Receivable or Rent Receivable. Thus, the appropriate adjusting entry increases assets and revenues earned.

8. This item involves an accrued expense. An accrued expense is an expense incurred but not yet paid. The salary for the last two work days of the year has been incurred because the employees have contributed their labor services for a period of time that has passed. The employees will not be paid until eleven calendar days after the balance sheet date. The accrued expense is recorded at the balance sheet date by a debit to an expense account and a credit to a liability account.

(b)

**OPEY'S EQUIPMENT RENTALS, INC.**
**Adjusted Trial Balance**
**December 31, 2010**

| | | Debit | Credit |
|---|---|---|---|
| | Cash | $ 16,500 | |
| * | Accounts Receivable | 1,400 | |
| | Prepaid Insurance | 3,360 | |
| | Supplies | 2,200 | |
| | Land | 62,000 | |
| | Building | 50,000 | |
| | Equipment | 130,000 | |
| | Accumulated Depreciation   Building | | $ 12,500 |
| | Accumulated Depreciation   Equipment | | 65,000 |
| | Note Payable | | 50,000 |
| | Accounts Payable | | 9,310 |
| * | Interest Payable | | 2,500 |
| * | Salaries Payable | | 640 |
| | Unearned Rent Revenue | | 8,500 |
| | Common Stock | | 30,000 |
| | Retained Earnings | | 60,660 |
| | Dividends | 31,000 | |
| | Rent Revenue | | 165,060 |
| | Salaries Expense | 71,240 | |
| | Interest Expense | 6,000 | |
| * | Supplies Expense | 11,000 | |
| * | Insurance Expense | 960 | |
| * | Depreciation Expense   Building | 2,500 | |
| * | Depreciation Expense   Equipment | 13,000 | |
| * | Miscellaneous Expense | 3,010 | |
| | | $404,170 | $404,170 |

\* Although these accounts are listed in a logical order on this adjusted trial balance when you consider the item's position on financial statements, account titles which are used in adjusting entries but that do **not** appear on the unadjusted trial balance are typically listed on the adjusted trial at the **end** of the listing of accounts which appeared on the unadjusted trial.

TIP:    Now that the adjusted trial balance is complete, think about where the account balances are to go in the preparation of financial statements. (See the next exercise to do just that).

## EXERCISE 3-7

**Purpose:** (L.O. 6)  This exercise illustrates how the items appearing on an adjusted trial balance get reported on the financial statements.

## Instructions

Using the items on the Adjusted Trial Balance at December 31, 2010 for Opey's Equipment Rentals, Inc., in the **SOLUTION TO EXERCISE 3-6**, prepare the following:

(a)  Income Statement for the year ended December 31, 2010.
(b)  Retained Earnings Statement for the year ended December 31, 2010.
(c)  Balance Sheet (unclassified) at December 31, 2010.

## SOLUTION TO EXERCISE 3-7

The solution shown here incorporates the Adjusted Trial Balance with arrows to help you to see the logical disposition of each item on the Adjusted Trial Balance as well as the "articulation" of these three basic financial statements.

# OPEY'S EQUIPMENT RENTALS, INC.
## Adjusted Trial Balance
### December 31, 2010

| Account | Debit | Credit |
|---|---|---|
| Cash | $ 16,500 | |
| Accounts Receivable | 1,400 | |
| Prepaid Insurance | 3,360 | |
| Supplies | 2,200 | |
| Land | 62,000 | |
| Building | 50,000 | |
| Equipment | 130,000 | |
| Accumulated Depreciation—Building | | $ 12,500 |
| Accumulated Depreciation—Equipment | | 65,000 |
| Note Payable | | 50,000 |
| Accounts Payable | | 9,310 |
| Interest Payable | | 2,500 |
| Salaries Payable | | 640 |
| Unearned Rent Revenue | | 8,500 |
| Common Stock | | 30,000 |
| Retained Earnings | | 60,660 |
| Dividends | 31,000 | |
| Rent Revenue | | 165,060 |
| Salaries Expense | 71,240 | |
| Interest Expense | 6,000 | |
| Supplies Expense | 11,000 | |
| Insurance Expense | 960 | |
| Depreciation Expense—Building | 2,500 | |
| Depreciation Expense—Equipment | 13,000 | |
| Miscellaneous Expense | 3,010 | |
| | $404,170 | $404,170 |

(a)

# OPEY'S EQUIPMENT RENTALS, INC.
## Income Statement
### For the Year Ended December 31, 2010

| | | |
|---|---|---|
| Revenues | | |
| Rent revenue | | $165,060 |
| Expenses | | |
| Salaries expense | $71,240 | |
| Interest expense | 6,000 | |
| Supplies expense | 11,000 | |
| Insurance expense | 960 | |
| Depreciation expense—building | 2,500 | |
| Depreciation expense—equipment | 13,000 | |
| Miscellaneous expense | 3,010 | |
| Total expenses | | 107,710 |
| Net income | | $ 57,350 |

(b)

# OPEY'S EQUIPMENT RENTALS, INC.
## Retained Earnings Statement
### For the Year Ended December 31, 2010

| | |
|---|---|
| Retained earnings, January 1 | $60,660 |
| Add: Net income | 57,350 |
| | 118,010 |
| Less: Dividends | 31,000 |
| Retained earnings, December 31 | $87,010 |

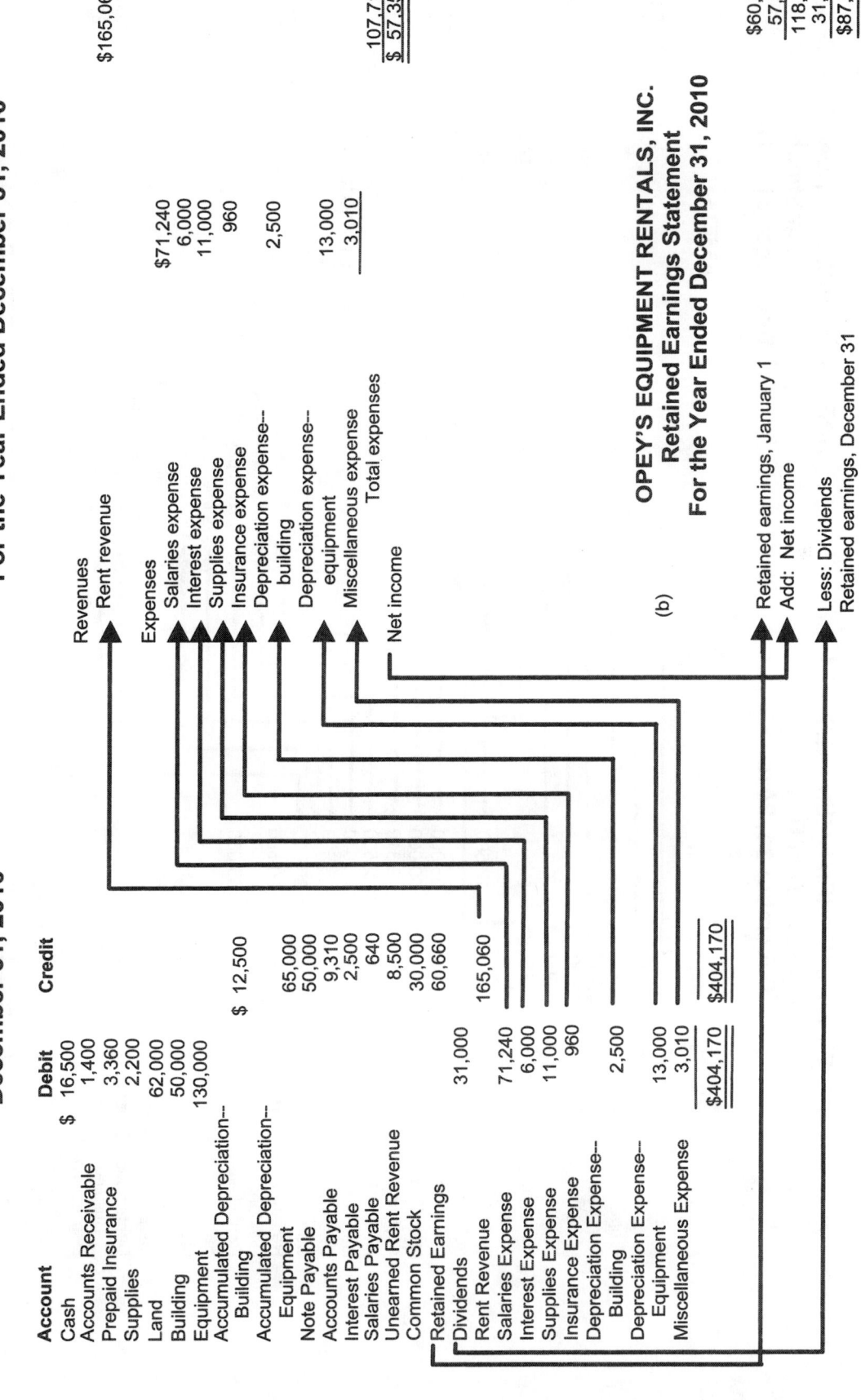

# OPEY'S EQUIPMENT RENTALS, INC.
## Adjusted Trial Balance
### December 31, 2010

| Account | Debit | Credit |
|---|---|---|
| Cash | $ 16,500 | |
| Accounts Receivable | 1,400 | |
| Prepaid Insurance | 3,360 | |
| Supplies | 2,200 | |
| Land | 62,000 | |
| Building | 50,000 | |
| Equipment | 130,000 | |
| Accumulated Depreciation—Building | | $ 12,500 |
| Accumulated Depreciation—Equipment | | 65,000 |
| Note Payable | | 50,000 |
| Accounts Payable | | 9,310 |
| Interest Payable | | 2,500 |
| Salaries Payable | | 640 |
| Unearned Rent Revenue | | 8,500 |
| Common Stock | | 30,000 |
| Retained Earnings | | 60,660 |
| Dividends | 31,000 | |
| Rent Revenue | | 165,060 |
| Salaries Expense | 71,240 | |
| Interest Expense | 6,000 | |
| Supplies Expense | 11,000 | |
| Insurance Expense | 960 | |
| Depreciation Expense—Building | 2,500 | |
| Depreciation Expense—Equipment | 13,000 | |
| Miscellaneous Expense | 3,010 | |
| | $404,170 | $404,170 |

(c)

# OPEY'S EQUIPMENT RENTALS, INC.
## Balance Sheet
### December 31, 2010

## ASSETS

| | | |
|---|---|---|
| Cash | | $ 16,500 |
| Accounts receivable | | 1,400 |
| Prepaid insurance | | 3,360 |
| Supplies | | 2,200 |
| Land | | 62,000 |
| Building | $ 50,000 | |
| Less: Accumulated depreciation | 12,500 | 37,500 |
| Equipment | 130,000 | |
| Less: Accumulated depreciation | 65,000 | 65,000 |
| Total assets | | $187,960 |

## LIABILITIES AND STOCKHOLDERS' EQUITY

| | | |
|---|---|---|
| Liabilities | | |
| Note payable | | $ 50,000 |
| Accounts payable | | 9,310 |
| Interest payable | | 2,500 |
| Salaries payable | | 640 |
| Unearned rent revenue | | 8,500 |
| Total liabilities | | 70,950 |
| Stockholders' equity | | |
| Common stock | | 30,000 |
| Retained earnings | | 87,010 |
| Total liabilities and stockholders' equity | | $187,960 |

Balance at Dec. 31
from Retained Earnings Statement

## EXERCISE 3-8

**Purpose:**   (L.O. 7) This exercise will review the preparation of closing entries.

The adjusted trial balance for the Ed & Mary Shuck Corporation at December 31, 2010 appears as follows:

**Ed & Mary Shuck Corporation**
**ADJUSTED TRIAL BALANCE**
**December 31, 2010**

| | Debit | Credit |
|---|---|---|
| Cash | $ 4,600 | |
| Accounts Receivable | 2,200 | |
| Supplies on Hand | 2,100 | |
| Accounts Payable | | $ 700 |
| Common Stock | | 5,000 |
| Retained Earnings (January 1, 2010) | | 1,300 |
| Service Revenue | | 4,900 |
| Rent Expense | 800 | |
| Advertising Expense | 300 | |
| Cleaning Expense | 200 | |
| Utilities Expense | 80 | |
| Utilities Payable | | 80 |
| Supplies Expense | 1,700 | |
| | $11,980 | $11,980 |

## Instructions
(a)   Prepare the appropriate closing entries at December 31, 2010.
(b)   Explain why closing entries are necessary.

## Solution to Exercise 3-8

(a)   Service Revenue ........ 4,900
      Income Summary ........ 4,900
        (To close the revenue account to Income Summary)

Income Summary ........ 3,080
      Rent Expense ........ 800
      Advertising Expense ........ 300
      Cleaning Expense ........ 200
      Utilities Expense ........ 80
      Supplies Expense ........ 1,700
        (To close expense accounts to Income Summary)

Income Summary ........ 1,820
      Retained Earnings ........ 1,820
        (To close Income Summary to Retained Earnings)
        ($4,900 total revenues - $3,080 total expenses = $1,820 credit balance in Income Summary before closing)

(b)     The major reason closing entries are needed is that they prepare the temporary (nominal) accounts for the recording of transactions of the next accounting period. Closing entries produce a zero balance in each of the temporary accounts so that they can be used to accumulate data pertaining to the next accounting period. Because of closing entries, the revenues of 2011 are not commingled with the revenues of the prior period (2010). A second reason closing entries are needed is that the Retained Earnings account will reflect a true balance only after closing entries have been completed. Closing entries formally recognize in the ledger the transfer of net income (or loss) and dividends declared to retained earnings as indicated in the statement of retained earnings.

> **TIP:**   The Income Summary account is used only in the closing process. Before it is closed, the balance in this account must equal the net income or net loss figure for the period.
>
> **TIP:**   Where do you look for the accounts (and their amounts) to be closed? If a work sheet is used, you can use the amounts listed in the Income Statement column pair and the balance of the Dividends Declared (or Owner's Drawing) account. If a work sheet is not used, you must refer to the temporary accounts (after adjustment) in the ledger to determine the balances to be closed.

## *ILLUSTRATION 3-2
## CONVERSION FROM CASH BASIS ACCOUNTING TO
## ACCRUAL BASIS ACCOUNTING (L.O. 8)

With the **cash basis of accounting,** a revenue item is reported in the time period when the related cash is received from the customer and an expense is recorded in the time period in which the related cash is paid. Cash basis financial statements are **not** in conformity with generally accepted accounting principles. Most companies use the **accrual basis of accounting**, whereby a revenue item is reported in the time period in which it is earned and an expense item is reported in the time period in which it is incurred.

Revenue that is earned during the period but not collected (accrued revenue) results in reporting an asset (receivable) on the balance sheet. Revenue that has been received but not earned (unearned or deferred revenue) results in reporting a liability (unearned revenue) on the balance sheet. Expense that is incurred but not paid (accrued expense) results in reporting a liability (payable) on the balance sheet. Expense that has paid but not incurred (prepaid or deferred expense) results in reporting an asset (prepaid expense).

**To Convert Cash Receipts to Revenues Earned:**

```
    Cash Received from Customers
-   Beginning Accounts Receivable
+   Ending Accounts Receivable
+   Beginning Unearned Revenues
-   Ending Unearned Revenues
=   Revenues Earned
```

**Explanation:** The balance of accounts receivable at the beginning of the period represents revenues earned in a prior period that are collected in the current period; ending accounts receivable stem from revenues earned in the current period that are not yet collected. Beginning unearned revenues represent cash collections in a prior period (not the current period) that are for revenues earned in the current period. Ending unearned revenues come from collections during the current period that are not yet recognized as earned revenues.

**To Convert Cash Payments to Operating Expenses:**

```
    Cash Paid for Operating Expenses
+   Beginning Prepaid Expenses
-   Ending Prepaid Expenses
-   Beginning Accrued Payables
+   Ending Accrued Payables
=   Operating Expenses Incurred
      (Excluding Depreciation and
      Bad Debt Expense)
```

**Explanation:** Beginning prepaid expenses represent amounts recognized as expense in the current period for which cash payments are not made in the current period. (The cash payments occurred in a prior period.) Ending prepaids stem from cash payments in the current period for expenses not recognized in the current period. (The expense recognition is being deferred to a future period.) Beginning accrued payables come from expenses recognized in a prior period (not the current year) that require cash payments during the current period. Ending accrued payables stem from expenses recognized during the current year that have not yet been paid.

> **TIP:** Noncash expenses such as depreciation on plant assets, bad debt expense, amortization of intangibles, and amortization of discount on notes payable are ignored in the above format. These items would also have to be considered in computing total operating expenses incurred or in computing net income on an accrual basis.

## EXERCISE 3-9

**Purpose:** (L.O. 5, 8) This exercise will point out the relationships that exist between cash data and accrual amounts when certain balance sheet accounts increase during the period.

### Instructions

Complete each of the blanks below with one of the following, whichever is appropriate:

>    >    symbol for "is greater than"
>    <    symbol for "is less than"
> or   =    symbol for "equals."

1. On a comparative balance sheet, if an accrued receivable increased, then revenue earned _____ cash received so net income on the accrual basis _____ income on a cash basis.

2. On a comparative balance sheet, if an unearned revenue increased, then revenue earned _____ cash received so net income on the accrual basis _____ income on a cash basis.

3. On a comparative balance sheet, if a prepaid expense increased, then expense incurred _____ cash paid so net income on the accrual basis _____ income on a cash basis.

4. On a comparative balance sheet, if an accrued payable increased, then expense incurred _____ cash paid so net income on the accrual basis _____ income on a cash basis.

### Solution to Exercise 3-9

| 1. | > | 2. | < | 3. | < | 4. | > |
|----|---|----|---|----|---|----|---|
|    | > |    | < |    | > |    | < |

| | |
|---|---|
| **TIP:** | Revenue that is earned during the period but not collected (accrued revenue) results in reporting an asset (receivable) on the balance sheet. Revenue that has been received but not earned (unearned or deferred revenue) results in reporting a liability (unearned revenue) on the balance sheet. Expense that is incurred but not paid (accrued expense) results in reporting a liability (payable) on the balance sheet. Expense that has been paid but not incurred (prepaid or deferred expense) results in reporting an asset (prepaid expense). |
| **TIP:** | Notice that the signs are the **same** in the answers to 1 and 2 but the signs are **different** in the answers to 3 and 4. The reason is that **revenue** is a **positive** component of income and **expense** is a **negative** component of income. |
| **TIP:** | A comparative balance sheet is a balance sheet with amounts shown for at least two different dates; for example, at the end of the current period (December 31, 2010) and at the end of the prior period (December 31, 2009). The date at the end of the prior period (end of day December 31, 2009) is the same as the date of the beginning of the current period (beginning of day January 1, 2010). |

## *EXERCISE 3-10

**Purpose:**     (L.O. 8) This exercise illustrates the different results that are obtained when the accrual and the cash methods of accounting are used.

Annabell's Specialty Service Shop, a proprietorship business, conducted the following transactions during the first week in March.

1.  Purchased supplies for $1,800. Paid 20% down; remaining 80% to be paid in 10 days.
2.  Paid $30 for newspaper advertising to appear this week.
3.  Collected $1,400 from customers on account.
4.  Performed services at a $1,620 charge to customers; however, cash payment is not due until next week.
5.  Paid $600 rent for the month of March.
6.  Performed services for $280 cash.
7.  Paid part-time sales clerk $40 wages for the week.
8.  Wrote a check for $100 to the owner for her personal use.
9.  Consumed supplies of $1,400.

### Instructions
(a)     Compute the net income for the week, using the cash method of accounting.
(b)     Compute the net income for the week, using the accrual method of accounting.
Show your computations in good form.

### Solution to Exercise 3-10

(a)     **Cash Method:**

| | | |
|---|---:|---:|
| Cash Received from Customers ($1,400 + $280) | | $1,680 |
| Less:  Payment for Supplies ($1,800 x 20%) | $ 360 | |
|        Payment for Advertising | 30 | |
|        Payment for Rent | 600 | |
|        Payment to Employee | 40 | 1,030 |
| Net Income (cash method) | | $   650 |

> **TIP:**     Using the **cash basis** (method) of accounting, revenues are recognized (reported) in the period in which they are **received** and expenses are recognized in the period in which they are **paid**. The cash basis is **not** in accordance with generally accepted accounting principles.

(b)  **Accrual Method:**

| | | |
|---|---:|---:|
| Service Revenue ($1,620 + $280) | | $ 1,900 |
| Less: Operating Expenses | | |
| Supplies Expense | $1,400 | |
| Advertising Expense | 30 | |
| Rent Expense ($600 ÷ 4) | 150 | |
| Wages Expense | 40 | 1,620 |
| Net Income (accrual method) | | $   280 |

> **TIP:** Withdrawals by owner ($100) do **not** enter into the income computations.
>
> **TIP:** Using the **accrual basis** (method) of accounting, revenues are recognized in the period in which they are **earned** and expenses are recognized in the period in which they are **incurred**.
>
> Accrual basis accounting is theoretically preferable to the cash basis because it provides information about future cash inflows and outflows associated with earnings activities as soon as a company can estimate these cash flows with an acceptable degree of certainty. That is, accrual basis accounting aids in predicting future cash flows by reporting transactions and events with cash consequences at the time the transactions and events occur, rather than when the cash is received and paid.

## *EXERCISE 3-11

**Purpose:** (L.O. 8) This exercise will illustrate the conversion of cash data to accrual data.

Dr. Jeffrey Prickett, M.D., maintains the accounting records of the Holistic Center on a cash basis. During 2010, Dr. Prickett collected $305,400 from his patients and paid $91,200 in expenses. Information regarding the amount of receivables (accrued revenues), unearned revenues, payables for accrued expenses, and prepaid expenses is as follows:

| | Balance at December 31, 2009 | Balance at December 31, 2010 |
|---|---:|---:|
| Accounts receivable | $45,000 | $51,000 |
| Unearned revenues | 2,000 | 2,800 |
| Accrued payables | 5,200 | 4,980 |
| Prepaid expenses | 3,000 | 8,000 |

## Instructions
(a)  Prepare a schedule to convert Dr. Prickett's cash basis income of $214,200 (excess of $305,400 cash collections over $91,200 cash disbursements) for the year 2010 to net income on an accrual basis.

(b)  Describe any items other than the above that may have to be considered in converting cash basis income to accrual basis income.

## Solution to Exercise 3-11

(a)
| | |
|---|---:|
| Cash collections from patients | $305,400 |
| Accounts receivable, beginning of year | (45,000) |
| Accounts receivable, end of year | 51,000 |
| Unearned revenue, beginning of year | 2,000 |
| Unearned revenue, end of year | (2,800) |
| Revenues earned during 2010 | $310,600 |
| | |
| Cash payments for expense items | $91,200 |
| Accrued payables, beginning of year | (5,200) |
| Accrued payables, end of year | 4,980 |
| Prepaid expenses, beginning of year | 3,000 |
| Prepaid expenses, end of year | (8,000) |
| Expenses incurred during 2010 | 85,980 |
| | |
| Revenues earned during 2010 | 310,600 |
| Expenses incurred during 2010 | 85,980 |
| Net income on accrual basis for 2010 | $224,620 |

**TIP:** An alternate schedule would be as follows:

| | |
|---|---:|
| Cash basis income for 2010 | $214,200 |
| Accounts receivable, beginning of year | (45,000) |
| Accounts receivable end of year | 51,000 |
| Unearned revenues, beginning of year | 2,000 |
| Unearned revenues, end of year | (2,800) |
| Accrued payables, beginning of year | 5,200 |
| Accrued payables, end of year | (4,980) |
| Prepaid expenses, beginning of year | (3,000) |
| Prepaid expenses, end of year | 8,000 |
| Net income on accrual basis for 2010 | $224,620 |

Notice the differences between this computation and the first solution. When converting cash basis income to net income, the balances of accounts stemming from revenue type transactions (Accounts Receivable and Unearned Revenues) are handled the same exact way as they were treated in the conversion of cash collections to revenues earned because revenues are a positive component of net income. However, when converting cash basis income to net income, the balances of accounts stemming from expense type transactions (Accrued Payable and Prepaid Expense) are handled the opposite of the way they were treated in the conversion of cash payments to expenses incurred because expenses are a negative component of net income.

Therefore, the accounts receivable balance of $45,000 at the beginning of the year is deducted from cash collections in 2010 to arrive at revenue earned in 2010 because that $45,000 was collected in 2010 but earned in a prior period. Likewise, the accounts receivable balance of $45,000 at the beginning of the year is also **deducted** from the cash basis income to arrive at net income because that $45,000 was collected in 2010 and reflected in the cash basis income of $214,200 but should not be reflected as revenue earned in the net income on an accrual basis figure.

> In comparison, the accrued payables balance of $5,200 at the beginning of the year 2010 is deducted from cash payments in 2010 to arrive at expenses incurred in 2010 because that $5,200 was paid in 2010 but incurred in a prior period. Thus, the accrued payable balance at the beginning of the year is **added** to the cash basis income figure to arrive at net income on an accrual basis because that $5,200 was paid in 2010 and reflected as a deduction in the cash basis income of $214,200 but should not be reflected as an expense incurred in the net income on an accrual basis figure. An addition is made to negate the negative number reflected in the cash basis income figure.

(b)    In addition to the items above, expense items **not** currently requiring a cash outlay such as:
● depreciation expense
● amortization of intangible assets (patents, etc.)
● amortization of discount on bonds payable
would also have to be added to cash payments to arrive at expenses incurred on an accrual basis. Thus, they would reduce the net income calculation.

## **EXERCISE 3-12

**Purpose:**   (L.O. 9) This exercise will provide practice in determining which adjusting entries may be reversed.

## Instructions
The following represent adjusting entries prepared for the Bent Tree Company at December 31, 2010 (end of the accounting period). The company has the policy of using reversing entries when appropriate. For each adjusting entry below, indicate if it would be appropriate to reverse it at the beginning of 2011. Indicate your answer by circling "yes" or "no."

Yes  No    1.    Deferred Advertising Expense...................... 4,500
                  Advertising Expense .......................... 4,500

Yes  No    2.    Interest Expense.......................... 800
                  Discount on Bonds Payable................ 800

Yes  No    3.    Interest Receivable...................... 690
                  Interest Revenue .................... 690

Yes  No    4.    Unearned Rental Income........................... 900
                  Rental Income.................................. 900

Yes  No    5.    Insurance Expense.................................... 1,600
                  Prepaid Insurance.............................. 1,600

Yes  No    6.    Salaries Expense.......................... 1,100
                  Salaries Payable................................ 1,100

## Solution to Exercise 3-12

| | | | | | |
|---|---|---|---|---|---|
| 1. | Yes | 3. | Yes | 5. | No |
| 2. | No | 4. | No | 6. | Yes |

> **TIP:** A **reversing entry** is an entry made at the very beginning of an accounting period that is the exact opposite of an adjusting entry made at the end of the previous period. The recording of reversing entries is an **optional** step in the accounting cycle. The **purpose** of a reversing entry is to simplify the recording of transactions in the new accounting period. The use of reversing entries does not change the amounts reported in financial statements.

**Approach:** Write down what the related reversing entry would look like and then (1) think about the effects that the reversing entry would have on the account balances in the accounting period that follows the one for which the adjustment was made, and (2) think about whether those effects are appropriate or not. It is appropriate to reverse an adjusting entry involving a deferral (prepaid expense or unearned revenue) **only if** the adjustment increases (rather than decreases) a balance sheet account. It is **always** appropriate to reverse an adjusting entry involving an accrual. It is **never** appropriate to reverse an adjusting entry for depreciation or amortization or bad debts.

**Explanation:**
1. An adjustment for a deferred expense can be reversed if the adjustment increases an asset or liability account. This adjustment increases a prepaid expense (asset) account.
2. Never reverse an adjustment for amortization of a discount or premium.
3. An accrual type adjustment can always be reversed.
4. A reversal of this entry would put back into the Unearned Rental Revenue account the amount that the adjustment indicated has been earned.
5. An adjustment for a deferral can be reversed only if it increases a balance sheet account. This adjustment decreases an asset account.
6. An accrual type adjustment can always be reversed. You can tell the adjusting entry is for an accrued expense because the debit is to an expense account and the credit is to a payable account.

---

## **EXERCISE 3-13

**Purpose:**    (L.O. 9) This exercise will give you practice in identifying adjusting entries that may be reversed.

### Instructions

Refer to **Exercise 3-6** and the **Solution to Exercise 3-6**. Indicate the adjusting entries that can be reversed.

### Solution to Exercise 3-13

Adjusting entries that may be reversed: 6, 7, 8
Adjusting entries that are **not** to be reversed: 1, 2, 3, 4, 5

**Approach and Explanation:**    Think of the types of adjustments and whether they can be reversed. Accrual type adjusting entries can always be reversed. Therefore, items 6, 7, and 8 can be reversed. Items such as depreciation of plant assets, the recognition of bad debts, and amortization of intangibles and discounts and premiums on receivables and payables should never be reversed. Therefore, items 4 and 5 should **not** be reversed. Adjustments involving deferrals can be reversed **if** the original cash entry involved a nominal account (revenue or expense account) rather than a prepaid or unearned account (a real account) and the adjustment **increases** a prepaid expense or unearned revenue account. Therefore, items 1, 2, and 3 should **not** be reversed.

## **ILLUSTRATION 3-3
## SUMMARY OF ADJUSTMENT RELATIONSHIPS
## AND EXPLANATIONS (L.O. 5, 9)

| Type of Adjustment | Account Relationship | Reason for Adjustment | Account Balances Before Adjustment | Adjusting Entry |
|---|---|---|---|---|
| 1. Prepaid Expense | Asset and Expense | (a) Prepaid expense initially recorded in asset account has been consumed; or, | Asset overstated Expense understated | Dr. Expense Cr. Asset |
| | | **(b) Prepaid expense initially recorded in expense account has not been consumed. | Asset understated Expense overstated | Dr. Asset Cr. Expense |
| 2. Unearned Revenue | Liability and Revenue | (a) Unearned revenue initially recorded in liability account has been earned; or, | Liability overstated Revenue understated | Dr. Liability Cr. Revenue |
| | | **(b) Unearned revenue initially recorded in revenue account has not been earned. | Liability understated Revenue overstated | Dr. Revenue Cr. Liability |
| 3. Accrued Expense | Expense and Liability | Expense incurred has not been billed nor paid nor recorded. | Expense understated Liability understated | Dr. Expense Cr. Liability |
| 4. Accrued Revenues | Asset and Revenue | Revenue earned has not been billed nor collected nor recorded. | Asset understated Revenue understated | Dr. Asset Cr. Revenue |

**These situations are addressed in **Appendix 3B** in the text.

**Explanation:**

1.   When expenses are paid for before they are incurred, the payment may either be recorded by a debit to an asset account (prepaid expense) or by a debit to an expense account. At the end of the accounting period, the accounts are adjusted as needed. If the prepayment was initially recorded by use of a prepaid (asset) account, the consumed portion is transferred to an expense account in the adjusting entry. Whereas, if the prepayment was initially recorded by use of an expense account, an adjusting entry is required only if a portion of the expense remains prepaid at the end of the accounting period (in which case the unconsumed portion is transferred to an asset account). (See **Illustration 3-4** for an example.)

2.   When revenues are received before they are earned, the receipt may either be recorded by a credit to a liability account (unearned revenue) or by a credit to a revenue account. At the end of the accounting period, the accounts are adjusted as needed. If the collection was initially recorded by a credit to a liability account (unearned revenue), the earned portion is transferred to a revenue account in the adjusting entry. Whereas, if the collection was initially recorded by use of a revenue account, an adjusting entry is required only if a portion of the revenue remains unearned at the end of the accounting period (in which case the unearned portion is transferred to a liability account). (See **Illustration 3-4** for an example.)

## ILLUSTRATION 3-3 (Continued)

3.   Expenses are often incurred before they are paid. An expense incurred but not yet paid is called an **accrued expense**. If at the end of an accounting period this accrued expense has not been recorded (which is often the case because it usually has not been billed yet by the vendor), it must be recorded by way of an adjusting entry. Expense that accrues with the passage of time (such as interest expense) is a good example of a reason to need an accrued expense (or accrued liability) type adjusting entry.

4.   Revenues are often earned before they are collected. A revenue earned but not received is called an **accrued revenue**. If at the end of an accounting period this accrued revenue has not been recorded (which is often the case because it usually has not been billed yet), it must be recorded by way of an adjusting entry. Revenue that accrues with the passage of time (such as interest revenue) is a good example of a reason to need an accrued revenue (or accrued asset) type adjusting entry.

**TIP:**   Examine each type of adjustment explained above and notice the logic of the resulting entry. For example, an adjustment to recognize supplies used (when the supplies were recorded in an asset account when purchased) should reduce assets and increase expenses.

**TIP:**   Keep in mind that for accrued items (accrued revenues and accrued expenses), the related cash flow **follows** the period in which the relevant revenue or expense is recognized; whereas, with prepayment type items (unearned revenues and prepaid expenses), the related cash flow **precedes** the period in which the relevant revenue or expense is recognized.

For example, assume the accounting period is the calendar year. Consider an accrued expense such as accrued salaries at the end of 2010. An adjusting entry will be recorded at the end of 2010 so the expense will get reported on the 2010 income statement. The related cash payment to employees will take place in the following accounting period (2011, in this case). For another example, consider a prepaid expense such as the prepayment of rent in December 2010 for January 2011 occupancy. The cash payment occurs in December 2010. The expense is incurred and recognized in the following accounting period (January 2011).

## **ILLUSTRATION 3-4
## ALTERNATIVE TREATMENTS OF PREPAID EXPENSES
## AND UNEARNED REVENUES (L.O. 5, 9)

When a company writes a check to pay for an item that affects expense in at least two different time periods (such as for an insurance premium or a license or dues), the bookkeeper may record the payment in one of two ways. Either as a prepaid expense (asset) or as an expense. The first way is used most often in introductory accounting textbooks; the second is used most often in the real world. Regardless of the way the payment is recorded, an appropriate adjusting entry will be made at the end of the accounting period so that correct balances appear on the income statement and the balance sheet. For example, a $1,200 payment is made on April 1, 2010, for a twelve-month insurance premium covering the time between April 1, 2010 and March 31, 2011. (Assume a calendar year reporting period.) A comparison of the two possible approaches appears below.

| Prepayment (Cash Paid) Initially Debited to Asset Account | | | OR | Prepayment (Cash Paid) Initially Debited to Expense Account | | |
|---|---|---|---|---|---|---|
| 4/1 | Prepaid Insurance | 1,200 | | 4/1 | Insurance Expense | 1,200 |
| | Cash | | 1,200 | | Cash | | 1,200 |
| 12/31 | Insurance Expense | 900 | | 12/31 | Prepaid Insurance | 300 |
| | Prepaid Insurance | | 900 | | Insurance Expense | | 300 |

After posting the entries, the accounts appear as follows:

| Prepaid Insurance | | | | | Prepaid Insurance | | | |
|---|---|---|---|---|---|---|---|---|
| 4/1 | 1,200 | 12/31 Adj. | 900 | | 12/31 Adj. | 300 | | |
| 12/31 Bal. | 300 | | | | | | | |

| Insurance Expense | | | | | Insurance Expense | | | |
|---|---|---|---|---|---|---|---|---|
| 12/31 Adj. | 900 | | | | 4/1 | 1,200 | 12/31 Adj. | 300 |
| | | | | | 12/31 Bal. | 900 | | |

Notice that regardless of the path, you end up at the same place—with a balance of $300 in Prepaid Insurance and a balance of $900 in Insurance Expense. That was your objective—to report balances in accordance with the accrual basis of accounting.

> **TIP:** Reversing entries are never required. But if it is company policy to use reversing entries where appropriate, would either or both of the above adjusting entries get reversed? The adjusting entry illustrated in the left column would **not** get reversed since to do so would result in reestablishing an asset amount that the adjusting entry indicated had expired. The adjusting entry illustrated in the right column **can be** reversed since a reversing entry will record $300 of insurance expense in the new accounting period (2011) which is the period we expect the remaining $300 of premium to pertain.

## Illustration 3-4 (Continued)

When a company receives cash from a customer in advance of earning the related revenue, the bookkeeper may record the receipt in one of two ways. Either as an unearned revenue (liability) or as an earned revenue. The first way is used most often in introductory accounting textbooks; the second is used most often in the real world. Regardless of the way the receipt is recorded, an appropriate adjusting entry will be made at the end of the accounting period so that correct balances appear on the income statement and the balance sheet. For example, $1,200 is received on May 1, 2010, for a twelve-month magazine subscription covering the time between May 1, 2010 and April 30, 2011. (Assume a calendar year reporting period.) A comparison of the two possible approaches appears below:

| Unearned Revenue (Cash Received) Initially Credited to Liability Account | | | OR | Unearned Revenue (Cash Received) Initially Credited to Revenue Account | | |
|---|---|---|---|---|---|---|
| 5/1 | Cash | 1,200 | | 5/1 | Cash | 1,200 |
| | Unearned Sub. Rev. | 1,200 | | | Subscription Revenue | 1,200 |
| 12/31 | Unearned Sub. Rev. | 800 | | 12/31 | Subscription Revenue | 400 |
| | Subscription Revenue | 800 | | | Unearned Sub Rev. | 400 |

After posting the entries, the accounts appear as follows:

| Unearned Subscription Revenue | | | | Unearned Subscription Revenue | | |
|---|---|---|---|---|---|---|
| 12/31 Adj. | 800 | 5/1 | 1,200 | | 12/31 Adj. | 400 |
| | | 12/31 Bal. | 400 | | | |

| Subscription Revenue | | | | Subscription Revenue | | |
|---|---|---|---|---|---|---|
| | | 12/31 Adj. | 800 | 12/31 Adj. | 400 | 5/1 | 1,200 |
| | | | | | | 12/31 Bal. | 800 |

Notice that the balances in the accounts are the same regardless of the approach used; that is, Unearned Subscription Revenue is $400, and Subscription Revenue is $800 at December 31, 2010.

**TIP:** The adjusting entry illustrated in the left column would not be subject to reversal; a reversing entry can be used with the approach illustrated in the right column.

## **EXERCISE 3-14

**Purpose:**   (L.O. 5, 9) This exercise will provide you with examples of adjusting entries for:

(1)   Prepaid expenses when cash payments are recorded in an asset (real) account.

(2)   Prepaid expenses when cash payments are recorded in an expense (nominal) account.

(3)   Unearned revenues when cash receipts are recorded in a liability (real) account.

(4)   Unearned revenues when cash receipts are recorded in a revenue (nominal) account.

Thus, this exercise will review the alternative treatments of prepaid expenses and unearned revenues discussed in **Illustration 3-4**.

Each situation described below is **independent** of the others.

(1)   Office supplies are recorded in an asset account when acquired. There were $400 of supplies on hand at the beginning of the period. Cash purchases of office supplies during the period amount to $900. A count of supplies at the end of the period shows $320 worth to be on hand.

(2)   Office supplies are recorded in an expense account when acquired. There were $400 of supplies on hand at the beginning of the period. Cash purchases of office supplies during the period amount to $900. A count of supplies at the end of the period shows $320 worth to be on hand. No reversing entries are used.

(3)   Receipts from customers for magazine subscriptions are recorded as a liability when cash is collected in advance of delivery. The beginning balance in the liability account was $6,700. During the period, $54,000 was received for subscriptions. At the end of the period, it was determined that the balance of the Unearned Subscription Revenue account should be $8,000.

(4)   Receipts from customers for magazine subscriptions are recorded as revenue when cash is collected in advance of delivery. The beginning balance in the liability account was $6,700. During the period, $54,000 was received for subscriptions. At the end of the period, it was determined that the balance of the Unearned Subscription Revenue account should be $8,000. No reversing entries are used.

## Instructions

For each of the **independent** situations above:

(a)   Prepare the appropriate adjusting entry in general journal form.

(b)   Indicate the amount of revenue or expense which will appear on the income statement for the period.

(c)   Indicate the balance of the applicable asset or liability account at the end of the period.

(d)   Indicate the amount of cash received or paid during the period.

(e)   Indicate the change in the applicable asset or liability account from the beginning of the period to the end of the period.

## Solution to Exercise 3-14

(1)  a.  Office Supplies Expense ........................................ 980
           Office Supplies on Hand ............................... 980
     b.  Office Supplies Expense          $980
     c.  Office Supplies on Hand          $320
     d.  Cash paid                        $900
     e.  Decrease in Office Supplies on Hand   $ 80

**Approach:**

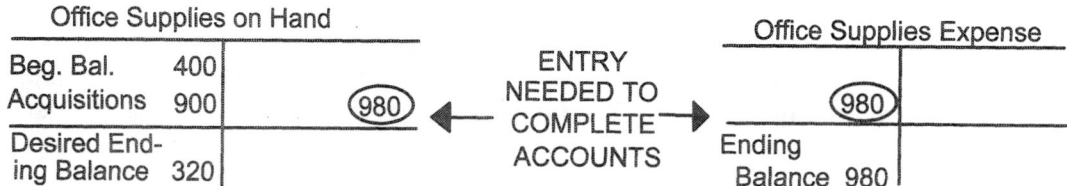

(2)  a.  Office Supplies Expense ........................................ 80
           Office Supplies on Hand ............................... 80
     b.  Office Supplies Expense          $980
     c.  Office Supplies on Hand          $320
     d.  Cash paid                        $900
     e.  Decrease in Office Supplies on Hand   $ 80

**Approach:**

(3)  a.  Unearned Subscription Revenue ............................ 52,700
           Subscription Revenue................................... 52,700
     b.  Subscription Revenue             $52,700
     c.  Unearned Subscription Revenue    $ 8,000
     d.  Cash received                    $54,000
     e.  Increase in Unearned Subscription Revenue   $ 1,300

**Approach:**

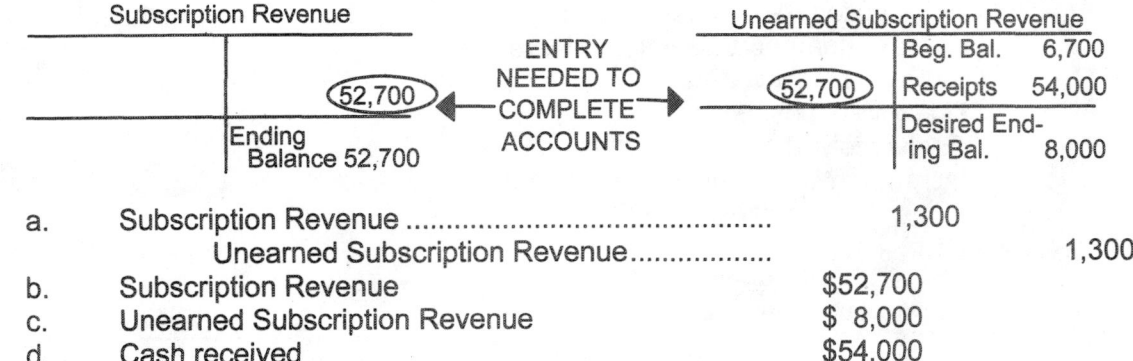

| | | | |
|---|---|---|---|
| (4) | a. | Subscription Revenue ............................................. | 1,300 | |
| | | Unearned Subscription Revenue................. | | 1,300 |
| | b. | Subscription Revenue | $52,700 |
| | c. | Unearned Subscription Revenue | $ 8,000 |
| | d. | Cash received | $54,000 |
| | e. | Increase in Unearned Subscription Revenue | $ 1,300 |

**Approach:**

---

**TIP:** Compare situation (3) with situation (4). Notice the facts are the same **except** for the account credited for receipt of revenue in advance of the period in which the revenue is earned. The solution is the same **except** for the adjusting entry required.

**TIP:** You should be able to handle what for most students can be the most challenging situations. Refer back to the descriptions of situations (2) and (4). Redo them, assuming that reversing entries **are** used. Reversing entries are described in **Appendix 3B** in the text. Those new solutions should appear as follows.

(2) Assuming reversing entries **are** used.

| | | | |
|---|---|---|---|
| | a. | Office Supplies on Hand ................................................ | 320 | |
| | | Office Supplies Expense..................................... | | 320 |
| | b. | Office Supplies Expense | $980 |
| | c. | Office Supplies on Hand | $320 |
| | d. | Cash paid | $900 |
| | e. | Decrease in Office Supplies on Hand | $ 80 |

**Approach:**

| Office Supplies Expense | | ENTRY NEEDED TO COMPLETE ACCOUNTS | Office Supplies on Hand | |
|---|---|---|---|---|
| Reversing 400 | | | Beg. Bal. 400 | |
| Acquisitions 900 | (320) | ← → | (320) Reversing 400 | |
| Ending Bal. 980 | | | Desired Ending Bal. 320 | |

---

| (4) | | Assuming reversing entries **are** used. | | |
|---|---|---|---|---|
| | a. | Subscription Revenue ............................................. | 8,000 | |
| | | Unearned Subscription Revenue................. | | 8,000 |
| | b. | Subscription Revenue | $52,700 | |
| | c. | Unearned Subscription Revenue | $ 8,000 | |
| | d. | Cash received | $54,000 | |
| | e. | Increase in Unearned Subscription Revenue | $ 1,300 | |

**Approach:**

| Unearned Subscription Revenue | | | Subscription Revenue | |
|---|---|---|---|---|
| | Beg. Bal. 6,700 | ENTRY | | Reversing 6,700 |
| Reversing 6,700 | 8,000 | NEEDED TO COMPLETE | 8,000 | Receipts 54,000 |
| | Desired End-ing Bal. 8,000 | ACCOUNTS | | Ending Balance 52,700 |

## ***EXERCISE 3-15

**Purpose:** (L.O. 10) This exercise will allow you to quickly check your knowledge of how items are extended on a 10-column work sheet.

### Instructions
The last six columns of an incomplete 10-column work sheet are illustrated below. Place an "X" in the appropriate columns to indicate the proper work sheet treatment of the balance in each of the accounts listed. (The accounts are not listed in their usual order, the work sheet is **only** partially illustrated, and the Trial Balance and Adjustments columns have been **omitted**.)

**Handy Dandy Hardware**
**WORK SHEET**
**For the Year Ended December 31, 2010**

| Account | Adjusted Trial Balance | | Income Statement | | Balance Sheet | |
|---|---|---|---|---|---|---|
| | Debit | Credit | Debit | Credit | Debit | Credit |
| Advertising Expense | | | | | | |
| Depreciation Expense | | | | | | |
| Land | | | | | | |
| Store Equipment | | | | | | |
| Wages and Salaries Expense | | | | | | |
| Mortgage Payable | | | | | | |
| Cash | | | | | | |
| Salaries Payable | | | | | | |
| Prepaid Insurance | | | | | | |
| Delivery Equipment | | | | | | |
| Accumulated Depreciation | | | | | | |
| Revenue Received in Advance | | | | | | |
| Rent Expense | | | | | | |
| Sales Revenue | | | | | | |
| Prepaid Rent | | | | | | |
| Dividends Declared | | | | | | |
| Repairs Expense | | | | | | |
| Wages Payable | | | | | | |
| Interest Receivable | | | | | | |
| Accounts Receivable | | | | | | |
| Net Income | | | | | | |
| Retained Earnings | | | | | | |

## Solution to Exercise 3-15

**Handy Dandy Hardware**
**WORK SHEET**
**For the Year Ended December 31, 2010**

| Account | Adjusted Trial Balance | | Income Statement | | Balance Sheet | |
|---|---|---|---|---|---|---|
| | Debit | Credit | Debit | Credit | Debit | Credit |
| Advertising Expense | X | | X | | | |
| Depreciation Expense | X | | X | | | |
| Land | X | | | | X | |
| Store Equipment | X | | | | X | |
| Wages and Salaries Expense | X | | X | | | |
| Mortgage Payable | | X | | | | X |
| Cash | X | | | | X | |
| Salaries Payable | | X | | | | X |
| Prepaid Insurance | X | | | | X | |
| Delivery Equipment | X | | | | X | |
| Accumulated Depreciation | | X | | | | X |
| Revenue Received in Advance | | X | | | | X |
| Rent Expense | X | | X | | | |
| Sales Revenue | | X | | X | | |
| Prepaid Rent | X | | | | X | |
| Dividends Declared | X | | | | X | |
| Repairs Expense | X | | X | | | |
| Wages Payable | | X | | | | X |
| Interest Receivable | X | | | | X | |
| Accounts Receivable | X | | | | X | |
| Net Income | | | X | | | X |
| Retained Earnings | | X | | | | X |

---

***TIP:** The amount shown for Retained Earnings on the work sheet above is the balance of that account **before** considering dividends declared during the period (determined by the fact that a separate Dividends Declared account appears on the same work sheet) and **before** considering net income for the period.

***TIP:** Every amount appearing in the Adjusted Trial Balance column pair must be extended to one of the four statement columns. Debit amounts go to a debit column further to the right and credit amounts go to a credit column further to the right of the adjusted trial balance column pair.

***TIP:** When a dollar amount is added to balance the income statement column pair of columns, the same amount must be added in an opposite debit or credit column in the balance sheet column pair. This amount in a balance sheet column indicates the impact of net income (or net loss) on owners' equity.

## ANALYSIS OF MULTIPLE-CHOICE TYPE QUESTIONS

**QUESTION**
1. (L.O. 1) Which of the following is a nominal account?
   a. Prepaid Insurance
   b. Unearned Revenue
   c. Insurance Expense
   d. Interest Receivable

**Approach and Explanation:** Read the question. Before looking at the answer selections, write down the meaning of the term "nominal account." Then answer "true" or "false" as you ask whether each answer selection is a nominal account. A nominal account is an account whose balance is closed at the end of an accounting period. Revenue and expense accounts are closed; real accounts (including asset and liability accounts) are never closed. Prepaid Insurance and Interest Receivable are asset accounts. Unearned Revenue is a liability account. Insurance Expense is a nominal account. (Solution = c.)

**QUESTION**
2. (L.O. 4) Which of the following errors will cause an imbalance in the trial balance?
   a. Omission of a transaction in the journal.
   b. Posting an entire journal entry twice to the ledger.
   c. Posting a credit of $720 to Accounts Payable as a credit of $720 to Accounts Receivable.
   d. Listing the balance of an account with a debit balance in the credit column of the trial balance.

**Approach and Explanation:** Analyze each error (answer selection) and write down whether or not the error will cause the trial balance to be out of balance. Look for the selection which will cause an imbalance (selection "d"). Selections "a," "b," and "c" do not cause an imbalance in the trial balance. (Solution = d.)

**QUESTION**
3. (L.O. 5) Which of the following statements is associated with the accrual basis of accounting?
   a. The timing of cash receipts and disbursements is emphasized.
   b. A minimum amount of record keeping is required.
   c. This method is used less frequently by businesses than the cash method of accounting.
   d. Revenues are recognized in the period they are earned, regardless of the time period the cash is received.

**Approach and Explanation:** Mentally define the accrual basis of accounting. Write down the key words and phrases of your definition. Compare each answer selection with your definition and choose the one that best matches. Using the **accrual basis of accounting**, events that change a company's financial statements are recorded in the periods in which the events occur. Thus, revenues are recognized in the period in which they are earned, and expenses are recognized in the period in which they are incurred, regardless of when the related cash is received or paid. Answer selections "a" and "b" refer to the cash basis of accounting which is not GAAP. (Solution = d.)

**QUESTION**

4.   (L.O. 5) An accrued expense is an expense that:
   a.   has been incurred but has not been paid.
   b.   has been paid but has not been incurred.
   c.   has been incurred for which payment is to be made in installments.
   d.   will never be paid.

**Approach and Explanation:** Write down a definition for accrued expense. Compare each answer selection with your definition and choose the best match. Expenses may be paid for in the same period in which they are incurred or they may be paid for in the period before or in the period after the one in which they are incurred. An **accrued expense** refers to an expense that has been incurred but has not yet been paid. It will be paid for in a period subsequent to the period in which it was incurred. (Solution = a.)

**QUESTION**

5.   (L.O. 5) In reviewing some adjusting entries, you observe an entry which contains a debit to Prepaid Insurance and a credit to Insurance Expense. The purpose of this journal entry is to record a(n):
   a.   accrued expense.
   b.   deferred expense.
   c.   expired cost.
   d.   prepaid revenue.

**Approach and Explanation:** Write down the entry so you can see what the entry does. Notice the entry records a prepaid expense (an asset). Then examine each answer selection one at a time. A debit to Prepaid Insurance records an increase in a prepaid expense. A prepaid expense is an expense that has been paid but has not been incurred. Another name for a prepaid expense is deferred expense. A deferred expense is an expense whose recognition is being deferred (put off) until a future period. An accrued expense is an expense incurred, but not paid. An expired cost is an expense or a loss. Prepaid revenue is a bad term for unearned revenue (or deferred revenue). (Solution = b.)

**QUESTION**

6.   (L.O. 5) An adjusting entry to record an accrued expense involves a debit to a(an):
   a.   expense account and a credit to a prepaid account.
   b.   expense account and a credit to Cash.
   c.   expense account and a credit to a liability account.
   d.   liability account and a credit to an expense account.

**Approach and Explanation:** Write down a definition for accrued expense and the types of accounts involved in an adjusting entry to accrue an expense. Find the answer selection that describes your entry.

   Dr.              Expenses
       Cr.                 Liabilities

Notice the logic of the entry. An **accrued expense** is an expense incurred but not yet paid. Thus, you record the incurrence by increasing an expense account and you record the "not paid" aspect by increasing a liability account. (Solution = c.)

**QUESTION**

7.  (L.O. 5) The failure to properly record an adjusting entry to accrue an expense will result in an:
    a.  understatement of expenses and an understatement of liabilities.
    b.  understatement of expenses and an overstatement of liabilities.
    c.  understatement of expenses and an overstatement of assets.
    d.  overstatement of expenses and an understatement of assets.

**Approach and Explanation:** Write down the adjusting entry to record an accrued expense. Analyze the effects of the entry. This will help you to determine the effects of the failure to properly make that entry.

> Dr.    Expenses             xx
>     Cr.        Liabilities              xx

This entry increases expenses and liabilities. Therefore, the failure to make this entry would result in an understatement of expenses and an understatement of liabilities. (Solution = a.)

**QUESTION**

8.  (L.O. 5) Which of the following properly describes a deferral?
    a.  Cash is received after revenue is earned.
    b.  Cash is received before revenue is earned.
    c.  Cash is paid after expense is incurred.
    d.  Cash is paid in the same time period that an expense is incurred.

**Approach and Explanation:**  Think about the nature of a deferral and the relative timing of revenue or expense recognition and the related cash flow. **Deferrals** result from cash flows that occur **before** expense or revenue recognition. That is, cash is paid for expenses that apply to more than one accounting period or cash is received for revenue that applies to more than one accounting period. The portion of the expense that applies to future periods is deferred by reporting a prepaid expense (asset) or the portion of the revenue that applies to future periods is deferred by reporting unearned revenue (liability) on the balance sheet.

**Accruals** result from cash flows that occur **after** expense or revenue recognition. That is, cash is to be paid or received in a future accounting period for an expense incurred or a revenue earned in the current period. Items a. and c. above are accrual situations. Item d. is neither an accrual or deferral situation. (Solution = b.)

**QUESTION**

9.  (L.O. 5) An adjusting entry to allocate a previously recorded asset to expense involves a debit to an:
    a.  asset account and a credit to Cash.
    b.  expense account and a credit to Cash.
    c.  expense account and a credit to an asset account.
    d.  asset account and a credit to an expense account.

**Approach and Explanation:**  Write down the sketch of an adjusting entry to transfer an asset to expense.  Compare each answer selection with your entry and choose the one that matches.

> Dr.        Expenses
>     Cr.        Assets

(Solution = c.)

**QUESTION**

10. (L.O. 5) Which of the following adjusting entries will cause an increase in revenues and a decrease in liabilities?
    a. Entry to record an accrued expense.
    b. Entry to record an accrued revenue.
    c. Entry to record the consumed portion of an expense paid in advance and initially recorded as an asset.
    d. Entry to record the earned portion of revenue received in advance and initially recorded as unearned revenue.

**Approach and Explanation:** For each answer selection, write down the sketch of the adjusting entry described and the effects of each half of the entry. Compare the stem of the question with your analyses to determine the correct answer. (Solution = d.)

The entry to record an accrued expense:
      Dr.            Expenses
            Cr.            Liabilities
The effects of the entry are to increase expenses and to increase liabilities.

The entry to record an accrued revenue:
      Dr.            Assets
            Cr.            Revenues
The effects of the entry are to increase assets and to increase revenues.

The entry to record the consumed portion of a prepaid expense initially recorded as an asset is:
      Dr.            Expenses
            Cr.            Assets
The effects of the entry are to increase expenses and to decrease assets.

The entry to record the earned portion of unearned revenue initially recorded as a liability is:
      Dr.            Liabilities
            Cr.            Revenues
The effects of the entry are to decrease liabilities and to increase revenues.

**QUESTION**

11. (L.O. 5) The failure to properly record an adjusting entry to accrue a revenue item will result in an:
    a. understatement of revenues and an understatement of liabilities.
    b. overstatement of revenues and an overstatement of liabilities.
    c. overstatement of revenues and an overstatement of assets.
    d. understatement of revenues and an understatement of assets.

**Approach and Explanation:** Write down the adjusting entry to record an accrued revenue. Analyze the effects of the entry. This will help you to determine the effects of the failure to properly make that entry.
      Dr.            Assets                              xx
            Cr.            Revenues                              xx
This entry increases assets and revenues. Therefore, the failure to make this entry would result in an understatement of assets and an understatement of revenues. (Solution = d.)

**QUESTION**
12.    (L.O. 5) The failure to properly record an adjusting entry for the expiration of insurance coverage will result in an (assume the account Prepaid Insurance was charged when the premiums were paid):
    a.    overstatement of assets and an overstatement of owners' equity.
    b.    understatement of assets and an understatement of owners' equity.
    c.    overstatement of assets and an overstatement of liabilities.
    d.    overstatement of liabilities and an understatement of owners' equity.

**Approach and Explanation:**  Analyze the effects of the adjusting entry that should have been made:
    Dr.                Insurance Expense                    xx
        Cr.                Prepaid Insurance                        xx
This entry increases expenses which decreases net income which gets closed into Retained Earnings which is a component of owners' equity; therefore, owners' equity will be overstated by the omission of the appropriate adjusting entry. The missing adjustment also reduces assets so assets are overstated by the failure to properly adjust the accounts. (Solution = a.)


**QUESTION**
13.    (L.O. 5) The omission of the adjusting entry to record depreciation expense will result in an:
    a.    overstatement of assets and an overstatement of owners' equity.
    b.    understatement of assets and an understatement of owners' equity.
    c.    overstatement of assets and an overstatement of liabilities.
    d.    overstatement of liabilities and an understatement of owners' equity.

**Explanation:**   The appropriate adjusting entry records an expense (Depreciation Expense) and an increase to a contra asset account (Accumulated Depreciation). Thus, the omission of that entry will cause an understatement of expenses and an overstatement of assets. The understatement of expense causes an overstatement of net income which causes an overstatement of Retained Earnings (a component of owners' equity on the balance sheet). (Solution = a.)


**QUESTION**
14.    (L.O. 5) An auditor is examining an adjusting entry that reduces liabilities and increases owners' equity. Which of the following adjusting entries could that be?
    a.    Entry to record an accrued revenue.
    b.    Entry to record the earned portion of revenue received in advance and previously recorded as Unearned Rent Revenue.
    c.    Entry to record an accrued expense.
    d.    Entry to record the expired portion of expense paid in advance and previously recorded as Prepaid Expense.
    e.    Entry to record bad debts expense.

**Explanation:**   The entry to record an accrued revenue increases receivables (assets) and increases revenues which increases owners' equity. The entry to record an accrued expense increases expenses (causing a decrease in owners' equity) and an increase in liabilities. The adjusting entry to record the expiration of an asset (items d and e above) will reduce assets and owners' equity. The entry to record the earning of previously recorded unearned revenue decreases liabilities and increases revenues (thus, increasing owners' equity). (Solution = b.)

---

**QUESTION**
15. (L.O. 5) The Office Supplies on Hand account had a balance at the beginning of year 3 of $1,600. Payments for acquisitions of office supplies during year 3 amounted to $10,000 and were recorded by a debit to the asset account. A physical count at the end of year 3 revealed supplies costing $1,900 were on hand. The required adjusting entry at the end of year 3 will include a debit to:
   a. Office Supplies Expense for $300.
   b. Office Supplies on Hand for $300.
   c. Office Supplies Expense for $9,700.
   d. Office Supplies on Hand for $1,900.

**Approach and Explanation:** Draw T-accounts. Enter the data given and solve for the adjusting entry. Compare each alternative answer to the adjusting entry you have sketched in the accounts. (Solution = c.)

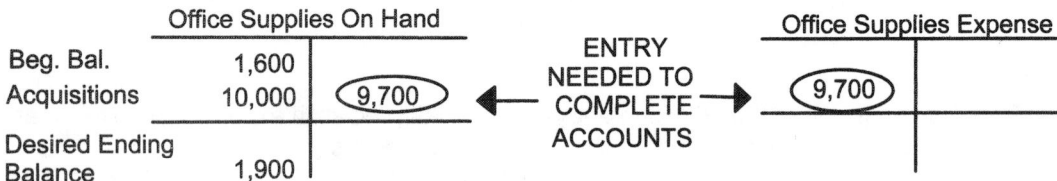

**QUESTION**
16. (L.O. 5) The book value of a piece of equipment is the:
   a. original cost of the equipment.
   b. current replacement cost of the used equipment.
   c. current market value of the used equipment.
   d. difference between the original cost of the equipment and its related accumulated depreciation.

**Explanation:** Equipment benefits the operations of several accounting periods; thus, in compliance with the matching principle, a portion of the cost of a long-lived asset should be reported as an expense during each period of the asset's useful life. Depreciation is the process of allocating the cost of an asset to expense over its useful life in a rational and systematic manner. The annual charge for depreciation is recorded by a debit to Depreciation Expense and a credit to Accumulated Depreciation. The Accumulated Depreciation - Office Equipment is a contra asset account and reflects the total depreciation to date. The difference between the balance in the Equipment account (the original cost of the asset) and balance in the related Accumulated Depreciation account at any given point in time represents the book value (often called carrying value or carrying amount) of the equipment. This amount will rarely equal the asset's current market value. (Solution = d.)

**QUESTION**
17. (L.O. 7) The purpose of recording closing entries is to:
   a. reduce the number of nominal accounts.
   b. enable the accountant to prepare financial statements at the end of an accounting period.
   c. prepare revenue and expense accounts for the recording of the next period's revenues and expenses.
   d. establish new balances in some asset and liability accounts.

**Approach and Explanation:** Cover up the answer selections while you read the question. Attempt to complete the statement started by the stem of the question. Think about when closing entries are made and what they do. Then go through the selections using a process of elimination approach. Closing entries clear out the balances of revenue and expense accounts so that the accounts are ready to accumulate data for a new accounting period. Selection "c" is correct. Selection "a" is incorrect; closing entries do not change the number of accounts. Selection "b" is incorrect; financial statements are prepared before closing entries are done. If closing entries were posted first, the income statement would include nothing but zero amounts. Selection "d" is incorrect, closing entries will affect only nominal accounts and owners' equity. (Solution = c.)

**QUESTION**

18.   (L.O. 8) If ending accounts receivable exceeds the beginning accounts receivable:
   a.   cash collections during the period exceed the amount of revenue earned.
   b.   net income for the period is less than the amount of cash basis income.
   c.   no cash was collected during the period.
   d.   cash collections during the year are less than the amount of revenue earned.

**Approach and Explanation:** Write down a format for reconciling the amount of cash receipts to the amount of revenue earned.

| | |
|---|---|
| Cash receipts | $ |
| Beginning accounts receivable | ( ) |
| Ending accounts receivable | + |
| Revenue earned | $ |

Fill in what you know from the question.

| | |
|---|---|
| Cash receipts | $  X |
| Beginning accounts receivable | ( ) |
| Ending accounts receivable | +____ More than beginning receivable |
| Revenue earned | $____ Greater than X |

An increase in accounts receivable indicates that the amount of revenue earned (and recognized) exceeds the amount of cash collected. Thus, net income for the period exceeds the amount of cash basis income. (Solution = d.)

**QUESTION**

19.   (L.O. 8)   The Camphor Company made cash sales of services of $5,000 and credit sales of services of $4,200 during the month of July. The company incurred expenses of $6,000 during July of which $2,000 was paid in cash and the remainder was expected to be paid in August. Using the accrual method of accounting, net income for July amounts to:
   a.   $7,200.
   b.   $5,200.
   c.   $3,200.
   d.   $200.

**Approach and Explanation:** Write down the essence of the accrual method: revenues are recorded when earned and expenses are recorded when incurred. Look for the figures to fit the description. Cash sales of $5,000 plus credit sales of $4,200 equals $9,200 total revenue earned during July. Revenues earned of $9,200 minus expenses incurred of $6,000 equals net income of $3,200. (Solution = c.)

**QUESTION**

20.   (L.O. 8) Dr. Hellinger keeps his accounting records on the cash basis. During 2010, Dr. Hellinger collected $660,000 in fees from his patients. At December 31, 2009, the good doctor had accounts receivable of $50,000 and unearned fees of $6,000. At December 31, 2010, he had accounts receivable of $68,000 and unearned fees of $4,000. The amount of fees earned on the accrual basis by Dr. Hellinger during 2010 was:
   a.   $640,000.
   b.   $676,000.
   c.   $680,000.
   d.   $724,000.
   e.   None of the above. The correct answer is $_____.

**Approach and Explanation:** Set up a schedule to reconcile cash collections with revenue earned. Fill in the amounts given and solve.

| | | |
|---|---:|---:|
| Cash collections during 2010 | | $660,000 |
| Accounts receivable, beginning of year | | (50,000) |
| Accounts receivable, end of year | | 6,000 |
| Unearned revenues, beginning of year | | 68,000 |
| Unearned revenues, end of year | (4,000) | |
| Fees earned during 2010 | | $680,000 |

Accounts receivable of $50,000 at the beginning of the year represent amounts earned last period and collected during the current year of 2010. Ending receivables of $6,000 represent amounts earned in 2010 but not collected yet. Beginning unearned revenues are part of earned revenues this current period but were not part of the current period's collections. Ending unearned revenues were collected this period but are not yet earned. (Solution = c.)

**QUESTION**

21. (L.O. 9) The Office Supplies on Hand account had a balance at the beginning of year 3 of $1,600. Payments for acquisitions of office supplies during year 3 amounted to $10,000 and were recorded as expense. A physical count at the end of year 3 revealed supplies costing $1,900 were on hand. Reversing entries are used by this company. The required adjusting entry at the end of year 3 will include a debit to:
   a.   Office Supplies Expense for $300.
   b.   Office Supplies on Hand for $300.
   c.   Office Supplies Expense for $9,700.
   d.   Office Supplies on Hand for $1,900.

**Approach and Explanation:** Draw T-accounts. Enter the data given and solve for the adjusting entry. Compare each alternative answer to the adjusting entry you have sketched in the accounts. (Solution = d.)

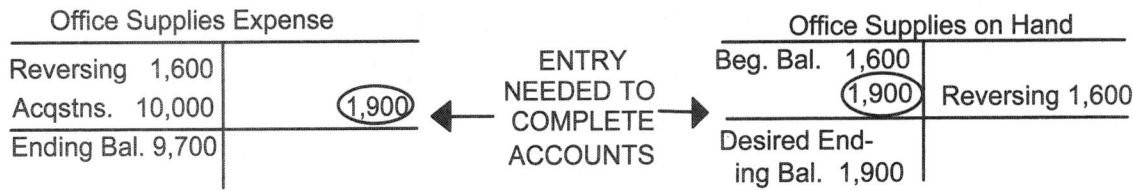

# CHAPTER 4

# INCOME STATEMENT AND RELATED INFORMATION

## OVERVIEW

An income statement reports on the results of operations of an entity for a period of time. It is important to classify revenues, expenses, gains, and losses properly on the income statement. In this chapter, we discuss the income statement classifications and the content of the statement of retained earnings along with related disclosure issues. It is imperative that charges and credits that represent elements of income determination be properly reflected in the financial statements. Errors in the determination of income cause errors on the income statement, statement of retained earnings, and balance sheet.

## SUMMARY OF LEARNING OBJECTIVES

1.  **Understand the uses and limitations of an income statement.** The income statement provides investors and creditors with information that helps them predict the amount, timing and uncertainty of future cash flows. Also, the income statement helps users determine the risk (level of uncertainty) of not achieving particular cash flows. The limitations of an income statement are: (1) The income statement does not include many items that contribute to general growth and well-being of an enterprise. (2) Income numbers are often affected by the accounting methods used. (3) Income measures are subject to estimates.

    The **transaction approach** focuses on the activities that have occurred during a given period; instead of presenting only a net change in net assets, it discloses the components of the change. The transaction approach to income measurement requires the use of revenue, expense, gain, and loss accounts.

2.  **Prepare a single-step income statement.** In a **single-step income statement**, just two groupings exist: revenues and expenses. Expenses are deducted from revenues to arrive at net income or net loss. The expression "single-step" is derived from the single subtraction necessary to arrive at net income. Frequently, however, companies report income taxes separately as the last item before net income to indicate their direct relationship to income before income taxes.

3.  **Prepare a multiple-step income statement.** A **multiple-step income statement** shows two further classifications: (1) a separation of operating results from those obtained through the subordinate or nonoperating activities of the company; and (2) a classification of expenses by functions, such as merchandising or manufacturing, selling, and administration.

4.  **Explain how to report irregular items.** Companies generally close irregular gains or losses or nonrecurring items to Income Summary and include them in the income statement as follows: (1) Discontinued operations of a component of a business is classified as a separate item, after continuing operations; (2) The unusual, material, nonrecurring items that are significantly different from the typical or customary business activities are shown in a separate section for extraordinary items, below discontinued operations; (3) Other items of a material amount that are of an unusual or nonrecurring nature and are not considered extraordinary are separately

disclosed as components of income from continuing operations. The cumulative adjustment that occurs when there is a correction of an error or a change in accounting principle is reported as an adjustment to beginning retained earnings in the retained earnings statement.

5.     **Explain intraperiod tax allocation.** Companies should relate the tax expense for the year should be related, where possible, to specific items on the income statement to provide a more informative disclosure to statement users. This procedure is called **intraperiod tax allocation**, that is, allocation within a period. Its main purpose is to relate the income tax expense for the fiscal period to the following items that affect the amount of the tax provisions: (1) income from continuing operations, (2) discontinued operations, and (3) extraordinary items.

6.     **Identify where to report earnings per share information.** Because of the inherent dangers of focusing attention solely on earnings per share, the profession concluded that companies must disclose earnings per share on the face of the income statement. A company that reports a discontinued operation or an extraordinary item must report per share amounts for these line items either on the face of the income statement or in the notes to the financial statements.

7.     **Prepare a retained earnings statement.** The retained earnings statement should disclose net income (loss), dividends, adjustments due to changes in accounting principles, adjustments due to error corrections, and transfers to and from unrestricted retained earnings (transfers to restricted retained earnings are often called appropriations of retained earnings).

8.     **Determine how to report other comprehensive income.** Companies report the components of other comprehensive income in a second income statement, a combined statement of comprehensive income, or in a statement of stockholders' equity.

## TIPS ON CHAPTER TOPICS

**TIP:**     The **income statement** or **statement of income** is often referred to as the statement of operations or the operating statement because it reports on the results of operations for a period of time. Other names include the "earnings statement," "statement of earnings," and "profit and loss statement" (or "P&L statement").

**TIP:**     The income statement is often referred to as a link between balance sheets because it explains one major reason why the balance of owners' equity changed during the period. Owners' equity (net assets) at the beginning of the period can be reconciled with ending owners' equity as follows:

|   | Owners' equity at the beginning of the period |
|---|---|
| + | Additional owner investments during the period |
| - | Owner withdrawals during the period |
| + | <u>Results of operations for the period (net income or net loss)</u> |
| = | Owners' equity at the end of the period |

This reconciliation of ending owner's equity with beginning owners' equity is oversimplistic in that it ignores the more complex situations discussed in this chapter such as (1) adjustments due to correction of errors in prior periods, (2) adjustments due to the effect on prior periods of a change in accounting principles, and (3) changes in accumulated other comprehensive income. The foregoing three items would also be part of this reconciliation if they were present in the situation.

**TIP:**   A **contra revenue** item has the same effect on net income as that of an expense; it decreases net income. Contra revenue accounts include Sales Discounts and Sales Returns and Allowances.

**TIP:**   It is often helpful to form an acronym when attempting to remember a list of items. In looking at the order of the things that can appear **after** the "Income from Continuing Operations" line on an income statement, you might come up with **DE** to help you to remember the exact order of these items:

> **D**iscontinued operations
> **E**xtraordinary items

Notice these two items appear in alphabetical order.

**TIP:**   The income tax consequences of all items appearing above the line "Income from continuing operations before income taxes" are summarized in the line "Income taxes." Revenues cause an increase in income taxes and expenses cause a decrease in income taxes. The income tax consequences of items appearing below the "income from continuing operations" line are reported right along with the items (hence, these items are reported "net of tax"). This procedure of allocating income taxes within a period is referred to as **intraperiod tax allocation**.

**TIP:**   An extraordinary item is reported "net of tax" by deducting the tax effect from the related gain or loss. For example, if the tax rate is 30%, an extraordinary gain of $400,000 will be reported at $280,000 net of tax. Likewise, an extraordinary loss of $400,000 will be reported at $280,000 net of tax. The gain situation increases net income, whereas the loss reduces it.

**TIP:**   A company normally provides **comparative financial statements** for its owners. That is, financial statements for the current period are shown side by side with the company's statements for one or two (or more) immediate prior periods.

**TIP:**   An error occurs as a result of a mathematical mistake, a mistake in the application of accounting principles, or an oversight or misuse of facts that existed at the time financial statements were prepared. When a company discovers that there was an error made in a prior period, a correction of that error entails making a proper entry(s) in the accounts and following specific reporting requirements in the preparation of financial statements. A correction for an error in the reporting of revenues or expenses in a prior period is accounted for as a **prior period adjustment** which is similar to the treatment accorded a change in accounting principle. The journal entry for a "catch-up adjustment" involves the Retained Earnings account and that amount is shown as an adjustment (**net** of the related income tax effect) to the beginning retained earnings balance on the financial statements.

If a company prepares comparative financial statements, it would restate the prior statements for the effects of the error; any effect on periods prior to the periods being shown would be reported as an adjustment to the beginning retained earnings balance for the earliest period being shown in the comparative reports.

**TIP:**   The **restatement** of prior period financial statements means the prior statements are recast. The statements for prior periods that are being reported again (such as in comparative reports) are changed to reflect items and balances as they would have (or should have) been in a prior period under other circumstances. For example, if the prior years' reports are restated because of an error in a prior year, the restated items and amounts will reflect what would have been reported had an error not occurred. When there is a change in accounting principle, the retrospective application of the new accounting method is similar to restatement in that the financial statements for prior periods are redone and presented again in the current period (for comparative purposes) as if the new principle had always been used.

---

**TIP:**   Net income minus preferred stock dividend requirements (i.e., income applicable to common stockholders) is divided by the weighted average of common stock shares outstanding to arrive at **earnings per share (EPS)**. This is a key ratio in financial analysis and must be disclosed on the face of the income statement. A per share amount must **always** be disclosed for "net income" on the face of the income statement. Also, a company that reports a discontinued operation or an extraordinary item must report per share amounts for these line items either on the face of the income statement or in the notes to the financial statements.

**TIP:**   In the EPS calculation, preferred dividends are deducted from net income if they were declared; however, if the preferred stock is cumulative, the preferred dividend preference for the current period is deducted whether or not the dividends were declared. Dividends declared on common stock have no effect on the EPS calculation.

## EXERCISE 4-1

**Purpose:**   (L.O. 1) This exercise reviews the basic accounting formula (Assets = Liabilities + Owners' Equity) and the connection between the income statement and the balance sheet (which is a change in owners' equity due to the net income or net loss for the period). This exercise focuses on the capital maintenance (or change in equity) approach to income determination.

The following data were extracted from the records of Dora Loesing's Cookies, a sole proprietorship:

| | | |
|---|---|---|
| Total assets, beginning of the period | $100,000 | |
| Total liabilities, beginning of the period | | 36,000 |
| Owner withdrawals during the period | 30,000 | |
| Total assets, end of the period | | 108,000 |
| Total liabilities, end of the period | | 38,000 |
| Owner's contributions during the period | | 10,000 |

## Instructions
Compute the amount of net income (or loss) for the period. Show computations.

## Solution to Exercise 4-1

| | |
|---|---|
| Beginning owner's equity | $ 64,000[a] |
| Additional owner contributions | 10,000 |
| Owner withdrawals during the period | (30,000) |
| Subtotal | 44,000 |
| Net income (loss) for the period | +   X |
| Ending owner's equity | $ 70,000[b] |
| | |
| Solving for X, net income | $ 26,000 |

[a]A = L + OE
$100,000 = $36,000 + ?
Beginning owner's equity = $64,000

[b]A = L + OE
$108,000 = $38,000 + ?
Ending owner's equity = $70,000

**Approach:** The question asks you to solve for net income; however, no information is given regarding revenues and expenses for the period. Only balance sheet data and transactions affecting owner's equity are given. Net income (or net loss) for a period is one reason for a change in the balance of owner's equity. Write down the items that reconcile the beginning owner's equity balance with the ending owner's equity balance, enter the amounts known, compute beginning and ending owner's equity balances by use of the basic accounting equation, and then solve for the amount of net income. Recall that assets - liabilities = net assets; that is, assets - liabilities = owner's equity at a point in time.

---

**TIP:** The basic accounting equation (A = L + OE) is applied at a specific point in time. When you have the facts for the equation components at two different points in time for the same entity (such as amounts as of the beginning of a year and amounts as of the end of a year), you can modify the basic accounting equation to reflect that total changes in assets equals total changes in liabilities + total changes in owners' equity. Using the symbol    to designate change, the following equation also holds true:

$$\Delta A = \Delta L + \Delta OE$$

Reasons for changes in owners' equity include:
   (1)    additional owner investments,
   (2)    owner withdrawals, and
   (3)    results of operations (net income or net loss).

**TIP:** When using the **capital maintenance** (or **change in equity**) approach, the amount of owners' equity is determined at the beginning and at the end of the period (using the same valuation method). The difference between these two amounts, adjusted for owner withdrawals and additional owner investments during the same period, is the measure of net income for the period. Net income (or net loss) is the change in owners' equity for a period of time, other than from capital transactions. (The foregoing sentence ignores any changes in owners' equity due to error corrections, changes in accounting principles, and changes in accumulated other comprehensive income). Capital transactions are those that involve owners acting in their capacity of being owners of the entity.

## ILLUSTRATION 4-1
## ELEMENTS OF THE INCOME STATEMENT (L.O. 1)

**REVENUES.** Inflows or other enhancements of assets of an entity or settlements of its liabilities during a period from delivering or producing goods, rendering services, or other activities that constitute the entity's ongoing major or central operations.

**EXPENSES.** Outflows or other using-up of assets or incurrences of liabilities during a period from delivering or producing goods, rendering services, or carrying out other activities that constitute the entity's ongoing major or central operations.

**GAINS.** Increases in equity (net assets) from peripheral or incidental transactions of an entity except those that result from revenues or investments by owners.

**LOSSES.** Decreases in equity (net assets) from peripheral or incidental transactions of an entity except those that result from expenses or distributions to owners.

Revenues take many forms, such as sales revenue, fees earned, dividend income, and rents earned. Expenses also take many forms, such as cost of goods sold, rent, salaries, depreciation, interest, and taxes.

---

Revenues and gains are similar (they both increase net income), and expenses and losses are similar (they both decrease net income). However, these terms are dissimilar in the fact that they convey significantly different information about an enterprise's performance. Revenues and expenses result from an entity's ongoing major or central operations and activities—that is, from activities such as producing or delivering goods, rendering services, lending, insuring, investing, and financing. In contrast, gains and losses result from incidental or peripheral or irregular transactions of an enterprise with other entities and from other events and circumstances affecting it. Gains and losses often arise from the sale of investments; disposal of plant assets; settlement of liabilities for an amount other than their book value; and write-offs of assets due to obsolescence, casualty, theft, or restructurings.

Revenues and expenses are commonly displayed as **gross** inflows or outflows of net assets; while gains and losses are usually displayed as **net** inflows or outflows. For example, assume a company buys an inventory item for $6,000, sells it for $10,000, and pays a sales representative a $1,000 commission. Further, the same company sells for $20,000 a plant asset with a book value (carrying value) of $15,000 and pays an outside agency $2,100 for finding the buyer. The various flows associated with the first transaction (the company's major activity or regular operations) will be reported gross on its income statement, and the various elements of the second transaction (a peripheral or incidental transaction) will be reported net. Assuming these were the only two transactions completed during the period and ignoring income taxes, the income statement would reflect the following:

| | |
|---|---:|
| Sales revenue | $ 10,000 |
| Cost of goods sold expense | ( 6,000) |
| Gross profit | 4,000 |
| Selling expense (sales commission) | (1,000) |
| Income from operations | 3,000 |
| Gain on sale of plant asset | 2,900[a] |
| Net income | $  5,900 |

[a]$20,000 proceeds - $15,000 book value - $2,100 finders fee = $2,900 gain on sale.

**TIP:** Net income results from revenue, expense, gain, and loss transactions. These transactions are summarized in the income statement. This method of income measurement is called the **transaction approach** because it focuses on the income-related activities (broken down into completed transactions) that have occurred during the period.

# ILLUSTRATION 4-2
# SECTIONS OF A MULTIPLE-STEP INCOME STATEMENT (L.O. 3)

1.  **OPERATING SECTION.** A report of the revenues and expenses of the company's principal operations. (This section may or may not be presented on a departmental basis.)
    (a)  **SALES OR REVENUE SECTION.** A subsection presenting sales, discounts, allowances, returns, and other related information. Its purpose is to arrive at the net amount of sales revenue.
    (b)  **COST OF GOODS SOLD SECTION.** A subsection that shows the cost of goods that were sold to produce the sales.
    (c)  **SELLING EXPENSES.** A subsection that lists expenses resulting from the company's efforts to make sales.
    (d)  **ADMINISTRATIVE OR GENERAL EXPENSES.** A subsection reporting expenses of general administration.

2.  **NONOPERATING SECTION.** A report of revenues and expenses resulting from secondary or auxiliary activities of the company. In addition, special gains and losses that are infrequent or unusual, but not both, are normally reported in this section. Generally these items break down into two main subsections:
    (a)  **OTHER REVENUES AND GAINS.** A list of the revenues earned or gains incurred, generally net of related expenses, from nonoperating transactions.
    (b)  **OTHER EXPENSES AND LOSSES.** A list of the expenses or losses incurred, generally net of any related incomes, from nonoperating transactions.

3.  **INCOME TAXES.** A short section reporting federal and state taxes levied on income from continuing operations.

4.  **DISCONTINUED OPERATIONS.** Material gains or losses resulting from the disposal of a component of the business. (Shown net of related income tax effect.)

5.  **EXTRAORDINARY ITEMS.** Unusual and infrequent material gains and losses. (Shown net of related income tax effect.)

6.  **EARNINGS PER SHARE.**

## EXERCISE 4-2

**Purpose:**     (L.O. 2, 3, 6) This exercise will allow you to contrast the multiple-step format and the single-step format for the income statement.

The accountant for Bubble Bath Products, Inc. has compiled the following information from the company's records as a basis for an income statement for the year ended December 31, 2010. (There was no change during the year in the 12,000 shares of common stock outstanding.)

| | |
|---|---:|
| Net sales | $ 970,000 |
| Depreciation on plant assets (60% selling, 40% administrative) | 70,000 |
| Dividends declared | 14,400 |
| Rent revenue | 30,000 |
| Interest on notes payable | 17,000 |
| Market appreciation on land held as an investment | 44,000 |
| Merchandise purchases | 421,000 |
| Transportation-in—merchandise | 37,000 |
| Merchandise inventory, January 1, 2010 | 82,000 |
| Merchandise inventory, December 31, 2010 | 81,000 |
| Purchase returns and allowances | 11,000 |
| Wages and salaries—sales | 95,000 |
| Materials and supplies—sales | 11,400 |
| Income taxes | 45,000 |
| Wages and salaries—administrative | 135,900 |
| Other administrative expenses | 46,700 |
| Advertising expense | 20,000 |
| Express mail | 6,000 |

## Instructions
(a)     Prepare a multiple-step income statement.
(b)     Prepare a single-step income statement.

# Solution to Exercise 4-2

(a)

**Bubble Bath Products, Inc.**
**INCOME STATEMENT**
**For the Year Ending December 31, 2010**

| | | | |
|---|---:|---:|---:|
| <u>Sales Revenue</u> | | | |
| Net sales revenue | | | $970,000 |
| | | | |
| <u>Cost of Goods Sold</u> | | | |
| Merchandise inventory, Jan. 1 | | $ 82,000 | |
| Purchases | $ 421,000 | | |
| Less purchase returns & allowances | <u>11,000</u> | | |
| Net purchases | 410,000 | | |
| Transportation-in | <u>37,000</u> | <u>447,000</u> | |
| Total merchandise available for sale | | 529,000 | |
| Less merchandise inventory, Dec. 31 | | <u>81,000</u> | |
| Cost of goods sold | | | <u>448,000</u> |
| | | | |
| Gross profit | | | 522,000 |
| | | | |
| <u>Operating Expenses</u> | | | |
| Selling expenses | | | |
| Wages and salaries | 95,000 | | |
| Advertising | 20,000 | | |
| Materials and supplies | 11,400 | | |
| Depreciation (60% x $70,000) | 42,000 | | |
| Express mail | <u>6,000</u> | 174,400 | |
| Administrative expenses | | | |
| Wages and salaries | 135,900 | | |
| Depreciation (40% x $70,000) | 28,000 | | |
| Other administrative expenses | <u>46,700</u> | <u>210,600</u> | <u>385,000</u> |
| | | | |
| Income from operations | | | 137,000 |
| | | | |
| <u>Other Revenues and Gains</u> | | | |
| Rent revenue | | | <u>30,000</u> |
| | | | 167,000 |
| | | | |
| <u>Other Expenses and Losses</u> | | | |
| Interest expense | | | <u>17,000</u> |
| | | | |
| Income before taxes | | | 150,000 |
| Income taxes | | | <u>45,000</u> |
| Net income | | | <u>$105,000</u> |
| | | | |
| Earnings per share ($105,000 ÷ 12,000) | | | <u>$8.75</u> |

> **TIP:** Dividends declared do not appear on the income statement. They are a distribution of corporate income—**not** a determinant of net income. Increases in the market value of assets held (such as plant assets, inventory, and most investments) are generally not recognized in the accounts until they are realized through the sale of the assets. Hence, the market appreciation on the land held as an investment does **not** appear on the income statement.

(b)

**Bubble Bath Products, Inc.**
**INCOME STATEMENT**
**For the Year Ending December 31, 2010**

| | |
|---|---:|
| Revenues | |
| Net sales | $ 970,000 |
| Rent revenue | 30,000 |
| Total revenue | 1,000,000 |
| | |
| Expenses | |
| Cost of goods sold | 448,000 |
| Selling expenses | 174,400 |
| Administrative expenses | 210,600 |
| Interest expense | 17,000 |
| Total expenses | 850,000 |
| | |
| Income before taxes | 150,000 |
| Income taxes | 45,000 |
| Net income | $ 105,000 |
| | |
| Earnings per share | $8.75 |

> **TIP:** In the single-step income statement, just two groupings exist: revenues and expenses. Expenses are deducted from revenues to arrive at net income or loss. The expression "single-step" is derived from the single subtraction necessary to arrive at net income. Frequently, however, income taxes are reported separately to indicate their direct relationship to income before income taxes.
>
> **TIP:** In the multiple-step income statement, there are three major subtotals presented before arriving at net income. They are: net sales revenue, gross profit, and income from operations. These subtotals emphasize (1) a classification of expenses by **function**, such as merchandising or manufacturing (cost of goods sold), selling, and administration, and (2) a separation of operating and subordinate or nonoperating activities of the company. The "other revenues and gains" and "other expenses and losses" sections include (1) investing and financing revenues and expenses such as interest revenue, dividend revenue (from dividends received), and interest expense, and (2) the results of nonoperating items such as the sale of plant assets and investments.

| TIP: | The nature of an entity's typical operations is critical in determining whether the results of a transaction should be classified as an operating or a nonoperating revenue, gain, expense, or loss. For example, consider rental activities. A business specializing in equipment rentals will classify rent revenue as an operating revenue. Whereas, a retail establishment that occasionally rents its temporarily idle assets to others will classify rent revenue as a nonoperating (other) revenue. For a second example, consider the sale of an investment. An investment dealer will report the revenue from a sale as an operating revenue. Whereas, a retail entity that occasionally sells an investment will report the difference between the proceeds from the sale and the investment's carrying value as a nonoperating gain or loss. |
|---|---|
| TIP: | There is no specific order in which the individual selling expenses and administrative expenses are to be listed in the multiple-step income statement. Very often, they appear in order of decreasing magnitude. |
| TIP: | Some accountants prefer to use a multiple-step income statement format because it discloses the amount of income from operations. Thus, by this disclosure, the difference between regular and irregular or incidental activities is highlighted. Irregular activities encompass transactions and other events that are derived from developments outside the normal operations of the business. Thus, they may not be expected to continue at the same level in future periods. |
| TIP: | The item "Income taxes" is sometimes called "Income tax expense." Accountants refer to it as the **tax provision** and may even use the caption "Provision for income taxes" on the income statement. |

# EXERCISE 4-3

**Purpose:**    (L.O. 2, 7) This exercise will give you practice in identifying components of net income and the order of items appearing on a single-step income statement and on a retained earnings statement.

Presented below is the adjusted trial balance of the Limp Bizkit Corporation at December 31, 2010. The account titles and balances are **not** in the customary order.

## Limp Bizkit Corporation
### ADJUSTED TRIAL BALANCE
### December 31, 2010

|  | Debits | Credits |
|---|---:|---:|
| Sales |  | $ 958,500 |
| Notes Receivable | $  80,000 |  |
| Investments | 88,500 |  |
| Accounts Payable |  | 51,000 |
| Accumulated Depreciation—Equipment |  | 31,000 |
| Sales Discounts | 10,500 |  |
| Sales Returns | 17,500 |  |
| Purchase Discounts |  | 8,000 |
| Cash | 190,000 |  |
| Accounts Receivable | 95,000 |  |
| Rent Revenue |  | 14,000 |
| Retained Earnings |  | 240,000 |
| Salaries Payable |  | 22,000 |
| Notes Payable | 75,000 |  |
| Common Stock, $15 par |  | 300,000 |
| Income Tax Expense | 68,000 |  |
| Cash Dividends Declared | 70,000 |  |
| Allowance for Doubtful Accounts |  | 6,500 |
| Supplies on Hand | 11,000 |  |
| Freight-In | 16,000 |  |
| Selling Expenses | 212,000 |  |
| Administrative Expenses | 114,000 |  |
| Land | 65,000 |  |
| Equipment | 130,000 |  |
| Merchandise Inventory | 79,000 |  |
| Building | 104,000 |  |
| Purchases | 500,000 |  |
| Dividend Income |  | 10,000 |
| Loss on Sale of Investment | 13,000 |  |
| Interest Revenue |  | 9,000 |
| Interest Expense | 12,500 |  |
| Bonds Payable |  | 100,000 |
| Gain on Sale of Land |  | 24,500 |
| Accumulated Depreciation—Building | 26,500 |  |
| Totals | $ 1,876,000 | $ 1,876,000 |

The company uses the periodic inventory system. A physical count of inventory on December 31 resulted in an inventory amount of $100,000.

## Instructions

(a)  Prepare an income statement for the year ending December 31, 2010 using the single-step form.  Assume that twenty thousand shares of common stock were outstanding the entire year.

(b)  Prepare a retained earnings statement for the year ending December 31, 2010.  Assume that the only changes in retained earnings during the current year were from net income and dividends.

## Solution to Exercise 4-3

(a)

**Limp Bizkit Corporation**
**INCOME STATEMENT**
**For the Year Ended December 31, 2010**

| | |
|---|---:|
| Revenues | |
| Net sales * | $ 930,500 |
| Gain on sale of land | 24,500 |
| Rent revenue | 14,000 |
| Dividend income | 10,000 |
| Interest revenue | 9,000 |
| Total revenues | 988,000 |
| Expenses | |
| Cost of goods sold** | 487,000 |
| Selling expenses | 212,000 |
| Administrative expenses | 114,000 |
| Loss on sale of investment | 13,000 |
| Interest expense | 12,500 |
| Total expenses | 838,500 |
| Income before taxes | 149,500 |
| Income taxes | 68,000 |
| Net income | $ 81,500 |
| | |
| Earnings per common share ($81,500 ÷ 20,000) | $ 4.08 |

| | | | |
|---|---|---:|---:|
| *Net sales: | | | |
| Sales | | | $ 958,500 |
| Less: | Sales discounts | $ 10,500 | |
| | Sales returns | 17,500 | 28,000 |
| | Net sales | | $ 930,500 |

| | | | |
|---|---|---:|---:|
| **Cost of goods sold: | | | |
| Merchandise inventory, Jan. 1 | | | $ 79,000 |
| Purchases | | $ 500,000 | |
| Less purchase discounts | | 8,000 | |
| Net purchases | | | 492,000 |
| Add freight-in | | | 16,000 |
| Merchandise available for sale | | | 587,000 |
| Less merchandise inventory, Dec. 31 | | | 100,000 |
| Cost of merchandise sold | | | $ 487,000 |

> **TIP:** The solution presented here reports income taxes separately as the last item before net income to indicate their relationship to income before taxes. It is acceptable to list the income taxes in the expenses classification and omit the subtotal and caption for "income before taxes."

(b)

### Limp Bizkit Corporation
### RETAINED EARNINGS STATEMENT
### For the Year Ended December 31, 2010

| | |
|---|---:|
| Balance, January 1 | $240,000 |
| Add: Net income | 81,500 |
| | 321,500 |
| Less: Cash dividends declared | 70,000 |
| Balance, December 31 | $251,500 |

## Approach:

(1)   Go through the adjusted trial balance and lightly cross through any account title that does **not** pertain to the computation of net income. With the exception of the balance of Merchandise Inventory (which is used to compute cost of goods sold when a periodic inventory system is in use), balance sheet account balances are not used in determining net income.

(2)   Compute intermediate subtotals for items such as (a) net sales, (b) cost of goods sold, (c) selling expenses, and (d) administrative expenses. Show your computations for these subtotals. (In this particular exercise, selling expenses and administrative expenses are already summarized.)

(3)   Identify revenue and gain items.

(4)   Identify expense and loss items.

(5)   Identify income taxes for the period.

(6)   Identify any discontinued operations and extraordinary items (none of these appear in this exercise).

(7)   Compute net income.

(8)   Compute earnings per share.

(9)   Identify the retained earnings balance at the beginning of the period.

(10)   Include any adjustments to prior periods on the statement of retained earnings (none are identified in this exercise).

(11)   Add net income for the period.

(12)   Deduct dividends declared.

(13)   Arrive at the retained earnings balance at the end of the period.

> **TIP:** The account balances in the adjusted trial balance that are **not** used for the solution requested are as follows: Notes Receivable, Investments, Accounts Payable, Accumulated Depreciation—Equipment, Cash, Accounts Receivable, Salaries Payable, Notes Payable, Common Stock, Allowance for Doubtful Accounts, Supplies on Hand, Land, Equipment, Building, Bonds Payable, and Accumulated Depreciation—Building.

## ILLUSTRATION 4-3
## TREATMENT OF IRREGULAR ITEMS (L.O. 4)

1. **DISCONTINUED OPERATIONS.** The (1) results of operations (income or loss) of a component of business that has been or will be disposed of, and (2) gain or loss on disposal of the discontinued component are reported in a separate income statement category called "Discontinued operations." This category appears **after** continuing operations but **before** extraordinary items. The gain or loss in this category is reported net of the related income tax effect.

   A component of an entity may be a reportable segment or operating segment, a reporting unit, a subsidiary, or an asset group. A segment of a business is either a separate line of business or a separate class of customer. A discontinued component of an entity comprises operations and cash flows that can be clearly distinguished operationally and for financial reporting purposes, from the rest of the entity and that will be eliminated from the ongoing operations of the entity.

2. **EXTRAORDINARY ITEMS.** Extraordinary items are reported individually in a separate category (immediately after discontinued operations, if any) net of any related income tax effect. Extraordinary items are defined as nonrecurring (infrequent) material items that differ significantly from the entity's typical business activities. In addition to being material in amount, a transaction or event must meet **both** of the following criteria to be classified as extraordinary:

   (a) **UNUSUAL NATURE.** The underlying event or transaction should possess a high degree of abnormality and be of a type clearly unrelated to, or only incidentally related to, the ordinary and typical activities of the entity, taking into account the environment in which the entity operates.

   (b) **INFREQUENCY OF OCCURRENCE.** The underlying event or transaction should be of a type that would not reasonably be expected to recur in the foreseeable future, taking into account the environment in which the entity operates.

   Examples of items that are **not** classified as extraordinary:

   (a) Writedown or writeoff of receivables, inventories, equipment leased to others, deferred research and development costs, or other intangible assets.
   (b) Gains or losses from exchange or translation of foreign currencies, including those relating to major devaluations and revaluations.
   (c) Gains or losses on disposal of a segment of a business.
   (d) Other gains or losses from sale or abandonment of property, plant, or equipment used in the business.
   (e) Effects of a strike, including those against competitors and major suppliers.
   (f) Adjustment of accruals on long-term contracts.
   (g) Gains or losses from restructurings.
   (h) Gains or losses from refunding or extinguishments of debt.

   Examples of items that **are** classified as extraordinary:
   An event or transaction that clearly meets both criteria (unusual in nature and infrequent in occurrence) and gives rise to a gain or loss from the writedown or writeoff of assets or to a gain or loss from disposal of assets and is a **direct result** of one of the following:

# ILLUSTRATION 4-3 (Continued)

      (a)     A **major casualty** (such as an earthquake, tornado, hurricane, flood, or hail storm).

      (b)     An **expropriation** (such as the confiscation of assets by a government or the exercise of eminent domain or condemnation).

      (c)     A **prohibition** under a newly enacted law or regulation.

3.    **UNUSUAL GAINS AND LOSSES.** A gain or loss that arises from a transaction that is unusual or infrequent, but not both, should be reported in the income statement as part of "income from continuing operations" (or "income before extraordinary items"). If the amount is material, it should be separately disclosed; if the amount is immaterial, it may be combined with other items on the income statement. In a multiple-step income statement, unusual gains and losses normally are classified in the "other revenues and gains" or "other expenses and losses" section, although a separate unusual items section may be displayed. Unusual gains and losses are **not** to be reported net of tax; rather, the tax consequences of these items are combined with the tax effects of all other components of income from continuing operations in the line called "income taxes."

4.    **CHANGES IN ACCOUNTING PRINCIPLE.** A change in accounting principle occurs when a company changes from one generally accepted method to another generally accepted method. Because such a change violates consistency and, therefore, reduces or destroys comparability of successive financial statements, a change in principle should only be made when the newly adopted principle is preferable (e.g., for better matching of revenues and expenses). An entity shall report a change in accounting principle through retrospective application of the new accounting principle to all prior periods. Retrospective application requires the financial statements for each individual prior period to be adjusted (recast) to reflect the application of the new principle. Any cumulative effect on periods prior to the earliest period being reported upon shall be shown as an adjustment to the opening balance of retained earnings for that period on the retained earnings statement. That is, the effect on prior periods of using the old method is compared to the effect that would have occurred if the new method had been used for prior periods; the difference is the cumulative effect of the change on prior periods. (This subject is more thoroughly discussed in **Chapter 22.**)

5.    **CHANGES IN ACCOUNTING ESTIMATE (Normal Recurring Corrections and Adjustments).** A change from one good faith estimate to another good faith estimate because of new information or experience constitutes a change in accounting estimate. A change in an estimate will affect the amount of related revenue or expense reported in the period of change if the change affects only that period, or in the period of change (called the current period) and future periods if the change affects both. Examples are a change in the estimate of uncollectible accounts receivable (bad debts expense) and a change in the estimated service life of a plant (fixed) asset (depreciation expense). A change in estimate is **not** considered a correction of an error (prior period adjustment); therefore, it is **not** handled retroactively.

# EXERCISE 4-4

**Purpose:** (L.O. 3, 4, 5, 6, 7) This exercise is designed to give you practice in preparing a condensed multiple-step income statement and a retained earnings statement when discontinued operations, an extraordinary item, a change in accounting principle, and a correction of an error are to be reported.

Presented below is information related to Chelsea Clinton Corp., for the year 2010.

| | |
|---|---|
| Net sales | $ 650,000 |
| Cost of goods sold | 400,000 |
| Selling expenses | 32,000 |
| Administrative expenses | 24,000 |
| Dividend revenue | 10,000 |
| Interest revenue | 7,000 |
| Interest expense | 15,000 |
| Write-off of goodwill due to impairment | 25,000 |
| Depreciation expense omitted in 2008 | 35,000 |
| Uninsured loss due to flood (unusual and infrequent) | 60,000 |
| Dividends declared | 42,000 |
| Retained earnings at December 31, 2009 | 1,800,000 |
| Effect on prior years of change in accounting principle (credit) | 75,000 |
| Loss from operations of discontinued segment of business | 81,000 |
| Gain from disposal of segment of business | 100,000 |
| Federal tax rate of 30% on all items | |

## Instructions
(a) Prepare a multiple-step income statement for 2010. Assume that 50,000 shares of common stock were outstanding during 2010.
(b) Prepare a retained earnings statement for 2010.

## Solution to Exercise 4-4

(a)

**Chelsea Clinton Corp.**
**INCOME STATEMENT**
**For the Year Ended December 31, 2010**

| | | |
|---|---:|---:|
| Net sales | | $ 650,000 |
| Cost of goods sold | | 400,000 |
| Gross profit | | 250,000 |
| Operating expenses | | |
|     Selling expenses | $ 32,000 | |
|     Administrative expenses | 24,000 | 56,000 |
| Income from operations | | 194,000 |
| Other revenues and gains | | |
|     Dividend revenue | 10,000 | |
|     Interest revenue | 7,000 | 17,000 |
| | | 211,000 |
| Other expenses and losses | | |
|     Interest expense | 15,000 | |
|     Loss due to write-off of goodwill | 25,000 | 40,000 |
| Income before taxes and discontinued | | |
|   operations and extraordinary item | | 171,000 |
|     Income taxes | | 51,300 |
| Income before discontinued operations and | | |
|   extraordinary item | | 119,700 |
| Discontinued operations | | |
|   Loss from operations of discontinued segment of | | |
|     business (net of $24,300 income tax effect) | 56,700 | |
|   Gain from disposal of segment of business | | |
|     (net of $30,000 income tax effect) | 70,000 | 13,300 |
| Extraordinary item | | |
|   Loss from flood (net of $18,000 income tax effect) | | 42,000 |
| Net income | | $ 91,000 |
| | | |
| Per share of common stock: | | |
|     Income before discontinued operations and | | |
|       extraordinary item | | $2.39[a] |
|     Discontinued operations | | .27[b] |
|     Extraordinary item (net of tax) | | (.84)[c] |
|     Net income | | $1.82[d] |

[a]$119,700    50,000 shares = $2.39
[b]$13,300    50,000 shares = .27
[c]$42,000    50,000 shares (.84)
[d]$91,000    50,000 shares = 1.82

**TIP:** The total income taxes pertaining to 2010 for this company was $39,000. This amount resulted from a tax bill of $51,300 that relates to the tax consequences of all items reportable on the 2010 tax return **before** considering the casualty loss of $60,000, the loss of $81,000 from operations of a discontinued segment, and the $100,000 gain from disposal of a segment of business. The $81,000 loss from operations of the discontinued segment caused a reduction in taxes of $24,300 and the $100,000 gain caused an increase in taxes of $30,000. The casualty loss caused a tax savings of $18,000. Because the casualty loss is reported as an extraordinary item on the income statement, the requirement for a net-of-tax presentation calls for the $18,000 tax reduction to be reported along with the extraordinary loss. Also, net of tax presentations are required for discontinued operations, leaving income taxes of $51,300 to be matched with income before discontinued operations and before extraordinary items. The income tax effect of the accounting change involves deferred income taxes which are discussed in **Chapter 19.** The $10,500 income tax effect of the error correction would relate to an amended tax return for a prior year.

**TIP:** In this case, the change in accounting principle caused an increase in the reported amount of Retained earnings (because it was a credit). Sometimes the cumulative effect of a change in accounting principle is a charge (debit) to Retained Earnings.

(b)

**Chelsea Clinton Corp.**
**RETAINED EARNINGS STATEMENT**
**For the Year Ended December 31, 2010**

| | | |
|---|---:|---:|
| Retained earnings, Jan. 1, 2010, as previously reported | | $ 1,800,000 |
| Correction of an error in depreciation in prior period (net of $10,500 income tax effect) | (24,500) | |
| Effect on prior periods of a change in accounting principle (net of $22,500 income tax effect) | | 52,500 |
| Adjusted balance of retained earnings at Jan. 1, 2010 | | 1,828,000 |
| Net income | | 91,000 |
| | | 1,919,000 |
| Dividends declared | | 42,000 |
| Retained earnings, December 31, 2010 | | $ 1,877,000 |

## EXERCISE 4-5

**Purpose:**    (L.O. 4) This exercise will test your knowledge of the elements and arrangement of the major sections of the income statement.

## Instructions

The following list represents captions that would appear on an income statement (single-step format) for a company reporting an extraordinary gain, an extraordinary loss, and losses from discontinued operations, as well as the results of continuing operations for the period. You are to "unscramble" the list and prepare a skeleton income statement using the captions given. (If you do not wish to write out each caption above, you may still test your knowledge by listing the appropriate letters in the correct order.)

(a)    Income before extraordinary item
(b)    Revenues
(c)    Extraordinary loss (net of tax)
(d)    Income taxes
(e)    Discontinued operations:
(f)    Extraordinary gain (net of tax)
(g)    Expenses
(h)    Loss from disposal of discontinued component of business (net of tax)
(i)    Net income
(j)    Income from continuing operations before income taxes
(k)    Loss from operations of discontinued component of business (net of tax)
(l)    Income from continuing operations

## Solution to Exercise 4-5

**Company Name**
**INCOME STATEMENT**
**For the Year Ended December 31, 20XX**

(b)    Revenues
(g)    Expenses
(j)    Income from continuing operations before income taxes
(d)    Income taxes
(l)    Income from continuing operations
(e)    Discontinued operations:
(k)        Loss from operations of discontinued component of business (net of tax)
(h)        Loss from disposal of discontinued component of business (net of tax)
(a)    Income before extraordinary item
(c)    Extraordinary loss (net of tax)
(f)    Extraordinary gain (net of tax)
(i)    Net income

# EXERCISE 4-6

**Purpose:**     (L.O. 3, 4, 5, 6, 7) This exercise will enable you to practice identifying the proper classification for items on an income statement. It will also give you an example of how the tax effects of various items are reflected in the income statement.

Margaret Moylan had the following selected transactions and events occur during 2010. The corporation is subject to a 30% tax rate on all items. All amounts are material. The corporation is engaged in the sale of energy products. The company does not report comparative financial statements.

1.     The corporation experienced an uninsured flood loss in the amount of $60,000 during the year. A flood is unusual and infrequent in the region where the corporation resides.

2.     At the beginning of 2008, the corporation purchased an office machine for $108,000 (salvage value of $18,000) that has a useful life of six years. The bookkeeper used straight-line depreciation for 2008 and 2009, but failed to deduct the salvage value in computing the depreciable base. The same depreciation calculations were used for tax purposes.

3.     Sale of securities held as a part of Moylan's portfolio resulted in a loss of $62,200 (pretax).

4.     When its president died, the corporation realized $100,000 from an insurance policy. The cash surrender value of this policy had been carried on the books as an investment in the amount of $34,000 (the gain is nontaxable).

5.     The corporation disposed of a component of business at a loss of $140,000 before taxes.

6.     The corporation decided to change its method of inventory pricing from average cost to the FIFO method. The effect of this change on prior years would be to increase 2008 income by $64,000 and decrease 2009 income by $20,000 before taxes. The FIFO method has been used for 2010.

## Instructions:

Describe how each of the items above will be reported in a multiple-step income statement for 2010. Indicate the amount that will be reported and the section of the income statement in which the amount will appear.

## Solution to Exercise 4-6

1.   A loss of $42,000 ($60,000 minus 30% of $60,000) will be reported in the extraordinary items section of the income statement.

2.   Depreciation expense of $15,000 [($108,000 - $18,000) ÷ 6 years] will appear in the administrative expense (an operating expense) section of the 2010 income statement. The correction of an error in computing prior periods' depreciation (a prior period adjustment) will **not** appear on the income statement. Rather, a credit of $4,200 will appear on the retained earnings statement for 2010 as an adjustment to the beginning balance of retained earnings (assuming single-period rather than comparative financial statements are presented). The prior period adjustment is reported net of tax. Computations:

       $108,000 ÷ 6 = $18,000 depreciation taken in 2008.
       $108,000 ÷ 6 = $18,000 depreciation taken in 2009.
       ($108,000 - $18,000) ÷ 6 = $15,000 correct annual depreciation.
       $15,000 x 2 = $30,000 correct depreciation for 2008 & 2009.
       ($18,000 + $18,000) - $30,000 = $6,000 overstated expense in prior years.
       $6,000 - 30%($6,000) = $4,200 addition to retained earnings.

3.   A loss of $62,200 will be reported in the other expenses and losses section of the income statement. It is **not** reported net of tax.

4.   A gain of $66,000 ($100,000 - $34,000) will appear in the other revenues and gains section of the income statement. It is **not** reported net of tax (in this case, it had no tax effect anyway). A good caption for this item is "Gain from proceeds of life insurance policy."

5.   A loss of $98,000 ($140,000 minus 30% of $140,000) will appear as a loss in the discontinued operations section of the income statement.

6.   A cumulative effect on prior periods of a change in accounting principle from average cost to FIFO will appear as a $30,800 credit adjustment to retained earnings balance at the beginning of 2010 on the retained earnings statement. The 2010 income statement will report amounts based on application of the new (FIFO) method. Computations:

       $64,000 credit (increase in prior period income)
        20,000 debit (decrease in prior period income)
        44,000 credit (net catch-up adjustment needed)
          70% net of tax rate
       $30,800 credit (cumulative effect, net of tax)

## ILLUSTRATION 4-4
## NET INCOME AND COMPREHENSIVE INCOME (L.O. 8)

**Comprehensive income** includes all changes in stockholders' equity except those resulting from investments by owners and distributions to owners. Comprehensive income therefore includes all revenues, gains, expenses, and losses reported in net income. In addition, it includes gains and losses that bypass net income but are included as part of comprehensive income. These gains and losses are referred to as **other comprehensive income.**

An example of a gain or loss that is reported as other comprehensive income is an unrealized gain or loss on available-for-sale securities held as an investment. Excluding this type of gain or loss from net income and disclosing it separately reduces the volatility of net income due to changes in fair value yet informs the financial statement user of the gain or loss that would occur if the securities were sold at fair value. This subject is discussed further in **Chapter 17.** Other examples of other comprehensive income items are translation gains and losses on foreign currency (a subject in an advanced accounting text) and excess of additional pension liability over unrecognized prior service cost (a subject of **Chapter 20**).

The FASB requires that components of other comprehensive income be reported in one of three ways: (1) in a separate (second) income statement, (2) in a combined statement of comprehensive income, or (3) as a part of the statement of stockholders' equity. To illustrate these three presentation formats, assume Rosie O'Donnell Inc. reports the following information for 2010: sales revenues, $1,600,000, cost of goods sold $1,200,000, operating expenses $180,000, and an unrealized holding gain on available-for-sale securities of $60,000.

The first approach is to provide information in a two income statement format. It is shown below:

**Rosie O'Donnell Inc.**
**Income Statement**
**For the Year Ended December 31, 2010**

| | |
|---|---:|
| Sales revenue | $1,600,000 |
| Cost of goods sold | 1,200,000 |
| Gross profit | 400,000 |
| Operating expenses | 180,000 |
| Net income | $ 220,000 |

**Rosie O'Donnell Inc.**
**Comprehensive Income Statement**
**For the Year Ended December 31, 2010**

| | |
|---|---:|
| Net income | $220,000 |
| Other comprehensive income | |
|     Unrealized holding gains | 60,000 |
| Comprehensive income | $280,000 |

## ILLUSTRATION 4-4 (Continued)

–

Reporting comprehensive income in a separate statement indicates that the gains and losses identified as other comprehensive income do not have the same status as traditional gains and losses. In addition, the relationship of the traditional income statement to the new statement is apparent because net income is the starting point in the new statement.

The second approach is to provide a combined statement. It is shown below:

**Rosie O'Donnell Inc.**
**Combined Statement of Comprehensive Income**
**For the Year Ended December 31, 2010**

| | |
|---|---:|
| Sales revenue | $1,600,000 |
| Cost of goods sold | 1,200,000 |
| Gross profit | 400,000 |
| Operating expenses | 180,000 |
| Net income | 220,000 |
| Unrealized holding gains, net of tax | 60,000 |
| Comprehensive income | $ 280,000 |

The combined statement has the advantage of not requiring the creation of a new financial statement. However, burying the traditional net income figure as a subtotal on the statement is a disadvantage.

A third approach is to report other comprehensive income items in a statement of stockholders' equity. This statement reports the changes in each stockholders' equity account and in total stockholders' equity during the year. The statement of stockholders' equity is prepared in columnar form with columns for each account and for total stockholders' equity. A statement of stockholders' equity for Rosie O'Donnell Inc. is shown below:

**Rosie O'Donnell Inc.**
**Statement of Stockholders' Equity**
**For the Year Ended December 31, 2010**

| | Total | Comprehensive Income | Retained Earnings | Accumulated Other Comprehensive Income | Common Stock |
|---|---|---|---|---|---|
| Beginning balance | $ 820,000 | | $100,000 | $120,000 | $600,000 |
| Issuance of stock | 150,000 | | | | 150,000 |
| Net income | 220,000 | $220,000 | 220,000 | | |
| Other comprehensive income | 60,000 | 60,000 | | 60,000 | |
| Ending balance | $1,250,000 | $280,000 | $320,000 | $180,000 | $750,000 |

The net income for a period of time is closed to Retained Earnings (a component of stockholders' equity). Other comprehensive income for a period is closed to Accumulated Other Comprehensive Income (a separate component of stockholders' equity). The accumulated other comprehensive income is reported in the stockholders' equity section of the balance sheet as follows:

## ILLUSTRATION 4-4 (Continued)

**Rosie O'Donnell Inc.**
**Balance Sheet (Partial)**
**As of December 31, 2010**

| | |
|---|---:|
| Stockholders' equity | |
| Common stock | $  750,000 |
| Retained earnings | 320,000 |
| Accumulated other comprehensive income | 180,000 |
| Total stockholders' equity | $1,250,000 |

**TIP:** By providing a comprehensive income statement and a stockholders' equity statement, the company reports information about all changes in net assets (owners' equity). With this information, users will be better able to understand the quality of the company's earnings. This information should help users to predict the amount, timing, and uncertainty of future cash flows.

**TIP:** The **statement of stockholders' equity** is often called the **statement of changes in stockholders' equity** or **stockholders' equity statement.**

**TIP:** If a company chooses to report the components of other comprehensive income in a statement of stockholders' equity, that statement must be displayed as a primary financial statement.

**TIP:** A company is required to display the components of other comprehensive income either (1) net of related tax effects or (2) before related tax effects with one amount shown for the aggregate amount of tax related to the total amount of other comprehensive income. Under either alternative, each component of other comprehensive income must be shown, net of related taxes, either on the face of the statement or in the notes.

## ANALYSIS OF MULTIPLE-CHOICE TYPE QUESTIONS

**QUESTION**

1. (L.O. 3) In a multiple-step income statement, the excess of gross profit over operating expenses is called:
   a. net margin.
   b. income from operations.
   c. net profit.
   d. earnings.

**Approach and Explanation:** Visualize a multiple-step income statement. Net sales less cost of goods sold yields gross profit (sometimes called gross margin). Gross profit less operating expenses equals income from operations. From there, other revenues and gains are added, other expenses and losses are deducted, and income tax expense is deducted to arrive at net income. Another popular name for net income is earnings. Net profit would likely refer to net income. Net margin is not a term applied to the income statement. (Solution = b.)

**QUESTION**

2. (L.O. 3) The following expenses and loss were among those incurred by Mitzer Company during 2010:

| | |
|---|---|
| Rent for office space | $ 660,000 |
| Loss on sale of office furniture | 55,000 |
| Interest | 132,000 |
| Accounting and legal fees | 352,000 |
| Freight-out | 70,000 |

One-half of the rented premises is occupied by the sales department. How much of the items listed above should be classified as general and administrative expenses in Mitzer's income statement for 2010?
   a. $682,000
   b. $869,000
   c. $884,000
   d. $939,000

**Approach and Explanation:** For each item listed, identify where it is reported. Then collect together the ones that you identify as general and administrative (G&A) expenses.

| | |
|---|---|
| Rent for office space: | One-half selling; one-half G&A |
| Loss on sale of equipment: | Other expenses and losses |
| Interest: | Other expenses and losses |
| Accounting and legal fees: | G&A expenses |
| Freight-out: | Selling expenses |

| | | |
|---|---|---|
| One-half of office space (.5 x $660,000) | $330,000 | |
| Accounting and legal fees | 352,000 | |
| General and administrative expenses | $682,000 | (Solution = a.) |

**QUESTION**

3. (L.O. 3) Which of the following is **not** a selling expense?
   a. Advertising expense
   b. Office salaries expense
   c. Freight-out
   d. Store supplies consumed

**Approach and Explanation:** Take each account and determine its classification. Items "a," "c," and "d" are selling expenses because they are associated with the sales function. Office salaries are related to normal operations, but they are not related to the sales function of the business. Therefore, they are not classified as a selling expense. (Solution = b.)

## QUESTION

4.  (L.O. 3) The accountant for the Orion Sales Company is preparing the income statement for 2010 and the balance sheet at December 31, 2010. The January 1, 2010 merchandise inventory balance will appear:
    a.  only as an asset on the balance sheet.
    b.  only in the cost of goods sold section of the income statement.
    c.  as a deduction in the cost of goods sold section of the income statement and as a current asset on the balance sheet.
    d.  as an addition in the cost of goods sold section of the income statement and as a current asset on the balance sheet.

**Explanation:** The January 1, 2010 inventory amount is the beginning inventory figure. Beginning inventory is a component of the cost of goods available for sale for the period which is a component of cost of goods sold. (Solution = b.)

> **TIP:** If the question asked about the December 31, 2010 merchandise inventory balance (ending inventory) rather than the beginning inventory balance, the correct answer would have been "c" (as a deduction in computing cost of sales and as a current asset).

## QUESTION

5.  (L.O. 2, 3) The following amounts relate to the current year for the Ira Company:

| | |
|---|---|
| Beginning inventory | $ 20,000 |
| Ending inventory | 28,000 |
| Purchases | 166,000 |
| Purchase returns | 4,800 |
| Transportation-out | 6,000 |

The amount of cost of goods sold for the period is:
    a.  $169,200.
    b.  $162,800.
    c.  $153,200.
    d.  $147,200.

**Approach and Explanation:** Write down the computation model for cost of goods sold. Enter the amounts given and solve for the unknown.

| | | |
|---|---|---|
| $ 20,000 | | Beginning Inventory |
| + 166,000 | + | Purchases |
| - 4,800 | - | Purchase Returns and Allowances |
| | - | Purchase Discounts |
| _____ | + | Freight-in |
| 181,200 | = | Cost of Goods Available for Sale |
| - 28,000 | - | Ending Inventory |
| $ 153,200 | = | Cost of Goods Sold |

(Solution = c.)

> **TIP:** Transportation-out is classified as a selling expense, not a component of cost of goods sold. "Transportation-out" is often called "freight-out;" "transportation-in" is another name for "freight-in."

**QUESTION**

6.    (L.O. 4) A loss from the disposal of component of an entity should be reported in the income statement:
   a.    after extraordinary items and it should be reflected net of the related income tax effect.
   b.    before extraordinary items and it should be reflected net of the related income tax effect.
   c.    after extraordinary items and it should not be reflected net of the related income tax effect.
   d.    before extraordinary items and it should not be reflected net of the related income tax effect.

**Approach and Explanation:** Keep in mind the acronym **DE**. Write the items down in the proper order. Read each answer response to see if it properly describes the order in which you have listed the items.
      The correct order of the items involved in the question is as follows:
      (1)    **Discontinued operations**
      (2)   · **Extraordinary items**
Both discontinued operations and extraordinary items are to be reported net of the related income tax effect. (Solution = b.)

**QUESTION**

7.    (L.O. 4) A material loss should be presented separately as a component of income from continuing operations when it is:
   a.    unusual in nature and infrequent in occurrence.
   b.    unusual in nature but **not** infrequent in occurrence.
   c.    an extraordinary loss.
   d.    a cumulative effect of a change in accounting principle.

**Approach and Explanation:** Visualize an income statement and mentally identify the section that reports income from continuing operations. Read one answer at a time and determine if it correctly describes how the statement in the question stem can be completed. A material loss that is (1) unusual in nature **and** (2) infrequent in occurrence should be reported as an extraordinary item. A loss that meets one of the criteria for being classified as extraordinary, but not both, should be separately disclosed as a component of income from continuing operations. An extraordinary item is to be reported **after** (and not part of) income from continuing operations. A cumulative effect of a change in accounting principle does not affect the income statement. (Solution = b.)

**QUESTION**

8.    (L.O. 4) During the year ended December 31, 2010, Schmelya Corporation incurred the following infrequent losses:
      1.    A factory was shut down during a major strike by employees; costs were $120,000.
      2.    A loss of $50,000 was incurred on the abandonment of computer equipment used in the business.
      3.    A restructuring charge of $75,000.
      4.    A loss of $82,000 was incurred as a result of flood damage to a warehouse.
   How much total loss should Schmelya report in the extraordinary item section of its 2010 income statement?
   a.    $82,000
   b.    $120,000
   c.    $202,000
   d.    $252,000

**Approach and Explanation:** It is wise to review the list of items that are classified as extraordinary items and the list of items that are not extraordinary items (see **Illustration 4-3**) until you can readily recognize items that appear in the list. In the question at hand, the first three items are on the list of items that are **not** extraordinary. Therefore, the only possible one being extraordinary is the loss from flood damage. A flood would be considered infrequent in some locations but not others. The stem of the question indicates it is deemed infrequent for Schmelya. To be classified as extraordinary, an item needs to be unusual in nature and infrequent in occurrence. However, there are certain items that do **not** constitute extraordinary items. (Solution = a.)

**QUESTION**
9.  (L.O. 4) Which of the following should be classified as an extraordinary item?
    a.  Loss from excess of book value of assets over amount of condemnation award.
    b.  Loss from exchange of foreign currencies.
    c.  Loss from abandonment of plant assets.
    d.  Loss from writedown of goodwill.

**Explanation:** Answer selections "b.", "c.", and "d." involve transactions that appear on the list of items that are **not** to be classified as extraordinary items on the income statement. A gain or loss from an expropriation is to be classified as an extraordinary item. When a government exercises its right to eminent domain, a condemnation award is given to the owner of the property. An excess of the asset's book value over its condemnation award results in a loss. (Solution = a.)

**QUESTION**
10. (L.O. 4) When a piece of equipment is sold at a gain of $700,000 less related taxes of $280,000, and the gain is **not** considered unusual or infrequent, the income statement for the period would show these effects as:
    a.  an extraordinary item net of applicable income taxes, $420,000.
    b.  a prior period adjustment net of applicable income taxes, $420,000.
    c.  an other gain net of applicable income taxes, $420,000.
    d.  an other gain of $700,000 and an increase in income tax expense of $280,000.

**Explanation:** A gain or loss on the disposal of property, plant and equipment that is **not** unusual and infrequent is **not** to be classified as an extraordinary item. Therefore, a gain from such a disposal goes in the "other revenues and gains" classification. The related tax effect is reflected in the "income tax expense" figure. The only items reported net of tax are extraordinary items, discontinued operations, changes in accounting principle, and prior period adjustments. The tax effects of all other transactions are summarized in the amount captioned "income tax expense." (Solution = d.)

**QUESTION**
11. (L.O. 7) A correction of an error in prior periods' income will be reported:

|     | In the income statement | Net of tax |
| --- | --- | --- |
| a.  | Yes | Yes |
| b.  | No | No |
| c.  | Yes | No |
| d.  | No | Yes |

**Approach and Explanation:** Write down what you know about the accounting for a correction of an error in computing income in a prior period. Then answer "yes" or "no" to each question posed at the top of the appropriate column. Find the combination that matches yours. A correction of an error is a prior period adjustment; it is reported net of tax as an adjustment to the beginning retained earnings balance on the statement of retained earnings in the period the error is corrected. (Solution = d.)

**QUESTION**

12.    (L.O. 7) The OVA Company had the following errors occur in its financial statements:

|  | 2009 | 2010 |
|---|---|---|
| Ending inventory | $12,000 Understated | $18,000 Overstated |
| Depreciation expense | $24,000 Overstated | $14,000 Overstated |

Ignoring any related income tax effect and assuming that none of the errors were detected or corrected, by what amount will retained earnings at December 31, 2010 be misstated?
a.    $18,000 overstated.
b.    $20,000 understated.
c.    $32,000 understated.
d.    $14,000 understated.
e.    None of the above.

**Approach and Explanation:** Explain the effects of each error separately and then combine your results. The $12,000 understatement of ending inventory for 2009 causes a $12,000 understatement of net income for 2009 and a $12,000 overstatement of net income for 2010 (because the ending inventory for 2009 is the beginning inventory for 2010); this nets to be a zero impact on the retained earnings balance at December 31, 2010. The $24,000 overstatement of depreciation expense in 2009 causes an understatement of net income for 2009 and a corresponding $24,000 understatement of retained earnings at December 31, 2009 and at December 31, 2010. The $18,000 overstatement of ending inventory for 2010 causes an overstatement of net income for 2010 and an $18,000 overstatement of retained earnings at December 31, 2010. A $14,000 overstatement of depreciation expense for 2010 causes a $14,000 understatement of net income for 2010 and a $14,000 understatement of retained earnings at December 31, 2010. The net effect on retained earnings at December 31, 2010 is therefore a $24,000 understatement + an $18,000 overstatement + a $14,000 understatement which equals a $20,000 understatement. (Solution = b.)

**QUESTION**

13.    (L.O. 8) Comprehensive income includes all of the following **except**:
a.    unrealized holding losses.
b.    dividends declared and paid.
c.    interest income.
d.    gains on disposal of assets.

**Approach and Explanation:**   Define comprehensive income before reading the answer selections. Then analyze each answer selection to see how it relates to the definition.   Comprehensive income includes all changes in stockholders' equity except those resulting from investments by owners and distributions to owners.  Dividends declared and paid are a distribution to owners.  Dividends received would be a component of comprehensive income. (Solution = b.)

# CHAPTER 5

# BALANCE SHEET AND
# STATEMENT OF CASH FLOWS

## OVERVIEW

A balance sheet reports on the financial position of an entity at a point in time. A statement of cash flows reports reasons for cash receipts and cash payments during the period. In this chapter, we discuss the classifications of a balance sheet and a statement of cash flows along with related disclosure issues. It is extremely important that items are properly classified. Errors in classification will result in incorrect ratio analyses which can lead to misinterpretations of the meaning of the information conveyed. This can affect the decisions that are being made based on that information.

## SUMMARY OF LEARNING OBJECTIVES

1.  **Explain the uses and limitations of a balance sheet.** The balance sheet provides information about the nature and amounts of investments in a company's resources, obligations to creditors, and the owners' equity in resources. The balance sheet contributes to financial reporting by providing a basis for: (1) computing rates of return, (2) evaluating the capital structure of the enterprise, and (3) assessing the liquidity, solvency, and financial flexibility of the enterprise. Three limitations of a balance sheet are: (1) The balance sheet does not reflect fair value because accountants use a historical cost basis in valuing and reporting most assets and liabilities. (2) Companies must use judgments and estimates to determine certain amounts, such as the collectibility of receivables and the useful life of long-term tangible and intangible assets. (3) The balance sheet omits many items that are of financial value to the business but cannot be recorded objectively, such as human resources, customer base, and reputation.

2.  **Identify the major classifications of the balance sheet.** The general elements of the balance sheet are assets, liabilities, and equity. The major classifications of assets are current assets; long-term investments; property, plant, and equipment; intangible assets; and other assets. The major classifications of liabilities are current liabilities and long-term liabilities. The balance sheet of a corporation generally classifies owners' equity as capital stock, additional paid-in capital, and retained earnings.

3.  **Prepare a classified balance sheet using the report and account formats.** The report form lists liabilities and stockholders' equity directly below assets on the same page. The account form lists assets, by sections, on the left side and liabilities and stockholders' equity, by sections, on the right side.

4.  **Determine which balance sheet information requries supplemental disclosure.** Four types of information normally are supplemental to account titles and amounts presented in the balance sheet: (1) **Contingencies:** Material events that have an uncertain outcome; (2) **Accounting policies:** Explanations of the valuation methods used or the basic assumptions made concerning inventory valuation, depreciation methods, investments in subsidiaries, etc.; (3) **Contractual situations:** Explanations of certain restrictions or covenants attached to specific assets or, more

likely, to liabilities; (4) **Fair values:** Disclosures related to the fair value information for certain types of assets and liabilities (particularly those that relate to financial instruments).

5.   **Describe the major disclosure techniques for the balance sheet.** Companies use four methods to disclose pertinent information in the balance sheet: (1) **Parenthetical explanations:** Parenthetical information provides additional information or description following the item; (2) **Notes:** A company uses notes if it cannot conveniently show additional explanations or descriptions as parenthetical explanations; (3) **Cross reference and contra items:** Companies "cross reference" a direct relationship between an asset and a liability on the balance sheet; (4) **Supporting schedules:** Often a company uses a separate schedule to present more detailed information shown in the balance sheet, than just the single summary item shown in the balance sheet.

6.   **Indicate the purpose of the statement of cash flows.** The primary purpose of a statement of cash flows is to provide relevant information about a company's cash receipts and cash payments during a period. Reporting the sources, uses, and net increase or decrease in cash enables financial statement readers to know what is happening to a company's most liquid resource.

7.   **Identify the content of the statement of cash flows.** In the statement of cash flows, companies classify the period's cash receipts and cash payments during a period into three different activities: (1) **Operating activities** include all transactions and other events that are not defined as investing or financing activities. Operating activities generally involve producing and delivering goods and providing services. Cash flows from operating activities are generally the cash effects of transactions that enter into the determination of net income. (2) **Investing activities** include making and collecting loans and acquiring and disposing of investments (both debt and equity) and property, plant, and equipment. (3) **Financing activities** include (a) obtaining resources from owners and providing them with a return on and a return of their investment, and (b) borrowing money from creditors and repaying the amounts borrowed.

8.   **Prepare a basic statement of cash flows.** The information to prepare a statement of cash flows usually comes from comparative balance sheets, the current income statement, and selected transaction data. Companies follow four steps to prepare the statement of cash flows from these sources: (1) Determine the net cash provided by or used in operating activities, (2) determine the net cash provided by or used in investing and financing activities, (3) determine the net change (increase or decrease) in cash during the period, and (4) reconcile the net change in cash with the beginning and the ending cash balances.

9.   **Understand the usefulness of the statement of cash flows.** Creditors examine the cash flow statement carefully because they are concerned about being paid. The amount and trend of net cash flow provided by operating activities in relation to the company's liabilities is helpful in making the assessment. Two ratios used in this regard are the current cash debt ratio and the cash debt ratio. In addition, the amount of free cash flow provides creditors and stockholders with a picture of the company's financial flexibility.

*10.   **Identify the major types of financial ratios and what they measure.** A ratio expresses the mathematical relationship between one quantity and another, in terms of either a percentage, a rate, or a proportion. **Liquidity ratios** measure the short-run ability to pay maturing obligations. **Activity ratios** measure the effectiveness of asset usage. **Profitability ratios** measure the success or failure of an enterprise. **Coverage** ratios measure the degree of protection for long-term creditors and investors.

   *This material is covered in Appendix 5A in the text.

# TIPS ON CHAPTER TOPICS

**TIP:** It is extremely important that items are properly classified on a balance sheet. Errors in classification can result in incorrect ratio analyses (discussed in **Appendix 5A**) which may lead to misrepresentations of the meaning of the information conveyed and can effect decisions that are based on those analyses.

**TIP:** The balance of liabilities and the balance of owners' equity at a point in time simply serve as scorecards of the total amounts of unspecified assets which have come about from creditor sources (liabilities) and owner sources (owners' equity). Thus, you can **not** determine the amount of cash (or any other specific asset) held by an entity by looking at the balance of owners' equity or liabilities. You must look at the listing of individual assets on the balance sheet to determine the amount of cash owned.

**TIP:** In answering questions regarding the classification of items on a balance sheet, always assume an individual item is material in amount unless it is apparent otherwise.

**TIP:** Current assets are presented in the balance sheet in order of liquidity. The five major items found in the current asset classification of the balance sheet and their bases of valuation are:

| Item | Basis of Valuation |
|---|---|
| Cash and cash equivalents | Fair value |
| Short-term investments | Fair value (generally) |
| Receivables | Estimated amount collectible (i.e., net realizable value) |
| Inventories | Lower of cost or market |
| Prepaid expenses | Cost |

**TIP:** For receivables arising from unusual transactions (such as sale of property, a loan to an affiliate, or loans to employees), companies should separately classify these as long-term assets unless collection is expected within one year. If collection is expected within one year, then these receivables must be shown separately from nontrade receivables.

**TIP:** To classify items in financial statements, companies group those items with similar characteristics and separate items that have different characteristics. For example, companies should report separately:

1. Assets that differ in their **type or expected function** in the company's central operations or other activities. For example merchandise inventories are to be reported separately from property, plant, and equipment.

2. Assets and liabilities with **different** implications for the company's **financial flexibility.** For example, equipment owned and used in operations should be separate from leased equipment used in operations (the leased items are subject to restrictions), and land supporting the company's office facilities should be separate from land held for investment.

3. Assets and liabilities with **different general liquidity** characteristics. For example, cash is reported separately from inventories.

## ILLUSTRATION 5-1
## BALANCE SHEET CLASSIFICATIONS (L.O. 2)

**CURRENT ASSETS:** includes cash (unrestricted) and items which are expected to be converted to cash or sold or consumed within the next year or operating cycle, whichever is longer. Includes cash and cash equivalents, short-term investments, net trade receivables, short-term notes receivable, inventories, prepaid expenses, and some deferred income taxes.

**LONG-TERM INVESTMENTS:** includes long-term receivables, restricted funds, investments in stocks and bonds of other companies, land held for future plant site, land held for speculation, investments set aside in special funds such as a sinking fund, pension fund, or plant expansion fund, cash surrender value of life insurance, and investments in nonconsolidated subsidiaries or affiliated companies.

**PROPERTY, PLANT AND EQUIPMENT:** includes long-lived tangible assets (land, building, equipment, machinery, and tools) that are currently being used in operations (used to produce goods and services for customers). Two items that do not meet this criteria (because they are not currently being used in operations) but are included in property, plant and equipment are Plant Under Construction and Deposits on Equipment. Assets in this category are often referred to as plant assets or fixed assets. They are not held for resale. Leasehold improvements are often included here.

**INTANGIBLE ASSETS:** includes assets that lack physical substance, such as a patent, copyright, franchise, trademark, or trade names that give the holder exclusive right of use for a specified period of time. Their value to a company is generally derived from the rights or privileges granted by governmental or other authority. Also includes goodwill, licenses, customer lists, and noncompete agreements.

**OTHER ASSETS:** includes assets that by common practice are not classified elsewhere. Can include long-term prepaid expenses, prepaid pension cost, some long-term receivables, restricted cash or other assets in special funds, deferred income taxes, and property held for sale that is not expected to be sold within the next year.

**CURRENT LIABILITIES:** obligations that are due within a year and are expected to require the use of current assets or the incurrence of other current liabilities to liquidate them. Includes short-term notes payable, accounts payable, taxes payable, salaries payable, warranty obligations, deferred income taxes, current maturities of long-term debt, unearned revenues, and accrued employee benefits payable.

**LONG-TERM LIABILITIES:** obligations that do not meet the criteria to be classified as current liabilities. Includes long-term notes payable, lease obligations, bonds payable, deferred income taxes, mortgage payable and pension obligations.

**CAPITAL STOCK:** the par or stated value of shares issued or about to be issued. Includes common stock and preferred stock.

## ILLUSTRATION 5-1 (continued)

**ADDITIONAL PAID-IN CAPITAL:** the excess of the issuance price over the par or stated value of stock issued or about to be issued. Includes paid-in capital in excess of par from various sources including treasury stock transactions.

**RETAINED EARNINGS:** Excess of net incomes over net losses and dividend distributions since inception of the business. An appropriation of retained earnings is a restricted portion of the total retained earnings figure.

---

**TIP:** Memorize the definition of current assets. **Current assets** are cash and other assets that are expected to be converted into cash, sold, or consumed within the year or operating cycle that immediately follows the balance sheet date, whichever is longer. Think about how various examples of current assets meet this definition. Accounts receivable are current assets because they will be converted to cash shortly after the balance sheet date; inventory is a current asset because it will be sold within the year that follows the balance sheet date; prepaid insurance is a current asset because it will be consumed (used up) within the next year.

**TIP:** A normal **operating cycle** is the length of time required to go from cash back to cash. That is, for an entity which sells products, the operating cycle is the time required to take cash out to buy (or to manufacture) inventory then sell the inventory and receive cash (either from a cash sale or the collection of an account receivable stemming from a credit sale). Thus, the length of an entity's operating cycle depends on the nature of its business. Unless otherwise indicated, always assume the operating cycle for an entity is less than a year so that the one-year test is used as the cutoff between current and noncurrent.

**TIP:** Memorize the definition of current liabilities. **Current liabilities** are obligations which are expected to require the use of current assets or the incurrence of other current liabilities. A liability may be due within a year of the balance sheet and **not** be a current liability. An example is a debt due in six months that will be liquidated by use of a noncurrent asset.

**TIP:** In a classified balance sheet, any asset that is not classified as a current asset is a noncurrent asset. There are four noncurrent asset classifications: long-term investments; property, plant and equipment; intangible assets; and other assets.

**TIP:** In a classified balance sheet, liabilities are classified either as current or noncurrent liabilities. The noncurrent liabilities are usually titled "long-term liabilities" or "long-term debt."

**TIP:** Current assets are listed in the order of their liquidity, with the most liquid ones being listed first. Current liabilities are not listed in any prescribed order; however, notes payable (short-term) is usually listed first followed by accounts payable (and the remainder of the current liabilities are often listed in descending order of amount). Property, plant and equipment items are listed in order of length of life, with the longest life first.

**TIP:** **"Short-term"** is synonymous with **"current,"** and **"long-term"** is synonymous with **"noncurrent."** Therefore, "short-term debt" can be used to refer to "current liabilities." Asset classifications are typically titled current and noncurrent; whereas, liability classifications are typically titled current and long-term.

**TIP:** All noncurrent assets (assets in classifications other than "current assets") are resources that are not expected to be converted into cash or fully consumed in operations within one year or the operating cycle, whichever is longer.

**TIP:**   An investment may be classified as a current asset (if it is a short-term investment) or as a noncurrent asset (if it is a long-term investment). For an investment to be classified as current: (1) it should be readily marketable, and (2) there should be a lack of management intent to hold it for a long-term purpose.

**TIP:**   A **valuation account** is an account whose balance is needed to properly value the item to which the valuation account relates. A **contra account** is a valuation account whose normal balance (debit versus credit) is opposite of the normal balance of the account to which the valuation account relates. An **adjunct account** is a valuation account whose normal balance is the same as the normal balance of the account to which it relates.

**TIP:**   Interest on debt is due annually or more frequently (semiannually or monthly, for example). Therefore, interest accrued on long-term debt is generally classified as a current liability. Likewise, interest receivable stemming from the accrual of interest on long-term receivables is generally classified as a current asset.

**TIP:**   A fund can consist of restricted cash or noncash assets such as stocks and bonds of other companies. Funds are reported in the long-term investment classification.

**TIP:**   If an account title starts with "Allowance for...," then it generally is a contra balance sheet account.

**TIP:**   If an account title starts with "Provision for...," it is generally an income statement account.

**TIP:**   An appropriation or restriction of retained earnings is a positive component of total retained earnings. An appropriation of retained earnings refers to a portion of retained earnings which for one reason or another is restricted, which simply means it cannot be used as a basis for the declaration of dividends.

**TIP:**   Regarding the valuation of balance sheet items, fair value information may be more useful than historical cost for valuation of certain types of assets and liabilities. This is particularly true for financial instruments (defined as cash, an ownership interest, or a contractual right to receive or obligation to deliver cash or another financial instrument where contractual rights represent assets and contractual obligations represent liabilities).

To increase consistency and comparability in the reporting of the ever expanding disclosures of fair value measures, companies follow a fair value hierarchy that provides insight into how to determine fair value. The hierarchy (depicted in **Illustration 2-5** in this book) has three levels. **Level 1** measures (the most reliable) are based on observable inputs, such as market prices for identical assets or liabilities. **Level 2** measures (less reliable) are based on market-based inputs other than those included in Level 1, such as those based on market prices for similar assets or liabilities. **Level 3** measures (least reliable) are based on unobservable inputs, such as a company's own data or assumptions.

For major groups of assets and liabilities, companies must make the following fair value disclosures: (1) the fair value measurement and (2) the fair value hierarchy level of the measurements as a whole, classified by Level 1, 2, or 3.

In addition, companies must provide significant additional disclosure related to Level 3 measurements. The disclosures related to Level 3 are substantial and must identify what assumptions the company used to generate the fair value numbers and any related income effects. Companies will want to use Level 1 and 2 measurements as much as possible. In most cases, these valuations should be very reliable, as the fair value measurements are based on market information. In contrast, a company that uses Level 3 measurements extensively must be carefully evaluated to understand the impact these valuations have on the financial statements.

Level 3 fair value measurements may be developed using expected cash flow and present value techniques, as described in Statement of Financial Accounting Concepts No. 7, "Using Cash Flow Information and Present Value in Accounting," as discussed in Chapter 6.

## EXERCISE 5-1

**Purpose:**     (L.O. 2) This exercise lists examples of balance sheet accounts and enables you to practice determining where they are classified.

## Instructions

Indicate which balance sheet classification is the most appropriate for reporting each account listed below by selecting the abbreviation of the corresponding section.

| | | | |
|---|---|---|---|
| CA | Current Assets | CL | Current Liabilities |
| INV | Long-term Investments | LTL | Long-term Liabilities |
| PPE | Property, Plant, and Equipment | CS | Capital Stock |
| ITG | Intangible Assets | APC | Additional Paid-in Capital |
| OA | Other Assets | RE | Retained Earnings |

If the account is a contra account, indicate that fact by putting the abbreviation in parenthesis. If the exact classification depends on facts which are not given, indicate your answer of "depends on" by the abbreviation **DEP** and the possible classifications. If the account is reported on the income statement rather than the balance sheet, indicate that fact with an **IS**. Assume all items are material.

| Classifi-cation | Account | Classifi-cation | Account |
|---|---|---|---|
| _____ | 1. Accounts Payable. | _____ | 11. Advances to Vendors. |
| _____ | 2. Accounts Receivable. | _____ | 12. Advertising Expense. |
| _____ | 3. Accrued Interest Receivable on Long-term Investments. | _____ | 13. Allowance for Bad Debts. |
| | | _____ | 14. Allowance for Depreciation. |
| _____ | 4. Accrued Interest Payable. | _____ | 15. Allowance for Doubtful Accounts. |
| _____ | 5. Accrued Taxes Payable. | _____ | 16. Allowance for Excess of Cost Over Market Value of Inventory. |
| _____ | 6. Accumulated Depreciation— Building. | | |
| _____ | 7. Accumulated Depreciation— Machinery. | _____ | 17. Allowance for Inventory Price Declines. |
| _____ | 8. Mineral Reserves. | _____ | 18. Allowance for Purchase Discounts. |
| _____ | 9. Advances by Customers. | _____ | 19. Allowance for Sales Discounts. |
| _____ | 10. Advances to Affiliates. | _____ | 20. Allowance for Uncollectible Accts. |

| Classifi-cation | Account | Classifi-cation | Account |
|---|---|---|---|
| _____ | 21. Appropriation for Bond Sinking Fund. | _____ | 39. Current Portion of Mortgage Payable. |
| _____ | 22. Appropriation for Contingencies. | _____ | 40. Current Portion of Long-term Debt. |
| _____ | 23. Appropriation for Future Plant Expansion. | _____ | 41. Customers' accounts with credit balances. |
| _____ | 24. Appropriation for Treasury Stock Purchased. | _____ | 42. Customers' Deposits. |
| _____ | 25. Bank Overdraft. | _____ | 43. Deferred Income Tax Asset. |
| _____ | 26. Bond Interest Payable. | _____ | 44. Deferred Income Tax Liability. |
| _____ | 27. Bond Interest Receivable. | _____ | 45. Deferred Property Tax Expense. |
| _____ | 28. Bond Sinking Fund. | _____ | 46. Deferred Office Supplies. |
| _____ | 29. Building. | _____ | 47. Deferred Rental Income. |
| _____ | 30. Cash. | _____ | 48. Deferred Subscription Revenue. |
| _____ | 31. Cash in Preferred Stock Redemption Fund. | _____ | 49. Deferred Service Contract Revenue. |
| _____ | 32. Cash Surrender Value of Life Insurance. | _____ | 50. Deposits on Equipment Purchases. |
| _____ | 33. Certificate of Deposit. | _____ | 51. Depreciation of Equipment. |
| _____ | 34. Common Stock. | _____ | 52. Discount on Bonds Payable. |
| _____ | 35. Construction in Process (entity's new plant under construction). | _____ | 53. Discount on Common Stock. |
| _____ | 36. Creditor's accounts with debit balances. | _____ | 54. Discount on Notes Payable. |
| _____ | 37. Current Maturities of Bonds Payable (to be paid from Bond Sinking Fund). | _____ | 55. Discount on Notes Receivable. |
| _____ | 38. Current Maturities of Bonds Payable (to be paid from general cash account). | _____ | 56. Dishonored Notes Receivable. |
| | | _____ | 57. Dividend Payable in Cash. |
| | | _____ | 58. Dividend Payable in Common Stock. |
| | | _____ | 59. Earned Rental Revenue. |
| | | _____ | 60. Accrued Pension Liability. |

| Classifi-<br>cation | Account | | Classifi-<br>cation | Account |
|---|---|---|---|---|
| _____ | 61. Estimated Liability for Income Taxes. | | _____ | 82. Leasehold Improvements. |
| _____ | 62. Estimated Liability for Warranties. | | _____ | 83. Leasehold Costs. |
| _____ | 63. Estimated Premium Claims Outstanding. | | _____ | 84. Loss on Sale of Marketable Securities. |
| _____ | 64. Factory Supplies. | | _____ | 85. Machinery and Equipment. |
| _____ | 65. Finished Goods Inventory. | | _____ | 86. Machinery and Equip. Sitting Idle. |
| _____ | 66. Furniture and Fixtures. | | _____ | 87. Marketable Securities. |
| _____ | 67. Gain on Sale of Equipment. | | _____ | 88. Merchandise Inventory. |
| _____ | 68. General and Administrative Expenses. | | _____ | 89. Mortgage Payable. |
| _____ | 69. Goodwill. | | _____ | 90. Notes Payable. |
| _____ | 70. Income Tax Payable. | | _____ | 91. Notes Payable to Banks. |
| _____ | 71. Income Tax Refund Receivable. | | _____ | 92. Notes Receivable. |
| _____ | 72. Income Tax Withheld (from employees). | | _____ | 93. Notes Receivable from Officers. |
| _____ | 73. Interest Payable. | | _____ | 94. Office Supplies on Hand. |
| _____ | 74. Interest Receivable. | | _____ | 95. Office Supplies Prepaid. |
| _____ | 75. Interest Revenue. | | _____ | 96. Office Supplies Expense. |
| _____ | 76. Investment in General Motors Stock. | | _____ | 97. Office Supplies Used. |
| _____ | 77. Investment in U.S. Gov. Bonds. | | _____ | 98. Patents. |
| _____ | 78. Investment in Unconsolidated Subsidiary. | | _____ | 99. Petty Cash Fund. |
| _____ | 79. Land. | | _____ | 100. Plant and Equipment. |
| _____ | 80. Land Held for Future Plant Site. | | _____ | 101. Plant Assets No Longer Used (and now Held for Sale). |
| _____ | 81. Land Used for Parking Lot. | | _____ | 102. Preferred Stock Redemption Fund. |
| | | | _____ | 103. Premium on Bonds Payable. |
| | | | _____ | 104. Premium on Common Stock. |

| Classifi-cation | Account | Classifi-cation | Account |
|---|---|---|---|
| _____ | 105. Prepaid Advertising. | _____ | 119. Store Supplies. |
| _____ | 106. Prepaid Insurance. | _____ | 120. Store Supplies Used. |
| _____ | 107. Prepaid Insurance Expense. | _____ | 121. Tools and Dies (5-year life). |
| _____ | 108. Prepaid Office Supplies. | _____ | 122. Tools and Dies (6-mos. life). |
| _____ | 109. Prepaid Royalty Payments. | _____ | 123. Treasury Stock Common (at cost). |
| _____ | 110. Prepaid Property Taxes. | _____ | 124. Unamortized Bond Issue Costs. |
| _____ | 111. Provision for Bad Debts. | _____ | 125. Unamortized Discount on Bonds Payable. |
| _____ | 112. Provision for Income Taxes. | | |
| _____ | 113. Rent Revenue. | _____ | 126. Unearned Rental Income. |
| _____ | 114. Salaries Payable. | _____ | 127. Unearned Royalties. |
| _____ | 115. Sales Discounts and Allowances. | _____ | 128. Unearned Subscription Income. |
| | | _____ | 129. Unexpired Insurance. |
| _____ | 116. Selling Expense Control. | _____ | 130. Vacation Pay Payable. |
| _____ | 117. Stock Dividends Distributable. | _____ | 131. Vouchers Payable. |
| _____ | 118. Stock Dividends Payable. | _____ | 132. Work in Process. |

## Solution to Exercise 5-1

| Solution | Explanation and/or Comment |
|---|---|
| CL | 1. These are trade payables usually due within 30 or 60 days. |
| CA | 2. These are trade receivables usually due within 30 or 60 days. |
| CA | 3. Interest is usually due annually or more frequently. |
| CL | 4. A better title is simply Interest Payable (item 73). |
| CL | 5. A better title is simply Taxes Payable. |
| (PPE) | 6. This is a contra account. It is another title for item 14 (item 6 is used more frequently). |
| (PPE) | 7. This is a contra account and an alternative title for item 14. |
| PPE | 8. Tracks of natural resources are classified in PPE. |
| DEP: CL or LTL | 9. These advances refer to revenue amounts received in advance from customers. |
| DEP: CA or INV or OA | 10. These advances are loans. |
| DEP: CA or INV or OA | 11. These advances can be prepayments or loans. |

| **Solution** | | **Explanation and/or Comment** |
|---|---|---|
| IS | 12. | This is a selling expense. |
| (CA) | 13. | This is another title for Allowance for Doubtful Accounts. |
| (PPE) | 14. | This is another title for Accumulated Depreciation (items 6 & 7). |
| (CA) | 15. | This is contra to Accounts Receivable. |
| (CA) | 16. | This account arises because of the use of the lower of cost or market rule. It is contra to Inventory. |
| (CA) | 17. | This is contra to Inventory; it is another title for item 16. |
| (CL) | 18. | This account reflects amounts included in Accounts Payable that will not be paid because of purchase discounts to be taken. |
| (CA) | 19. | This account reflects amounts included in Accounts Receivable that will not be collected because of sales discounts allowed. |
| (CA) | 20. | This is another title for Allowance for Doubtful Accounts. |
| RE | 21. | This is a restriction on retained earnings (portion of total retained earnings). |
| RE | 22. | This is a restriction on retained earnings (portion of total retained earnings). |
| RE | 23. | This is a restriction on retained earnings (portion of total retained earnings). |
| RE | 24. | This is a restriction on retained earnings (portion of total retained earnings). |
| CL | 25. | When the item exists, it is usually listed as the first item under current liabilities. It is a negative cash balance; an overdrawn bank account. |
| CL | 26. | The interest is usually payable semi annually. |
| CA | 27. | The interest is usually received semi annually. |
| INV | 28. | A fund can be comprised of restricted cash or securities. |
| PPE | 29. | This is a long-lived tangible asset used in operations. |
| CA | 30. | This is unrestricted cash. |
| INV | 31. | This cash is restricted for a long-term purpose. |
| INV or OA | 32. | The assumption is that the entity will continue the insurance coverage rather than take the cash surrender value. |
| DEP: CA or INV | 33. | Some CDs are for 90 days, 180 days, 30 months, or 60 months. |
| CS | 34. | This reflects the par or stated value of issued shares. |
| PPE | 35. | This is one of two exceptions to the general guidelines for items to be included in the PPE classification. |
| CA | 36. | A creditor has been overpaid or items purchased on account have been returned for credit after payment of account has been made. |
| LTL | 37. | This answer assumes that the Bond Sinking Fund is classified under long-term investments. |
| CL | 38. | This item will require current assets to settle the debt. |
| CL | 39. | "Current portion" refers to the portion that is coming due within a year of the balance sheet date. |
| CL | 40. | Some accountants list this item first in the list of current liabilities, others list it last. |
| CL | 41. | This arises when customers overpay or return goods after full payment is made. |
| DEP: CL or LTL | 42. | A deposit may be an advance payment for goods and services or a security deposit. |
| DEP: CA or OA | 43. | Deferred tax consequences of transactions reflected in the financial statements. |
| DEP: CL or LTL | 44. | Deferred tax consequences of transactions reflected in the financial statements. |

| Solution | Explanation and/or Comment |
|---|---|
| CA | 45. This is another title for item 110, Prepaid Property Taxes. |
| CA | 46. This is another title for items 94, 95, and 108. |
| DEP: CL or LTL | 47. This is another title for item 126, Unearned Rental Income. |
| DEP: CL or LTL | 48. Some subscriptions are for one year, others are for two or more years. This is another title for item 128, Unearned Subscription Revenue. |
| DEP: CL or LTL | 49. A service contract often covers two or more years; revenue has been collected but not earned. |
| PPE | 50. This is the second of two exceptions to the general guidelines for items to be included in the PPE classification. |
| IS | 51. This refers to the depreciation charges for the current period. |
| (LTL) | 52. In the rare instance where the bonds payable are classified as current, the discount would be current also. |
| (CS) | 53. It is rare that common stock is sold below par. |
| DEP: (CL) or (LTL) | 54. A discount occurs when the effective rate exceeds the stated rate. |
| DEP: (CA) or (INV) | 55. A discount results when the note is issued below par. |
| CA | 56. A dishonored note receivable is one that has reached its maturity date and remains uncollected. |
| CL | 57. A dividend is usually paid approximately three to four weeks after it is declared. |
| CS | 58. This is a bad title for Stock Dividend Distributable. This is the same as items 117 and 118. |
| IS | 59. This is another title for Rent Revenue. |
| LTL | 60. This item will be explained in Chapter 20. |
| CL | 61. This is another title for Income Tax Payable. |
| DEP: CL or LTL | 62. Some warranties are for more than one year. |
| DEP: CL or LTL | 63. Premiums in this context are similar to prizes. |
| CA | 64. This item is similar to a prepaid expense; these supplies will be part of factory overhead (hence, work in process inventory) when used. |
| CA | 65. This is one of three inventory accounts for a manufacturer. |
| PPE | 66. These are long-lived tangible assets used in operations. |
| IS | 67. This is classified as Other Gains on the income statement. |
| IS | 68. These are Operating Expenses on the income statement. |
| ITG | 69. This is referred to as an unidentifiable intangible asset with an indefinite life. The only time it appears on the balance sheet at a material dollar amount is when a company has purchased the goodwill in a business acquisition. |
| CL | 70. This is due and will require the use of current assets within a year. |
| CA | 71. This item will be collected normally within 8 to 10 weeks. |
| CL | 72. This is payable usually within a few days. |
| CL | 73. This is another title for item 4 (item 73 is the preferable title). |
| CA | 74. Interest is normally received monthly, semiannually or annually. |
| IS | 75. Interest revenue is an Other Revenue item on the income statement. |
| CA | 76. This answer assumes there is no reason to hold the stock for a long-term purpose. |
| DEP: CA or INV | 77. The maturity date and management's intention will dictate the classification. |
| INV | 78. The fact that the investee is a subsidiary means there is an intention to hold the investee's stock for a long-term purpose. |
| PPE | 79. Unless otherwise indicated, this refers to land used in operations. |
| INV | 80. This land is not used in operations so it is PPE or possibly OA. |
| PPE | 81. This land is currently being used in operations. |

| Solution | | Explanation and/or Comment |
|---|---|---|
| PPE | 82. | Some textbooks suggest classifying Leasehold Improvements as intangible assets. Most real life companies report them as PPE. |
| ITG | 83. | These are costs incurred in obtaining a lease. |
| IS | 84. | Classified as an Other Expense or Loss. |
| PPE | 85. | These are used in operations. |
| OA | 86. | These are not being used in operations. |
| CA or INV | 87. | This is a title often used to refer to short-term investments; it can also refer to securities (stocks and/or bonds of other entities) held for long-term purposes. |
| CA | 88. | This is another title for Inventory for a retailer. |
| LTL | 89. | The portion of this balance due within the next year will be reclassified and reported as a current liability. |
| DEP: CL or LTL | 90. | These may be short-term or long-term. |
| DEP: CL or LTL | 91. | These may be short-term or long-term. |
| DEP: CA or INV | 92. | The maturity date will dictate if it is current or not. |
| DEP: CA or INV | 93. | Separate disclosure must be made of related party transactions. |
| CA | 94. | This is another title for items 46, 95, and 108. |
| CA | 95. | This is another title for items 46, 94, and 108. |
| IS | 96. | This is an operating expense on the income statement. |
| IS | 97. | This is another title for Office Supplies Expense. |
| ITG | 98. | These offer long-term rights. |
| CA | 99. | This is one component of Cash. |
| PPE | 100. | These are long lived tangible assets used in operations. |
| DEP: CA or OA | 101. | Property previously used in operations and now held for sale is a current asset if the sale is expected to take place within a year; otherwise it is an Other Asset. |
| INV | 102. | This is cash or other assets restricted for a long-term purpose. |
| LTL | 103. | This is an adjunct type valuation account. If the related bonds payable are classified as a current liability, this valuation account will also be in current liabilities. |
| APC | 104. | This is an adjunct type valuation account. |
| CA | 105. | This is a prepaid expense. |
| CA | 106. | This is another title for items 107 and 129. |
| CA | 107. | This is another title for items 106 and 129. |
| CA | 108. | This is another title for items 46, 94, and 95. |
| CA | 109. | This is a prepaid expense. |
| CA | 110. | This is another title for item 45. |
| IS | 111. | This is another title for Uncollectible Accounts Expense or Bad Debt Expense. |
| IS | 112. | This is another title for Income Tax expense. |
| IS | 113. | This is classified as Other Revenue or Gains. |
| CL | 114. | This is another title for Accrued Salaries or Accrued Salaries Payable. Salaries Payable is the preferred title. |
| IS | 115. | This is contra to Sales Revenue. |
| IS | 116. | A control account is an account in the general ledger for which the details appear in a subsidiary ledger. |
| CS | 117. | This is another title for items 58 and 118. The title in item 117 is the preferred title. |
| CS | 118. | This is another title for items 58 and 117. This is a misleading title because the word "payable" suggests a liability, which a stock dividend is not. |

| Solution | | Explanation and/or Comment |
|---|---|---|
| CA | 119. | This answer assumes the supplies are on hand rather than used. |
| IS | 120. | This item refers to Store Supplies Expense. |
| PPE | 121. | These are used in operations and have a life longer than a year. |
| IS | 122. | The service life is so short that the benefits yielded do not extend beyond one year. Therefore, the expenditure is not capitalized. |
| (CS + APC + RE) | 123. | When the cost method is used to account for treasury stock, the treasury stock is shown contra to the total of all other stockholder equity items. |
| OA | 124. | This is usually called Bond Issue Costs. |
| (LTL) | 125. | This is another title for item 52. In the rare instance where the bonds payable are classified as a current liability, the discount would be contra current liability. |
| DEP: CL or LTL | 126. | This is another title for item 47. |
| DEP: CL or LTL | 127. | Revenue has been received, but not earned; hence, an obligation exists to provide a service or good or a refund. |
| DEP: CL or LTL | 128. | This is another title for item 48. |
| CA | 129. | This is another title for items 105 and 107. |
| CL | 130. | This is an accrued liability. |
| CL | 131. | This is another title for Accounts Payable when a voucher system is in use. |
| CA | 132. | This is an inventory account for a manufacturer. |

**Approach:** For each balance sheet classification, write down a definition or description of what is to be reported in that classification. Refer to those notes as you go down the list of items to be classified. Your notes should contain the guidelines summarized in **Illustration 4-1**.

# EXERCISE 5-2

**Purpose:**    (L.O. 3) This exercise will enable you to practice identifying errors and other deficiencies in a balance sheet.

Lee Cockerell Company has decided to expand its operations. The bookkeeper recently completed the balance sheet presented below to submit to the bank in order to obtain additional funds for expansion.

## Lee Cockerell Company
## BALANCE SHEET
### For the Year Ended 2010

Current assets

| | |
|---|---|
| Cash (net of bank overdraft of $15,000) | $ 180,000 |
| Accounts receivable (net) | 380,000 |
| Inventories, at lower of FIFO cost or market | 435,000 |
| Marketable securities—at cost (fair value $110,000) | 90,000 |

Property, plant, and equipment

| | |
|---|---|
| Building (net) | 590,000 |
| Office equipment (net) | 180,000 |
| Land held for future use | 75,000 |

Intangible assets

| | |
|---|---|
| Franchise | 90,000 |
| Cash surrender value of life insurance | 80,000 |
| Prepaid insurance | 6,000 |

Current liabilities

| | |
|---|---|
| Salaries payable | 18,000 |
| Accounts payable | 85,000 |
| Note payable, due June 30, 2012 | 100,000 |
| Pension obligation | 92,000 |
| Taxes payable | 40,000 |
| Note payable, due October 1, 2011 | 25,000 |
| Discount on bonds payable | 50,000 |

Long-term liabilities

| | |
|---|---|
| Bonds payable, 8%, due May 1, 2014 | 400,000 |

Stockholders' equity

| | |
|---|---|
| Common stock, $1 par, authorized 500,000 shares, issued 310,000 shares | 310,000 |
| Additional paid-in capital | 279,000 |
| Retained earnings | ? |

## Instructions

Prepare a revised balance sheet in good form. Correct any errors and weaknesses you find in the presentation above. Assume that the accumulated depreciation balance for the building is $150,000 and for the office equipment, $105,000. Marketable securities are classified as trading securities. The allowance for doubtful accounts has a balance of $20,000. The pension obligation is considered to be a long-term liability.

## Solution to Exercise 5-2

**Lee Cockerell Company**
**BALANCE SHEET**
**December 31, 2010**

### Assets

**Current Assets**

| | | | |
|---|---|---|---|
| Cash | | | $ 195,000 |
| Trading securities, at fair value (cost is $90,000) | | | 110,000 |
| Accounts receivable | | $ 400,000 | |
| Less allowance for doubtful accounts | | 20,000 | 380,000 |
| Inventories, at lower of FIFO cost or market | | | 435,000 |
| Prepaid insurance | | | 6,000 |
| Total current assets | | | 1,126,000 |

**Long-term Investments**

| | | | |
|---|---|---|---|
| Land held for future use | | 75,000 | |
| Cash surrender value of life insurance | | 80,000 | |
| Total long-term investments | | | 155,000 |

**Property, Plant, and Equipment**

| | | | |
|---|---|---|---|
| Building $ 740,000 | | | |
| Less accumulated depreciation—building | 150,000 | 590,000 | |
| Office equipment | 285,000 | | |
| Less accumulated depreciation—office equipment | 105,000 | 180,000 | |
| Total property, plant, and equipment | | | 770,000 |

**Intangible Assets**

| | | | |
|---|---|---|---|
| Franchise | | | 90,000 |
| Total assets | | | $ 2,141,000 |

### Liabilities and Stockholders' Equity

**Current Liabilities**

| | | | |
|---|---|---|---|
| Bank overdraft | | | $ 15,000 |
| Note payable, due October 1, 2011 | | | 25,000 |
| Accounts payable | | | 85,000 |
| Taxes payable | | | 40,000 |
| Salaries payable | | | 18,000 |
| Total current liabilities | | | 183,000 |

**Long-term Liabilities**

| | | | |
|---|---|---|---|
| Note payable, due June 30, 2012 | | $ 100,000 | |
| 8% Bonds payable, due May 1, 2014 | $ 400,000 | | |
| Less discount on bonds payable | 50,000 | 350,000 | |
| Pension obligation | | 92,000 | |
| Total long-term liabilities | | | 542,000 |
| Total liabilities | | | 725,000 |

**Stockholders' equity**

Paid-in capital

| | | | |
|---|---|---|---|
| Common stock, $1 par, authorized 500,000 shares, issued and outstanding 310,000 shares | 310,000 | | |
| Additional paid-in capital | 279,000 | 589,000 | |
| Retained earnings | | 827,000 | |
| Total stockholders' equity | | | 1,416,000 |
| Total liabilities and stockholders' equity | | | $ 2,141,000 |

**Explanation:**

1. A bank overdraft in one bank account should not be reflected as an offset to positive cash items (such as a positive balance in another account). A bank overdraft must be reported as a current liability. (The one exception to this rule is as follows: if an account with a positive balance exists in the same bank as the overdraft, the overdraft can be reflected as an offset to the extent of that positive balance.)

2. Marketable securities in a trading portfolio are to be reported on the balance sheet at their fair value. The difference between cost and fair value has been included as an element of income and is therefore reflected in the balance of Retained Earnings at the balance sheet date. (This topic will be more fully explained in **Chapter 17**.)

3. Land held for future use is not to be classified in the property, plant, and equipment section because the land is not currently being used in operations.

4. Cash surrender value of life insurance is an intangible item in a legal sense (because it lacks physical substance), but it is classified as a long-term investment for accounting purposes.

5. Prepaid expenses such as prepaid insurance represent prepayments that relate to benefits that are expected to be consumed within the year that follows the balance sheet date. Hence, they are current assets.

6. A pension obligation is generally not expected to become due in the near future and, therefore, is not expected to require the use of current assets within a year of the balance sheet date. Hence, it is a long-term liability.

7. Discount on Bonds Payable is a contra type valuation account. A valuation account should always be reported with the account to which it relates.

8. Bonds payable are always assumed to be a long-term liability unless the facts make them appear to meet the definition for a current liability.

9. The balance of retained earnings for this exercise can be derived by determining the amount needed to cause total liabilities and stockholders' equity to equal total assets. That is, it is a "plug" figure in this exercise.

# EXERCISE 5-3

**Purpose:**    (L.O. 3) This exercise will enable you to practice identifying errors and other deficiencies in a balance sheet.

Presented below is a balance sheet for the Gabby Corporation.

**Gabby Corporation**
**BALANCE SHEET**
**December 31, 2010**

| | | | |
|---|---|---|---|
| Current assets | $ 520,000 | Current liabilities | $ 365,000 |
| Investments | 700,000 | Long-term liabilities | 920,000 |
| Property, plant, & equipment | 2,185,000 | Stockholders' equity | 2,690,000 |
| Intangible assets | 570,000 | | |
| | $ 3,975,000 | | $ 3,975,000 |

The following information is available:

1.  The current asset section includes: cash $120,000, accounts receivable $190,000 less $10,000 for allowance for doubtful accounts, inventories $230,000, and unearned revenue $10,000 (credit balance). Inventories are stated at their replacement cost; original cost on a FIFO basis is $200,000.

2.  The investments section includes the cash surrender value of a life insurance contract $60,000; investments in common stock, short-term $70,000 and long-term $230,000; bond sinking fund $220,000; and land upon which a new plant is being constructed $120,000. Investments are all classified as available for sale and have fair values equal to their cost.

3.  Property, plant, and equipment includes buildings $1,600,000 less accumulated depreciation $375,000; equipment $400,000 less accumulated depreciation $240,000; land $500,000; and land held for future use $300,000. The building is stated at a recent appraisal value of $1,600,000; original cost was $1,250,000.

4.  Intangible assets include a franchise $140,000, goodwill $80,000 (from the acquisition of another business), discount on bonds payable $30,000, and construction in process $320,000 (a new plant is under construction and will be ready for operations within nine months).

5.  Current liabilities include accounts payable $80,000, notes payable—short-term $110,000, notes payable—long-term $150,000, and salaries payable $25,000. It does not include any amount for loss contingencies. The company's attorney states that it is probable the company will have to pay $60,000 in 2011 due to litigation pending at the balance sheet date.

6.  Long-term liabilities are composed of 10% bonds payable (due June 1, 2018) $800,000 and pension obligation $120,000.

7.  Stockholders' equity includes preferred stock, no par or stated value, 200,000 shares authorized with 70,000 shares issued for $450,000; and common stock, $2 par value, 300,000 shares authorized with 100,000 shares issued at an average price of $10. In addition, the corporation has retained earnings of $1,240,000.

## Instructions

Prepare a corrected balance sheet in good form.

# Solution to Exercise 5-3

**Gabby Corporation**
**BALANCE SHEET**
**December 31, 2010**

### Assets

| | | | |
|---|---|---|---|
| **Current Assets** | | | |
| Cash | | | $ 120,000 |
| Available-for-sale securities—at fair value | | | 70,000 |
| Accounts receivable | | $ 190,000 | |
| Less allowance for doubtful accounts | | 10,000 | 180,000 |
| Inventories, at lower of FIFO cost or market | | | 200,000 |
| Total current assets | | | 570,000 |
| | | | |
| **Investments** | | | |
| Available-for-sale securities—at fair value | | 230,000 | |
| Bond sinking fund | | 220,000 | |
| Cash surrender value of life insurance | | 60,000 | |
| Land held for future use | | 300,000 | |
| Total long-term investments | | | 810,000 |
| | | | |
| **Property, Plant, and Equipment** | | | |
| Land | | 620,000 | |
| Buildings | $ 1,250,000 | | |
| Less accumulated depreciation—building | 375,000 | 875,000 | |
| Construction in process | | 320,000 | |
| Equipment | 400,000 | | |
| Less accumulated depreciation—equip. | 240,000 | 160,000 | |
| Total property, plant, and equipment | | | 1,975,000 |
| | | | |
| **Intangible Assets** | | | |
| Franchise | | 140,000 | |
| Goodwill | | 80,000 | |
| Total intangible assets | | | 220,000 |
| Total assets | | | $ 3,575,000 |

**Gabby Corporation**
**BALANCE SHEET**
**December 31, 2010**
(Continued)

## Liabilities and Stockholders' Equity

Current Liabilities

| | | |
|---|---|---|
| Notes payable | | $ 110,000 |
| Accounts payable | | 80,000 |
| Estimated litigation obligation | | 60,000 |
| Salaries payable | | 25,000 |
| Unearned revenue | | 10,000 |
| Total current liabilities | | 285,000 |

Long-term Liabilities

| | | | |
|---|---|---|---|
| Notes payable | | $ 150,000 | |
| 10% bonds payable, due June 1, 2018 | $ 800,000 | | |
| Less discount on bonds payable | 30,000 | 770,000 | |
| Pension obligation | | 120,000 | |
| Total long-term liabilities | | | 1,040,000 |
| Total liabilities | | | 1,325,000 |

Stockholders' Equity
  Paid-in capital

| | | | |
|---|---|---|---|
| Preferred stock, no par value; 200,000 shares authorized, 70,000 issued and outstanding | | 450,000 | |
| Common stock, $2 par value; 300,000 shares authorized, 100,000 issued and outstanding | | 200,000 | |
| Paid-in capital in excess of par on common stock | | 800,000* | 1,450,000 |
| Retained earnings | | | 800,000** |
| Total stockholders' equity | | | 2,250,000 |
| Total Liabilities and Stockholders' Equity | | | $ 3,575,000 |

     *100,000 shares x ($10 - $2) = $800,000.

     **The corrected balance for the Retained Earnings account can be reconciled
       with the before corrected amount as follows:

| | |
|---|---|
| Retained Earnings, before corrections | $1,240,000 |
| Overstatement of inventory | (30,000) |
| Overstatement of buildings | (350,000) |
| Understatement of litigation liability | (60,000) |
| Corrected Retained Earnings balance | $ 800,000 |

      The errors that Gabby had on the balance sheet affected some income
      statement accounts (which were closed to Retained Earnings) or directly
      affected the Retained Earnings account.

**TIP:**    The $620,000 reported amount for land is comprised of land $500,000 plus land upon which a new plant is being constructed $120,000.

## ILLUSTRATION 5-2
## OPERATING, INVESTING, AND FINANCING ACTIVITIES (L.O. 7)

**DEFINITIONS:**

**Operating Activities:** include all transactions and other events that are not defined as investing or financing activities. Operating activities generally involve producing and delivering goods and providing services. Cash flows from operating activities are generally the cash effects of transactions and other events that enter into the determination of net income.

**Investing Activities:** include (a) making and collecting loans; (b) acquiring and disposing of debt and equity instruments of other entities; and (c) acquiring and disposing of property, plant, and equipment and other productive assets.

**Financing Activities:** include (a) obtaining resources from owners and providing them with a return on and a return of their investment; and (b) borrowing money and repaying the amounts borrowed, or otherwise settling the obligation.

**EXAMPLES:**

**Operating Activities:**
   **Cash inflows:**
      From sales of goods or services (includes cash sales and collections on account).
      From returns on loans (interest received) and on equity securities (dividends received).
      From other transactions, such as: Amounts received to settle lawsuits, and refunds
         from suppliers.
   **Cash outflows:**
      To suppliers for inventory and other goods and services (includes cash purchases
         and payments on account).
      To employees for services.
      To government for taxes.
      To lenders for interest.
      To others for items such as: Payments to settle lawsuits, refunds to customers, and
         contributions to charities.
**Investing Activities:**
   **Cash inflows:**
      From sale of property, plant, and equipment.
      From sale of debt or equity securities of other entities.
      From collection of principal on loans to other entities.
   **Cash outflows:**
      To purchase property, plant, and equipment.[a]
      To purchase debt or equity securities of other entities.
      To make loans to other entities.

## ILLUSTRATION 5-2 (Continued)

**EXAMPLES:**

**Financing Activities:**
    **Cash inflows:**
        From sale of equity securities (company's own stock).
        From issuance of debt instruments (bonds and notes).
    **Cash outflows:**
        To pay dividends to stockholders.
        To reacquire capital stock.
        To pay debt (both short-term and long-term) other than accounts payable.

[a]The cash outflows included in this category are payments at the time of purchase or soon before or after purchase to acquire property, plant, and equipment and other productive assets. Generally, only advance payments, the down payment, or other amounts paid at the time of purchase or soon before or after purchase of property, plant, and equipment and other productive assets are investing cash outflows. **Incurring directly related debt to the seller is a financing transaction and subsequent payments of principal on that debt thus are financing cash outflows.**

> **TIP:** Cash inflows and cash outflows from operating activities are usually netted together for presentation purposes. The net cash flow provided (used) by operating activities is usually determined by taking the net income (or net loss) figure and adjusting it for the amounts necessary to reconcile the accrual basis net income to a cash basis.

# EXERCISE 5-4

**Purpose:** (L.O. 7) The exercise enables you to practice identifying investing and financing activities.

## Instructions
Place the appropriate code in the blanks to identify each of the following transactions as giving rise to an:

**Code**

| | |
|---|---|
| II | inflow of cash due to an investing activity, or |
| IO | outflow of cash due to an investing activity, or |
| FI | inflow of cash due to a financing activity, or |
| FO | outflow of cash due to a financing activity. |

_____ 1. Sell common stock to new stockholders.

_____ 2. Purchase treasury stock.

_____ 3. Borrow money from bank by issuance of short-term note.

_____ 4. Repay money borrowed from bank.

_____ 5. Purchase bonds as an investment.

_____ 6. Sell investment in real estate.

_____ 7. Loan money to an affiliate.

_____ 8. Collect on loan to affiliate.

_____ 9. Buy equipment.

_____ 10. Sell a plant asset.

_____ 11. Pay cash dividends to stockholders.

## Solution to Exercise 5-4

| | | | | | | | |
|---|---|---|---|---|---|---|---|
| 1. | FI | 4. | FO | 7. | IO | 10. | II |
| 2. | FO | 5. | IO | 8. | II | 11. | FO |
| 3. | FI | 6. | II | 9. | IO | | |

**Approach:**

1. Reconstruct journal entries for the transactions. Examine each entry to identify if there is an inflow of cash (debit to Cash) or an outflow of cash (credit to Cash).

2. Write down the definitions for investing activities and financing activities (see below). Analyze each transaction to see if it fits one of these definitions.

   a) **Investing activities**—include (1) making and collecting loans, (2) acquiring and disposing of investments in debt and equity instruments, and (3) acquiring and disposing of property, plant, and equipment and other productive assets.

b) **Financing activities**—include (1) obtaining capital from owners and providing them with a return on and a return of their investment, and (2) borrowing money from creditors and repaying the amounts borrowed.

3. Assume purchases and sales of items are for cash, unless otherwise indicated.

> **TIP:** The journal entry to record a transaction that is an investing activity which results in a cash flow will involve: (1) Cash and (2) an asset account other than Cash, such as Investments (short-term or long-term), Land, Building, Equipment, Patent, Franchise, etc.
>
> **TIP:** The journal entry to record a transaction that is a financing activity which results in a cash flow will involve: (1) Cash and (2) a liability account or an owners' equity account, such as Bonds Payable, Note Payable, Dividends Payable, Common Stock, Additional Paid-in Capital, Treasury Stock, etc.

## EXERCISE 5-5

**Purpose:** (L.O. 8) This exercise will enable you to practice reconciling net income with net cash provided by operating activities.

The following data relate to the L. Heckenmueller Co. for 2010.

| | |
|---|---:|
| Net income | $ 75,000 |
| Increase in accounts receivable | 7,000 |
| Decrease in prepaid expenses | 3,200 |
| Increase in accounts payable | 5,000 |
| Decrease in taxes payable | 900 |
| Gain on sale of investment | 1,700 |
| Depreciation | 3,500 |
| Loss on sale of equipment | 600 |

## Instructions
Compute the net cash provided by operating activities for 2010.

> **TIP:** Refer to **Illustration 23-2** for guidance in reconciling net income (net loss) with net cash provided (used) by operating activities.

## Solution to Exercise 5-5

| | |
|---|---:|
| Net income | $ 75,000 |
| Increase in accounts receivable | (7,000) |
| Decrease in prepaid expenses | 3,200 |
| Increase in accounts payable | 5,000 |
| Decrease in taxes payable | (900) |
| Gain on sale of investment | (1,700) |
| Depreciation | 3,500 |
| Loss on sale of equipment | 600 |
| Net cash provided by operating activities | $ 77,700 |

**Explanation:**

1. Net income is a summary of all revenues earned, all expenses incurred, and all gains and losses recognized for a period. Most revenues earned during the year result in a cash inflow during the same period but there may be some cash and/or revenue flows that do not correspond. Most expenses incurred during the year result in a cash outflow during the same period but there may be some cash and/or expense flows that do not correspond.

2. An increase in accounts receivable indicates that revenues earned exceed cash collected from customers and, therefore, net income exceeds net cash provided by operating activities.

3. A decrease in prepaid expenses indicates that expenses incurred exceed cash paid and, therefore, net income is less than net cash provided by operating activities.

4. An increase in accounts payable indicates that expenses incurred exceed cash paid and, therefore, net income is less than net cash provided by operating activities.

5. A decrease in taxes payable indicates expenses incurred are less than the cash paid, and, therefore, net income is greater than net cash provided by operating activities.

6. When an investment is sold, the entire proceeds are to be displayed as an investing activity on the statement of cash flows. The gain included in net income must, therefore, be deducted from net income to arrive at the net cash provided by operating activities. If this adjustment was not made, there would be double counting for the gain amount. For example: An investment with a carrying value of $4,000 is sold for $7,000. The entire $7,000 proceeds is an investing inflow; the $7,000 includes the gain of $3,000 and a recovery of the investment's $4,000 carrying value; the $3,000 gain will be deducted from net income to arrive at the net cash from operating activities figure.

7. Depreciation is a noncash charge (debit) against income. It must be added to net income to arrive at the amount of net cash provided by operating activities.

8. A loss on the sale of equipment does not cause a cash outlay so it is added back to net income to arrive at the amount of net cash provided by operating activities. The cash proceeds from the sale of equipment are shown as a cash inflow from an investing activity.

## EXERCISE 5-6

**Purpose:**    (L.O. 8) This exercise will give you practice in preparing a statement of cash flows.

The comparative balance sheets of Spencer Corporation at the beginning and end of year 2010 appear below.

**Spencer Corporation**
**Balance Sheets**

|  | Dec. 31 2010 | Dec. 31 2009 | Inc./Dec. |
|---|---|---|---|
| **ASSETS** | | | |
| Cash | $10,500 | $7,100 | Inc.   3,400 |
| Accounts receivable | 18,000 | 9,400 | Inc.   8,600 |
| Prepaid expenses | 2,700 | 3,200 | Dec.    500 |
| Investments | -0- | 11,300 | Dec. 11,300 |
| Equipment | 56,000 | 42,000 | Inc.  14,000 |
| Less: Accumulated depreciation | (10,000) | (5,000) | Inc.   5,000 |
| Total | $77,200 | $68,000 | Inc.   9,200 |
| | | | |
| **LIABILITIES AND** | | | |
| **STOCKHOLDERS' EQUITY** | | | |
| Accounts payable | $ 4,900 | $ 4,500 | Inc.    400 |
| Unearned revenue | 1,700 | 6,000 | Dec.  4,300 |
| Common stock | 14,000 | 10,000 | Inc.   4,000 |
| Retained earnings | 56,600 | 47,500 | Inc.   9,100 |
| Total | $77,200 | $68,000 | Inc.   9,200 |

During the year 2010, Spencer purchased equipment for $14,000 cash, declared and paid cash dividends of $11,200, sold investments for $19,000, and reported net income of $20,300.

## Instructions
Prepare a statement of cash flows for Spencer Corporation for the year ending December 31, 2010.

---

**TIP:**    The statement of cash flows summarizes all of the transactions occurring during a period that have an impact on the cash balance. The activity format is used whereby cash inflows and cash outflows are summarized by the three categories: operating, investing and financing.

**TIP:**    Notice the increase (Inc.) in the Accumulated Depreciation account causes a decrease in the total assets figure.

## Solution to Exercise 5-6

**Spencer Corporation**
**Statement of Cash Flows**
**For the Year Ending December 31, 2010**

| | | |
|---|---:|---:|
| Cash flows from operating activities: | | |
|   Net income | | $20,300 |
|   Adjustments to reconcile net income | | |
|     to net cash provided by operating activities: | | |
|       Increase in accounts receivable | ($8,600) | |
|       Decrease in prepaid expenses | 500 | |
|       Increase in accounts payable | 400 | |
|       Decrease in unearned revenue | (4,300) | |
|       Depreciation expense | 5,000 | |
|       Gain on sale of investments | (7,700) | (14,700) |
| Net cash provided by operating activities | | 5,600 |
| | | |
| Cash flows from investing activities: | | |
|   Sale of investments | $19,000 | |
|   Purchase of equipment | (14,000) | |
| Net cash provided by investing activities | | 5,000 |
| | | |
| Cash flows from financing activities: | | |
|   Issuance of common stock | $4,000 | |
|   Payment of cash dividends | (11,200) | |
| Net cash used by financing activities | | (7,200) |
| | | |
| Net increase in cash | | 3,400 |
| Cash at beginning of the year | | 7,100 |
| Cash at end of the year | | $10,500 |

**Approach and Explanation:** The net change in cash for the year can easily be determined by taking the difference between the cash balance at the end of the year ($10,500) and the cash balance at the beginning of the year ($7,100) which yields a net increase of $3,400. The reasons for that net increase of $3,400 can be found by analyzing all of the transactions that caused changes in all of the balance sheet accounts other than Cash.

The changes in Accounts Receivable, Prepaid Expenses, Accounts Payable and Unearned Revenues are all due to accruals and deferrals which help to reconcile the net income figure with the amount of net cash provided (used) by operating activities. The changes in Investments and Equipment are due to transactions which constitute investing activities. The changes in Accumulated Depreciation are usually due to the recording of depreciation expense for the current period and disposals of plant assets. The changes in nontrade liability accounts (such as Mortgage Payable, Bonds Payable, Bank Note Payable) and most changes in stockholders' equity accounts are due to transactions which constitute financing activities.

An increase of $8,600 in Accounts Receivable indicates that sales revenue (on an accrual basis) exceeded cash collections from customers by $8,600. That in turn causes net income to exceed net cash provided by operating activities, so $8,600 is deducted from net income in reconciling net income to a cash basis figure. A decrease of $500 in Prepaid Expenses indicates that expenses incurred on an accrual basis exceeded the cash payments for expenses by $500 which in turn caused net income to be less than net cash provided by operating activities. (Remember that expenses are a negative component of net income so as expenses go up, net income goes down.) An increase in Accounts Payable of $400 results from an excess of expenses incurred over cash payments for expenses which causes net income to be less than net cash from operations.

Thus, both a decrease in Prepaid Expenses of $500 and an increase in Accounts Payable of $400 are added to net income to compute a cash basis income amount. A decrease in Unearned Revenue of $4,300 reflects an excess of revenue earned over cash collections from customers this period; this means net income exceeds net cash provided by operations. Thus, the $4,300 decrease in Unearned Revenue is deducted from net income in reconciling net income to net cash provided by operating activities.

It is helpful to reconstruct the journal entry for each transaction that caused a change in the remaining balance sheet accounts. You will be able to see the impact on Cash. Assume the most common transaction caused a change in a particular account. The entries and analyses are as follows:

| | | |
|---|---|---|
| Cash ............................................................ | 19,000 | |
|    Investments .............................................. | | 11,300 |
|    Gain on Sale of Investments............................ | | 7,700 |
|    (Sale of investments) | | |

There was an inflow of cash due to an investing activity — sale of investments — of $19,000. The $19,000 cash inflow represents a recovery of book value of the investment of $11,300 and a gain of $7,700. The entire $19,000 cash inflow is to be reported on the statement of cash flows as an investing activity. The gain is included in net income and net income is the starting point for determining the net cash provided by operating activities. Hence, the $7,700 gain must be deducted in determining the net cash provided by operations so as not to "double count" the $7,700 on the statement of cash flows.

| | | |
|---|---|---|
| Equipment.................................................... | 14,000 | |
|    Cash .......................................................... | | 14,000 |
|    (Purchase of equipment) | | |

There was an outflow of cash due to an investing activity — purchase of property, plant, and equipment.

| | | |
|---|---|---|
| Depreciation Expense................................... | 5,000 | |
|    Accumulated Depreciation............................. | | 5,000 |
|    (Recording of depreciation for current period) | | |

There was no impact on cash. There was an expense recorded but there was no cash outflow. Therefore, the amount of depreciation expense is added to net income in order to reconcile net income to net cash provided by operating activities.

| | | |
|---|---|---|
| Cash ............................................................ | 4,000 | |
|    Common Stock ............................................ | | 4,000 |
|    (Sale of common stock) | | |

There was an inflow of cash due to a financing activity    issuance of common stock (obtaining resources from owners).

| | | |
|---|---|---|
| Retained Earnings................................................... | 11,200 | |
|    Cash ............................................................... | | 11,200 |
|      (Declaration and payment of cash dividends) | | |

There was an outflow of cash due a financing activity    payment of dividends (giving owners a return on their investment).

| | | |
|---|---|---|
| Income Summary...................................................... | 20,300 | |
|    Retained Earnings ........................................... | | 20,300 |
|      (Net income amount is closed to Retained Earnings) | | |

The balance of the Income Summary account before closing is a summarized figure reflecting all revenues and all expenses; it is a summary of all transactions dealing with operations for the period. Most revenues increase cash and most expenses decrease cash so we use net income (a summary of all revenues and all expenses) as our starting point in computing cash provided by operating activities. The net income figure is then "adjusted" for the following items:
1.  revenue transactions that did not bring in cash this period.
2.  expense transactions that did not require a cash outlay this period.
3.  revenue items of another period that produced a cash inflow this period.
4.  expense items of another period that produced a cash outflow this period.

The result is the amount of net cash provided (used) by operating activities (a cash basis income figure).

| | |
|---|---|
| **TIP:** | In **Chapter 3,** we dealt extensively with the differences between the cash basis of accounting and the accrual basis of accounting because cash data gets recorded and the financial statements have to reflect accrual basis data: thus, the need for adjusting entries. A review of **Illustration 3-2** along with **Exercise 3-9, Exercise 3-10** and **Exercise 3-11** will likely help you here in your study of the statement of cash flows. |

# *ILLUSTRATION 5-3
# A SUMMARY OF FINANCIAL RATIOS (L.O. 10)

| Ratio | Formula for Computation | Purpose or Use |
|---|---|---|
| **I. Liquidity** | | |
| 1. Current ratio | $\dfrac{\text{Current assets}}{\text{Current liabilities}}$ | Measures short-term debt-paying ability. |
| 2. Quick or acid-test ratio | $\dfrac{\text{Cash, marketable securities, and receivables (net)}}{\text{Current liabilities}}$ | Measures immediate short-term liquidity. |
| 3. Current cash debt ratio | $\dfrac{\text{Net cash provided by operating activities}}{\text{Average current liabilities}}$ | Measures the company's ability to pay off its current liabilities out of its operations for a given year. |
| **II. Activity** | | |
| 4. Receivable turnover | $\dfrac{\text{Net sales}}{\text{Average trade receivables (net)}}$ | Measures liquidity of receivables |
| 5. Inventory turnover | $\dfrac{\text{Cost of goods sold}}{\text{Average inventory}}$ | Measures liquidity of inventory. |
| 6. Asset turnover | $\dfrac{\text{Net sales}}{\text{Average total assets}}$ | Measures how efficiently assets are used to generate sales. |
| **III. Profitability** | | |
| 7. Profit margin on sales | $\dfrac{\text{Net income}}{\text{Net sales}}$ | Measures net income generated by each dollar of sales. |
| 8. Rate of return on assets | $\dfrac{\text{Net income}}{\text{Average total assets}}$ | Measures overall profitability of assets. |
| 9. Rate of return on common stock equity | $\dfrac{\text{Net income minus preferred dividends}}{\text{Average common stockholders' equity}}$ | Measures profitability of owners' investment. |

## ILLUSTRATION 5-3 (Continued)

| Ratio | Formula for Computation | Purpose or Use |
|---|---|---|
| 10. Earnings per share | $\dfrac{\text{Net income minus preferred dividends}}{\text{Weighted shares outstanding}}$ | Measures net income earned on each share of common stock. |
| 11. Price earnings ratio | $\dfrac{\text{Market price of stock}}{\text{Earnings per share}}$ | Measures the ratio of the market price per share to earnings per share. |
| 12. Payout ratio | $\dfrac{\text{Cash dividends}}{\text{Net income}}$ | Measures percentage of earnings distributed in the form of cash dividends. |
| **IV. Coverage** | | |
| 13. Debt to total assets | $\dfrac{\text{Total debt}}{\text{Total assets or equities}}$ | Measures the percentage of total assets provided by creditors. |
| 14. Times interest earned | $\dfrac{\text{Income before interest charges and taxes}}{\text{Interest charges}}$ | Measures ability to meet interest payments as they come due. |
| 15. Cash debt coverage ratio | $\dfrac{\text{Net cash provided by operating activities}}{\text{Average total liabilities}}$ | Measures a company's ability to repay its total liabilities in a given year out of its operations. |
| 16. Book value per share | $\dfrac{\text{Common stock-holders' equity}}{\text{Outstanding shares}}$ | Measures the amount each share of common stock would receive if the company were liquidated at the amounts reported on the balance sheet. |

**TIP:** Throughout the remainder of the textbook, ratios are provided to help understand and interpret the information provided. Above, we provide you with the ratios that will be used throughout the text. You should find the chart helpful as you examine these ratios in more detail in the following chapters.

## ANALYSIS OF MULTIPLE-CHOICE TYPE QUESTIONS

**QUESTION**

1. (L.O. 1) The amount of time that is expected to elapse until an asset is realized or otherwise converted into cash is referred to as:
   a. solvency.
   b. financial flexibility.
   c. liquidity.
   d. exchangeability.

**Explanation:** Liquidity describes the amount of time that is expected to elapse until an asset is realized or otherwise converted into cash or until a liability has to be paid; liquidity refers to the "nearness to cash" of assets and liabilities. Current assets are listed in the order of liquidity (with the most liquid items first) on a balance sheet. Solvency refers to the ability of an enterprise to pay its debts as they mature. Liquidity and solvency affect an entity's financial flexibility which measures the ability of an enterprise to take effective actions to alter the amounts and timing of cash flows so it can respond and adapt to financial adversity and unexpected needs and opportunities. (Solution = c.)

**QUESTION**

2. (L.O.2) The Heather Miller Company has the following obligations at December 31, 2010:

| | | |
|---|---|---:|
| I. | Accounts payable | $ 72,000 |
| II. | Taxes payable | 60,000 |
| III. | Notes payable issued November 1, 2010, due October 31, 2011 | 80,000 |
| IV. | Bonds payable issued December 1, 2001, due November 30, 2011 (to be paid by use of a sinking fund) | 100,000 |

   The amount that should be reported for total current liabilities at December 31, 2010 is:
   a. $312,000.
   b. $212,000.
   c. $132,000.
   d. $72,000.

**Approach and Explanation:** Write down the definition (or key phrases therein) for a current liability. (A **current liability** is an obligation which is coming due within a year of the balance sheet date and is expected to require the use of current assets or the incurrence of another current liability to liquidate it.) Analyze each of the obligations listed to see if it meets the criteria for being classified as current.

Accounts payable and taxes payable will both be due shortly after the balance sheet date and will require cash to liquidate the debts. The notes payable are due within a year of the balance sheet date and there is no evidence to indicate that assets other than current assets will be used for settlement; thus, the notes payable are a current liability. The bonds payable are coming due within a year, but they will **not** require the use of current assets to liquidate the debt because a sinking fund (restricted cash or securities classified as a long-term investment) is to be used to extinguish that debt: $72,000 + $60,000 + $80,000 = $212,000. (Solution = b.)

**QUESTION**

3. (L.O. 2) Land held for a future plant site should be classified in the section for:
   a. current assets.
   b. long-term investments.
   c. property, plant, and equipment.
   d. intangible assets.

**Approach and Explanation:** Quickly review in your mind the descriptions of what goes in each of the asset classifications. Then read each answer selection and respond **True** or **False** if the selection answers the question. The land is not being used in operations, so it doesn't belong in property, plant, and equipment. It is not lacking physical existence, so it can't be an intangible asset. The land is not expected to be converted to cash or sold or consumed within the next year, so it is not a current asset. The land properly belongs in long-term investments. (Solution = b.)

**QUESTION**
4.   (L.O. 2) Working capital is:
     a.    current assets less current liabilities.
     b.    total assets less total liabilities.
     c.    the same as retained earnings.
     d.    capital which has been reinvested in the business.

**Explanation:** The excess of total current assets over total current liabilities is referred to as working capital. Working capital represents the net amount of a company's relatively liquid resources. That is, it is the liquid buffer available to meet the financial demands of the operating cycle. (Solution = a.)

**QUESTION**
5.   (L.O. 2) Treasury stock is classified as a(n):
     a.    current asset.
     b.    long-term investment.
     c.    other asset.
     d.    contra stockholders' equity item.

**Explanation:** Treasury stock is a company's own stock that has been issued, reacquired by the corporation, but not canceled. The acquisition of treasury stock represents a contraction of owners' equity; thus it is reported as a reduction of stockholders' equity. (Solution = d.)

**QUESTION**
6.   (L.O. 2) Which of the following is classified as an intangible asset on a balance sheet?
     a.    Long-term receivable.
     b.    Long-term investment in stock of another enterprise.
     c.    Licenses.
     d.    Accounts Receivable.

**Explanation:** Intangible assets lack physical substance and usually have a high degree of uncertainty concerning their future benefits. Although receivables and investments in stock lack physical existence, they are properly classifiable elsewhere so they are **not** classified for accounting purposes as intangible assets. Accounts receivable are classified as current assets, long-term receivables and long-term investments in stock are classified as long-term investments, and licenses are classified as intangible assets. (Solution = c.)

**QUESTION**
7.   (L.O.2) Which of the following should **not** be found in the long-term investment section of the balance sheet?
     a.    Land held for speculation.
     b.    Bond sinking fund.
     c.    Cash surrender value of life insurance.
     d.    Patent.

**Explanation:** A patent is classified as an intangible asset. Long-term investments, often referred to simply as investments, normally consist of one of four types:

1.  Investments in securities, such as bonds, common stock, or long-term notes receivable.
2.  Investments in tangible fixed assets not currently used in operations, such as land held for speculation or future plant site.
3.  Investments set aside in special funds such as a sinking fund, pension fund, or plant expansion fund. The cash surrender value of life insurance is included here.
4.  Investments in nonconsolidated subsidiaries or affiliated companies.

(Solution = d.)


**QUESTION**
8.  (L.O.3) Which of the following is a contra account?
    a.  Premium on bonds payable
    b.  Unearned revenue
    c.  Patents
    d.  Accumulated depreciation

**Approach and Explanation:** After reading the stem and before reading the answer selections, write down the description of the term "contra account". (A **contra account** is a valuation account whose normal balance is opposite of the balance of the account to which it relates.) Then take each answer selection and answer **True** or **False** whether it meets that description. Premium on bonds payable is a valuation account, but it is an adjunct type (its normal balance is the same as the normal balance of the account to which it relates). Unearned Revenue and Patents are not valuation accounts. Accumulated Depreciation is a valuation account for property, plant, and equipment. The normal balance of the Accumulated Depreciation account is a credit and the normal balance of a property, plant, and equipment account is a debit. Hence, Accumulated Depreciation is a contra account. (Solution = d.)


**QUESTION**
9.  (L.O. 2) The trial balance for Keller Corp. reflected the following account balances at December 31, 2010:

| | |
|---|---:|
| Cash | $33,000 |
| Accounts receivable (net of allowance) | 72,000 |
| Trading securities | 18,000 |
| Prepaid expenses | 6,000 |
| Patent | 12,000 |
| Land held for future business site | 54,000 |
| Inventory | 90,000 |
| Office equipment (fax, copiers, computers) | 75,000 |
| Accumulated depreciation on office equipment | 45,000 |

The current assets total at December 31, 2010 is:
a.  $219,000
b.  $231,000
c.  $261,000
d.  $303,000

**Approach and Explanation:** Take each account and determine its balance sheet classification according to the guidelines in **Illustration 5-1.** Total the items to be classified as current assets. The current assets classification includes cash and items which are expected to be converted to cash or sold or consumed within the next year or operating cycle, whichever is longer. Looking at the list we find the following to be current assets:

| Item | Why |
|---|---|
| $ 33,000 Cash | Cash |
| $ 72,000 Accounts receivable (net) | To be converted to cash in the next year. |
| $ 18,000 Trading securities | To be converted to cash in the next year. |
| $  6,000 Prepaid expenses | To be consumed in the next year. |
| $ 90,000 Inventory | To be sold in the next year. |
| $219,000 | |

(Solution = a.)

**QUESTION**

10. (L.O.7) Which of the following should be classified as an inflow of cash in the investing section of a statement of cash flows?
    a. Cash sale of merchandise inventory
    b. Sale of delivery equipment at a loss
    c. Sale of common stock
    d. Issuance of a note payable to a bank

**Approach and Explanation:** Read the stem and, before reading the answer selections, write down the items that appear in the definition of investing activities. (**Investing activities** include making and collecting loans to others, acquiring and disposing of stocks and bonds of other entities, acquiring and disposing of property, plant, and equipment and other productive assets.) Think of the items included in that definition that would produce a cash inflow (collecting loans, disposing of investments and property, plant, and equipment). Look for the answer selection that fits that analysis. As you analyze each answer selection, indicate what kind of activity it represents. A cash sale of merchandise inventory is an operating activity. The sale of common stock is a financing activity. The issuance of a note payable is a financing activity. A sale of equipment is an investing activity (regardless of whether the sale is at a gain, a loss, or at book value). (Solution = b.)

**QUESTION**

11. (L.O.7) An example of a cash flow from an operating activity is:
    a. payment to employees for services.
    b. payment of dividends to stockholders.
    c. receipt of proceeds from the sale of an investment.
    d. receipt of proceeds from the sale of common stock to stockholders.

**Explanation:** Operating activities include the cash effects of transactions that ultimately create revenues and expenses and thus enter into the determination of net income. Operating activities include collections from customers, collections of interest and dividends, payments for merchandise and other goods and services, and payments for interest and taxes. The payment of dividends is a financing activity. (The receipt of dividends is an operating activity [inflow].) The sale of an investment is an investing activity. The sale of common stock is a financing activity. (Solution = a.)

**QUESTION**

12. (L.O. 7) In preparing a statement of cash flows, the sale of property, plant and equipment at an amount greater than its carrying value will be classified as a(n):
    a. operating activity.
    b. investing activity.
    c. financing activity.
    d. extraordinary activity.

**Approach and Explanation:** Think about the nature of each of the three categories on a statement of cash flows and select the one involving disposal of plant assets:

1. operating activities    all transactions and other events that are not defined as investing, or financing activities. Cash flows from operating activities are generally the cash effects of transactions that enter into the determination of net income.
2. investing activities    include making and collecting loans, acquiring and disposing of investments (both debt and equity), and acquiring and disposing of property, plant, and equipment.
3. financing activities    include obtaining resources from owners and providing them with a return on and a return of their investment, borrowing money and repaying the amounts borrowed.

There is **no** category called "extraordinary activity" on a statement of cash flows. The fact that the asset was sold for a price exceeding the carrying value does not impact the answer because the entire proceeds from the sale are to be reported in the financing activity section. In the operating activity section, the amount of gain reflected in the net income figure is deducted from net income to arrive at "net cash provided by operating activities". (Solution = b.)

**QUESTION**
13.   (L.O. 7) In a statement of cash flows, proceeds from the issuance of common stock should be classified as a cash inflow from:
   a.   operating activities.
   b.   investing activities.
   c.   financing activities.
   d.   lending activities.

**Explanation:** The issuance of common stock by a corporation is the company's way of obtaining resources from an owner (i.e., owner investment into the business). Financing activities include obtaining resources from owners. There is no category called "lending activities". (Solution = c.)

**QUESTION**
14.   (L.O. 7) Which of the following would be classified as an investing activity on a statement of cash flows:
   a.   Issuance of bonds payable at a premium.
   b.   Purchase of land to be used in operations.
   c.   Issuance of common stock at a price equal to the par value of the stock.
   d.   Payment of dividends to stockholders.

**Approach and Explanation:**   Think about the types of items to be included in investing activities. Investing activities include making and collecting loans, acquiring and disposing of investments (both debt and equity) and acquiring and disposing of property, plant, and equipment. Take each of the answer choices and identify where it should go on a statement of cash flows. The issuance of bonds and the issuance of stock (regardless of price) are both financing activities that usually bring an inflow of cash. The payment of dividends is a financing outflow. The purchase of land (regardless of use) is an investing outflow. (Solution = b.)

**QUESTION**
15.   (L.O. 7) In preparing a statement of cash flows, the payment of interest to a creditor should be classified as a cash outflow due to:
   a.   operating activities.
   b.   investing activities.
   c.   financing activities.
   d.   borrowing activities.

**Explanation:** Borrowing money is a financing activity. Repaying amounts (the principal borrowed) is a financing activity. Paying interest on amounts borrowed is an operating activity because it is **not** included in the definition of financing activities and because the interest paid will be related to the interest incurred (interest expense) which is a transaction that enters into the determination of net income.  (Solution = a.)

## QUESTION

16.   (L.O. 8) Alley Cat Corporation had net income for 2010 of $5,000,000. Additional information is as follows:

| | |
|---|---|
| Depreciation of plant assets | $2,000,000 |
| Amortization of intangibles | $400,000 |
| Increase in accounts receivable | $700,000 |
| Increase in accounts payable | $900,000 |

Alley Cat's net cash provided by operating activities for 2010 was:
a.   $2,800,000.
b.   $7,200,000.
c.   $7,400,000.
d.   $7,600,000.

**Explanation:**  The depreciation and amortization amounts are items that reduce net income but do not cause a decrease in cash during the current period. The increase in accounts receivable indicates that sales revenue earned for the period exceeded the cash collections from customers, and therefore net income exceeded the net cash provided by operating activities. The increase in accounts payable indicates that expenses incurred exceeded cash payments for expense type items which caused net income to be less than net cash provided by operating activities. The solution is as follows:

| | |
|---|---|
| Net income | $5,000,000 |
| Depreciation of plant assets | 2,000,000 |
| Amortization of intangibles | 400,000 |
| Increase in accounts receivable | (700,000) |
| Increase in accounts payable | 900,000 |
| Net cash provided by operating activities     $7,600,000 | |

(Solution = d.)

## QUESTION

17.   (L.O. 8) Net cash flow from operating activities for 2010 for Graham Corporation was $75,000. The following items are reported on the financial statements for 2010:

| | |
|---|---|
| Depreciation and amortization | 5,000 |
| Cash dividends paid on common stock | 3,000 |
| Increase in accrued receivables | 6,000 |

Based only on the information above, Graham's net income for 2010 was:
a.   $64,000.
b.   $66,000.
c.   $74,000.
d.   $76,000.
e.   None of the above.

**Approach and Explanation:** Write down the format for the reconciliation of net income to net cash flow from operating activities. Fill in the information given. Solve for the unknown.

| | | |
|---|---|---|
| Net income | $ | X |
| Depreciation and amortization | | 5,000 |
| Increase in accrued receivables | | (6,000) |
| Net cash flow from operating activities | | $ 75,000 |

Solving for X, net income = $76,000. Cash dividends paid on common stock have no effect on this computation because cash dividends paid is not a component of net income and not an operating activity. Cash dividends paid is classified as a financing activity. (Solution = d.)

**QUESTION**

18. (L.O. 9) Free cash flow is:
    a.  net cash provided by operating activities minus capital expenditures and dividends.
    b.  net cash provided by operating activities minus retirement of debt and purchases of treasury stock.
    c.  the amount of cash obtained from donations.
    d.  the amount of net cash increase during the period.

**Explanation:** One method of examining a company's financial flexibility is to develop a free cash flow analysis. This analysis starts with net cash provided by operating activities and ends with free cash flow which is calculated as net cash provided by operating activities less capital expenditures and dividends. Free cash flow is the amount of discretionary cash flow a company has for purchasing additional investments, retiring its debt, purchasing treasury stock, or simply adding to its liquidity. This measure indicates a company's level of financial flexibility. (Solution = a.)

**QUESTION**

19. (L.O. 9) Net cash provided by operating activities divided by average total liabilities equals the:
    a.  Current cash debt coverage ratio.
    b.  Cash debt coverage ratio.
    c.  Free cash flow.
    d.  Current ratio.

**Approach and Explanation:** Visualize the computation of each ratio or computation referenced in the answer selections. The current cash debt coverage ratio equals net cash provided by operating activities provided by average current liabilities. The cash debt coverage ratio is computed by net cash provided by operating activities divided by average total liabilities. Free cash flow is calculated as net cash provided by operating activities less capital expenditures and dividends. The current ratio is current assets divided by current liabilities. (Solution = b.)

**QUESTION**

*20. (L.O. 10) Activity ratios measure the effectiveness of asset usage. One of the activity ratios is the:
    a.  inventory turnover ratio.
    b.  current ratio.
    c.  acid-test ratio.
    d.  rate of return on assets.

**Explanation:** The activity ratios include the (1) receivable turnover ratio, (2) inventory turnover ratio, and (3) asset turnover ratio. The current ratio and acid-test (or quick) ratio are both liquidity ratios. The rate of return on assets ratio is a profitability ratio. (Solution = a.)

**QUESTION**

*21. (L.O. 10) The current ratio is 3:1 for the Hamstock Company at December 31, 2010. What is the impact on that ratio of a collection of accounts receivable?
    a.  Current ratio is increased.
    b.  Current ratio is decreased.
    c.  Current ratio is unaffected.
    d.  Cannot be determined.

**Approach and Explanation:** Reconstruct the journal entry for the transaction. Analyze the effect of the debit portion of the entry on each element of the ratio and then analyze the effect of the credit portion of the entry on each element of the ratio. The entry to record the collection of accounts receivable involves a debit to Cash and a credit to Accounts Receivable. There is no change in the total amount of current assets. There is no change in the total amount of current liabilities. Thus, there is no change in the current ratio which is current assets divided by current liabilities. (Solution = c.)

# CHAPTER 6

# ACCOUNTING AND THE TIME VALUE OF MONEY

## OVERVIEW

Due to the time value of money, a certain sum today is not equal to the same sum at a future point in time. We must consider the compound interest factor for the time between two given dates in order to determine what amount in the future is equivalent to a given sum today or what amount today is equivalent to a given sum in the future. We compound the dollar amount forward in time in the former case and discount the dollar amount from the future to the present time in the latter case. In this chapter we discuss both of these procedures for a single sum and the appropriate procedures for compounding and discounting annuities. Interest tables appear at the end of this chapter.

## SUMMARY OF LEARNING OBJECTIVES

1.   **Identify accounting topics where the time value of money is relevant.**  Some of the applications of present-value-based measurements to accounting topics are: (1) notes, (2) leases, (3) pensions and other postretirement benefits, (4) long-term assets, (5) sinking funds, (6) business combinations, (7) disclosures, and (8) installment contracts.

2.   **Distinguish between simple and compound interest.** Interest is a payment for the use of money. It is the excess cash received or repaid over and above the amount lent (invested) or borrowed (principal). Simple interest is interest that is computed on the amount of the principal only. It is the return on (or growth of) the principal for one time period. Simple interest is commonly expressed as follows:

$$\text{Interest} = p \times i \times n$$

where:  $p$ = principal
$i$ = rate of interest for a single period
$n$ = number of periods

Compound interest is computed on principal **and** on any interest earned to date on that principal that has not been paid or withdrawn.

3.   **Use appropriate compound interest tables.** In order to identify which of the five compound interest tables to use, determine whether you are solving for (1) the future value of a single sum, (2) the present value of a single sum, (3) the future value of a series of sums (an annuity), or (4) the present value of a series of sums (an annuity). In addition, when a series of equal payments or receipts that occur at equal intervals of time (an annuity) is involved, identify whether these sums are received or paid (1) at the **beginning** of each period (annuity due) or (2) at the **end** of each period (ordinary annuity).

4.    **Identify variables fundamental to solving interest problems.** The following four variables are fundamental to all compound interest problems: (1) **Rate of interest:** unless otherwise stated, an annual rate that must be adjusted to reflect the length of the compounding period if less than a year. (2) **Number of time periods:** the number of compounding periods (a period may be equal to or less than a year). (3) **Future value:** the value at a future date of a given sum or sums invested assuming compound interest. (4) **Present value:** the value now (present time) of a future sum or sums discounted back to the present assuming compound interest.

5.    **Solve future and present value of 1 problems.** The future value (or future amount) of a single sum is the value at a future point in time of a given amount to be deposited (or invested) today using compound interest. The present value of a single sum is the current worth of a given future sum. In determining the future value, we move forward in time using a process of accumulation; in determining present value, we move backward in time using a process of discounting. The present value is always a smaller amount than a known future amount because interest will be earned and accumulated on the present value to the future date.

6.    **Solve future value of ordinary and annuity due problems.** The future value of an annuity is the future value (accumulated total) of a series of equal deposits at regular intervals at compound interest. Both deposits and interest increase the accumulation. Thus, the future value of an annuity is the sum of all the rents plus the accumulated compound interest on them.

7.    **Solve present value of ordinary and annuity due problems.** The present value of an annuity is the present value (worth) of a series of equal rents due in the future, all discounted at compound interest; in other words, it is the sum when invested today at compound interest that will permit a series of equal withdrawals at regular intervals.

8.    **Solve present value problems related to deferred annuities and bonds.** Deferred annuities are annuities in which rents begin after a specified number of periods. The future value of a deferred annuity is computed the same as the future value of an annuity not deferred. To find the present value of a deferred annuity, compute the present value of an ordinary annuity of 1 as if the rents had occurred for the entire period, and then subtract the present value of rents not received during the deferral period. The current market value of bonds is the combined present values of the interest annuity and the principal amount. The preferred procedure for amortization of bond discount or premium is the effective interest method, which (1) computes bond interest expense using the effective interest method (this is done by multiplying the carrying value of he bonds at the beginning of the period by the effective interest rate), (2) computes the cash amount of bond interest (this is done by multiplying the face amount of the bonds by the stated interest rate), and (3) compares those two items to determine the amount of amortization.

9.    **Apply expected cash flows to present value measurement.** The expected cash flow approach uses a range of cash flows and the probabilities of those cash flows to provide the most likely estimate of expected cash flows. The proper interest rate used to discount the cash flows is the risk-free rate of return.

## TIPS ON CHAPTER TOPICS

**TIP:**  Tables for future value and present value factors appear at the end of this chapter.

**TIP:**  The **future value of 1** (a single sum) is often referred to as the **future amount of 1**, and the **future value of an annuity** is often called the **future amount of an annuity**.

**TIP:**  Anytime you have a present value or a future value problem to solve, it is wise to draw a time diagram (or time line). This picture will help you to determine:
1.  if you are given present value or future value data or both.
2.  if you are dealing with a single sum or an annuity situation.
3.  what you are to solve for—present value, future value, $n$ (number of periods), $i$ (interest rate) or rent.

**TIP:**  Future value involves finding the value at a future date of a given amount today; that is, finding the amount a given sum today will accumulate to be at a future date. Present value involves finding the value today of a given amount specified at future date; that is, finding the amount which if invested today at a specified rate would grow to be that given amount.

**TIP:**  The present value of a single sum is based on three variables: (1) the dollar amount to be received or paid (future value), (2) the length of time until the amount is received or paid (number of periods), and (3) the interest rate (the discount rate). The process of determining the present value is referred to as discounting the future value. The relationship of these fundamental variables is depicted in the following diagram.

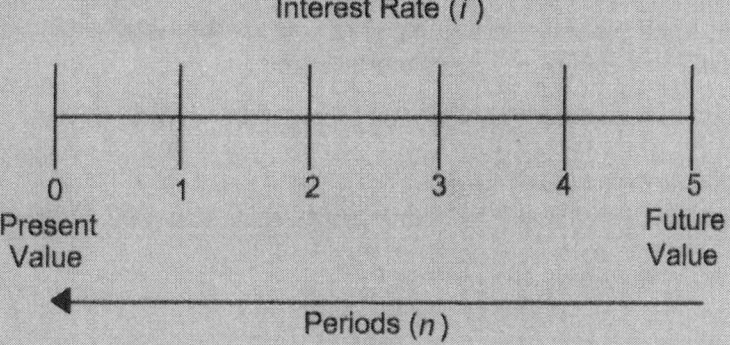

Interest Rate ($i$)

0  1  2  3  4  5
Present Value    Future Value

Periods ($n$)

Unless otherwise indicated, an interest rate is stated on an annual basis. To convert an annual interest rate into a compounding period interest rate, divide the annual rate by the number of compounding periods per year. The total number of periods is determined by multiplying the number of years involved by the number of compounding periods per year.

**TIP:**  The **interest rate** is often referred to as the **discount rate** in computing present value. The **higher** the discount rate (interest rate) is, the **lower** the present value will be

**TIP:**  One payment (or receipt) involved in an annuity is called a **rent**.

**TIP:**  The factor for the "present value of 1" is the reciprocal (inverse) of the factor for the "future value of 1." Thus, if you are given the factor from the Future Value of 1 Table for $n = 3$, $i = 8\%$ which is 1.25971, you can compute the factor for the "present value of 1" for $n = 3$, $i = 8\%$ by dividing 1 by 1.25971. This division yields a factor of .79383, which does agree with the factor for $n = 3$, $i = 8\%$ in the Present Value of 1 Table.

**TIP:**  The factor for the present value of an ordinary annuity of 1 for $n$ periods is the sum of factors for the present value of 1 for each of the $n$ periods. For example, the factor for the present value of an ordinary annuity of 1 for $n = 3$, $i = 8\%$ (which is 2.57710) is equal to sum of the factors from the 8% column of the Present Value of 1 Table for $n = 1$, $n = 2$, $n = 3$ (.92593 + .85734 + .79383 = 2.57710).

**TIP:**  The factor for the future value of an ordinary annuity of 1 for $n = 3$, $i = 8\%$ is 3.24640. It reflects interest on the first rent for two periods, interest on the second rent for one period, and no interest on the third rent. The factor for the future value of an annuity due of 1 for $n = 3$, $i = 8\%$ is 3.50611. It reflects interest on the first rent for three periods, interest on the second rent for two periods, and interest for one period on the third rent.  Thus, for a given $n$ and $i$, the factor for an annuity due is greater than the factor for an ordinary annuity.

**TIP:**  Referring to the TIP immediately above, we can see that the future value of an annuity due factor can be found by multiplying the future value of an ordinary annuity factor by 1 plus the interest rate. Likewise, the present value of an annuity due factor can be found by multiplying the present value of an ordinary annuity factor by 1 plus the interest rate.

**TIP:**  A deferred annuity is an annuity in which the rents begin after a specified number of periods. A deferred annuity does not begin to produce rents until two or more periods have expired.

**TIP:**  A factor for the present value or the future value of an annuity reflects one rent per period. Therefore, if an annuity involves a delay before the rents begin, the factor for $n$ must be adjusted before the problem can be solved.

**TIP:**  Any present value or future value problem is an application (or variation) of one or more of the following formulas: (parentheses indicate multiplication)

Future Value of an Amount = Present Value (Future Value of 1 Factor)
Present Value of an Amount = Future Value (Present Value of 1 Factor)
Future Value of an Annuity = Rent (Future Value of an Annuity Factor)
Present Value of an Annuity = Rent (Present Value of an Annuity Factor)

## ILLUSTRATION 6-1
## PRESENT VALUE-BASED ACCOUNTING MEASUREMENTS
## (L.O. 1)

Financial reporting uses different measurements in different situations—historical cost for equipment, net realizable value for inventories, fair value for investments. As was discussed in **Chapter 2,** the FASB increasingly is requiring the use of fair values in the measurement of assets and liabilities. According to the FASB's recent guidance on fair value measurements, the most useful fair value measures are based on market prices in active markets. Within the fair value hierarchy these are referred to as Level 1. Recall that Level 1 fair value measures are the most reliable because they are based on quoted prices, such as a closing stock price in the Wall Street Journal.

However, for many assets and liabilities, market-based fair value information is not readily available. In these cases, fair value can be estimated based on the expected future cash flows related to the asset or liability. Such fair value estimates are generally considered Level 3 (least reliable) in the fair value hierarchy because they are based on unobservable inputs, such as a company's own data or assumptions related to the expected future cash flows associated with the asset or liability. As discussed in the fair value guidance, present value techniques are used to convert expected cash flows into present values, which represent an estimated of fair value.

Because of the increased use of present values in this and other contexts, it is important to understand present value techniques. Some of the applications of present value-based measurements to accounting topics are listed below. Many of these will be discussed in detail in the following chapters.

1.   **Notes.** Valuing noncurrent receivables and payables that carry no stated interest rate or a lower than market interest rate.

2.   **Leases.** Valuing assets and obligations to be capitalized under long-term leases and measuring the amount of the lease payments and annual leasehold amortization.

3.   **Pensions** and Other Postretirement Benefits. Measuring service cost components of employers' postretirement benefits expense and postretirement benefits obligation.

4.   **Long-term assets.** Evaluating alternative long-term investments by discounting future cash flows. Determining the value of assets acquired under deferred payment contracts. Measuring impairments of assets.

5.   **Sinking funds.** Determining the contributions necessary to accumulate a fund for debt retirements.

6.   **Business combinations.** Determining the value of receivables, payables, liabilities, accruals, and commitments acquired or assumed in a "purchase."

7.   **Disclosures.** Measuring the value of future cash flows from oil and gas reserves for disclosure in supplementary information.

8.    **Installment contracts.** Measuring periodic payments on long-term purchase contracts.

---

> **TIP:** In addition to accounting and business applications, compound interest, annuity, and present value concepts apply to personal finance and investment decisions. In purchasing a home or car, planning for retirement, and evaluating alternative investments, you will need to understand time value of money concepts.

## ILLUSTRATION 6-2
## FUNDAMENTAL CONCEPTS UNDERLYING
## FUTURE VALUE AND PRESENT VALUE PROBLEMS (L.O. 2, 3, 4)

---

1.    **Simple Interest.** Interest on principal only, regardless of interest that may have accrued in the past.

2.    **Compound Interest.** Interest accrues on the unpaid interest of past periods as well as on the principal.

3.    **Rate of Interest.** Interest is usually expressed as an annual rate.   When the interest period is shorter than one year, the interest rate for the shorter period must be determined.

4.    **Annuity.**  A series of payments or receipts (called rents) that occur at equal intervals of time.
Types of annuities:
a.  **Ordinary Annuity.** Each rent is payable (receivable) at the end of the period.
b.  **Annuity Due.** Each rent is payable (receivable) at the beginning of the period.

5.    **Future Value.** Value at a later date of a single sum that is invested at compound interest.
a.  **Future Value of 1** (or value of a single sum). The future value of $1.00 (or a single given sum), *FV*, at the end of *n* periods at *i* compound interest rate (Table 1).
b.  **Future Value of an Annuity.**  The future value of a series of rents invested at compound interest; in other words, the accumulated total that results from a series of equal deposits at regular intervals invested at compound interest. Both deposits and interest increase the accumulation.
    1.  **Future Value of an Ordinary Annuity.** The future value on the date of the last rent.
    2.  **Future Value of an Annuity Due.** The future value one period after the date of the last rent. When an annuity due table is not available, use Table 3 with the following formula:

## ILLUSTRATION 6-2 (Continued)

$$\begin{array}{c} \text{Value of annuity due of 1} \\ \text{for } n \text{ rents} \end{array} = \begin{array}{c} \text{(Value of ordinary annuity for} \\ n \text{ rents)} \times (1 + \text{interest rate)} \end{array}$$

6.  **Present Value.** The value at an earlier date (usually now) of a given future sum discounted at compound interest.

    a.  **Present Value of 1** (or present value of a single sum). The present value (worth) of $1.00 (or a given sum), due $n$ periods hence, discounted at $i$ compound interest (Table 2).

    b.  **Present Value of an Annuity.** The present value (worth) of a series of rents discounted at compound interest; in other words, it is the sum when invested at compound interest that will permit a series of equal withdrawals at regular intervals.

        1.  **Present Value of an Ordinary Annuity.** The value now of $1.00 to be received or paid at the end of each period (rents) for $n$ periods, discounted at $i$ compound interest (Table 4).

        2.  **Present Value of an Annuity Due.** The value now of $1.00 to be received or paid at the beginning of each period (rents) for the $n$ periods, discounted at $i$ compound interest (Table 5). To use Table 4 for an annuity due, apply this formula:

$$\begin{array}{c} \text{Present value of annuity due} \\ \text{of 1 for } n \text{ rents} \end{array} = \begin{array}{c} \text{(Present value of an ordinary annuity} \\ \text{of } n \text{ rents)} \times (1 + \text{interest rate).} \end{array}$$

# ILLUSTRATION 6-3
# STEPS IN SOLVING FUTURE VALUE AND
# PRESENT VALUE PROBLEMS (L.O. 5, 6, 7)

Step 1:    Classify the problem into one of six types:
   a.  Future value of a single sum.
   b.  Present value of a single sum.
   c.  Future value of an ordinary annuity.
   d.  Present value of an ordinary annuity.
   e.  Future value of an annuity due.
   f.  Present value of an annuity due.

Step 2:    Determine $n$, the number of compounding periods, and $i$, the interest rate per period.
   a.  Draw a time diagram. This is helpful when the number of periods or number of rents must be figured out from the dates given in the problem.
   b.  If interest is compounded more than once a year:
       1)  To find $n$: **multiply** the number of years by the number of compounding periods per year.
       2)  To find $i$: **divide** the annual interest rate by the number of compounding periods per year.

Step 3:    Use $n$ and $i$ (if known) to choose the proper interest factor from the interest table indicated in Step 1.

Step 4:    Solve for the missing quantity. A summary of the possibilities appears in **Illustration 6-5.**. Abbreviations used in that summary are explained at the end of the summary.

---

**TIP:**    Many situations require that a business estimate expected future cash flows. The FASB takes the position that after computing the expected cash flows, a company should discount those cash flows by the **risk-free rate of return**. That rate is defined as the **pure rate of return plus the expected inflation rate**. Any credit risk is already incorporated in the determination of the probability of receipt or payment used in the computation of the expected cash flow. Therefore, the rate used to discount the expected cash flows should consider only the pure rate of interest along with the inflation rate.

# ILLUSTRATION 6-4
## STEPS IN SOLVING FUTURE VALUE AND
## PRESENT VALUE PROBLEMS ILLUSTRATED (L.O. 5, 6, 7)

The steps in solving future value and present value problems (listed in **Illustration A-3** are illustrated below and on the following pages:

1. **If $10,000 is deposited in the bank today at 8% interest compounded annually, what will be the balance in 5 years?**

   Step 1:   This is a future value of a single sum problem.
   Step 2:   $n = 5$; $i = 8\%$

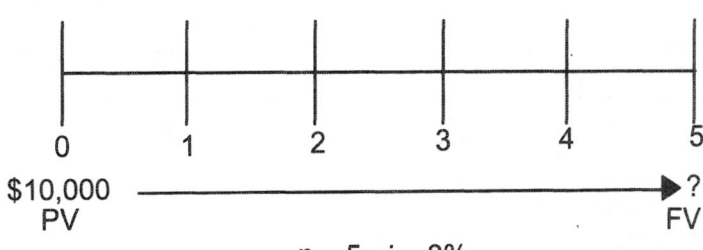

$$n = 5; \quad i = 8\%$$

   Step 3:   The interest factor from Table 1 is 1.46933.
   Step 4:   Future Value = Present Value x $FVF_{n,i}$
   Future Value = $10,000 x 1.46933
   Future Value = $\underline{\$14,693.30}$

2. **A company needs $100,000 to retire debt when the debt matures two years from now. What amount must be deposited on January 1, 2010 at 8% interest compounded quarterly in order to accumulate the desired sum by January 1, 2012?**

   Step 1:   This is a present value of a single sum problem.
   Step 2:   It is 2 years from 1/1/10 to 1/1/12. The annual interest rate is 8%. $n = 2 \times 4 = 8$; $i = 8\% \div 4 = 2\%$.

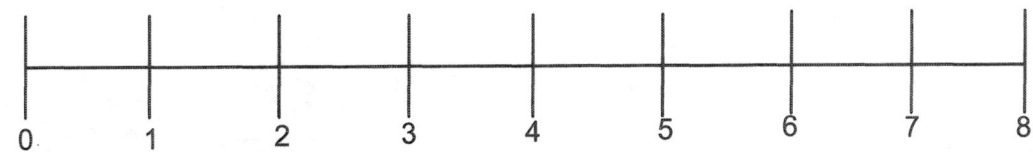
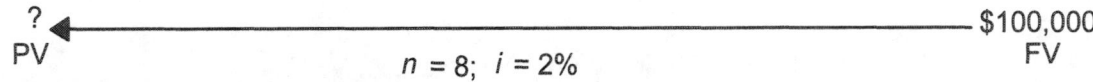

$$n = 8; \quad i = 2\%$$

   Step 3:   The interest factor from Table 2 is .85349.
   Step 4:   Present Value = Future Value x $PVF_{n,i}$
   Present Value = $100,000 x .85349
   Present Value = $\underline{\$85,349.00}$

## ILLUSTRATION 6-4 (Continued)

3.    **If $71,178 can be invested now, what annual interest rate must be earned in order to accumulate $100,000 three years from now?**

Step 1:   This can be solved either as a future value or as a present value of a single sum problem. This solution illustrates the present value approach.

Step 2:   $n = 3$; $i$ must be solved for.

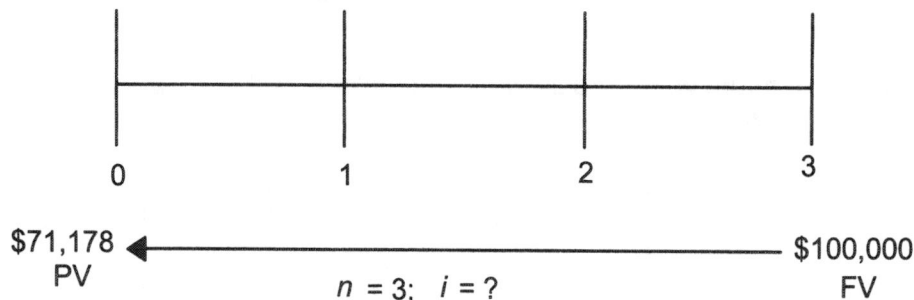

Step 3:   $i$ must be solved for.

Step 4:   Present Value = Future Value x $PVF_{n,i}$

$71,178 = $100,000 x $PVF_{n,i}$

$71,178 ÷ $100,000 = $PVF_{n,i}$

.71178 = $PVF_{n,i}$

Refer to Table 2 in the 3 period row.

$i = 12\%$

4.    **If $1,000 is deposited into an account at the end of every year for six years, what will be the balance in the account after the sixth deposit if all amounts on deposit earn 6% interest?**

Step 1:   This is a future value of an ordinary annuity problem.

Step 2:   $n = 6$; $i = 6\%$

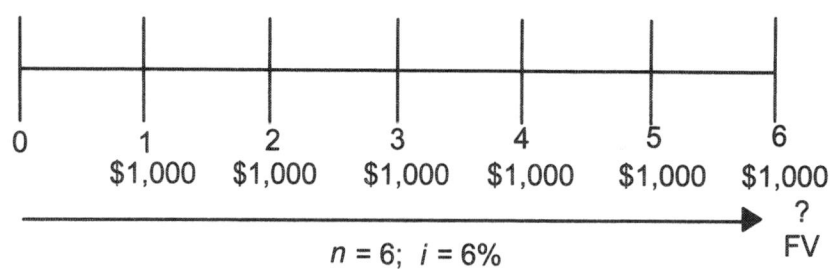

Step 3:   The interest factor from Table 3 is 6.97532.

Step 4:   Future Value of an Ordinary Annuity = Rent x $FVF\text{-}OA_{n,i}$

Future Value of an Ordinary Annuity = $1,000 x 6.97532

Future Value of an Ordinary Annuity = $6,975.32

## ILLUSTRATION 6-4 (Continued)

5.  **What amount must be deposited at 10% in an account on January 1, 2010 if it is desired to make equal annual withdrawals of $10,000 each, beginning on January 1, 2011 and ending on January 1, 2014?**

Step 1:   This is a present value of an ordinary annuity problem.
Step 2:   The time diagram shows 4 withdrawals. $n = 4$; $i = 10\%$

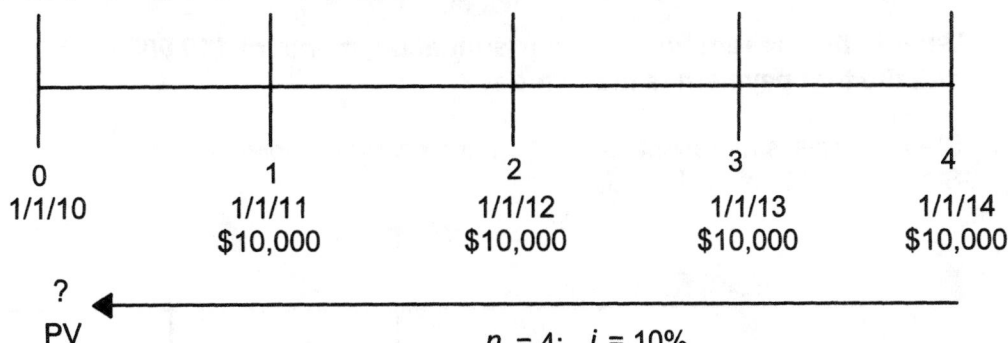

Step 3:   The interest factor from Table 4 is 3.16986.
Step 4:   Present Value of an Ordinary Annuity = Rent x PVF-OA$_{n,i}$
          Present Value of an Ordinary Annuity = $10,000 x 3.16986
          Present Value of an Ordinary Annuity = <u>$31,698.60</u>

6.  **Beginning today, six annual deposits of $1,000 each will be made into an account paying 6%. What will be the balance in the account one year after the sixth deposit is made?**

Step 1:   This is a future value of an annuity due problem.
Step 2:   $n = 6$; $i = 6\%$.

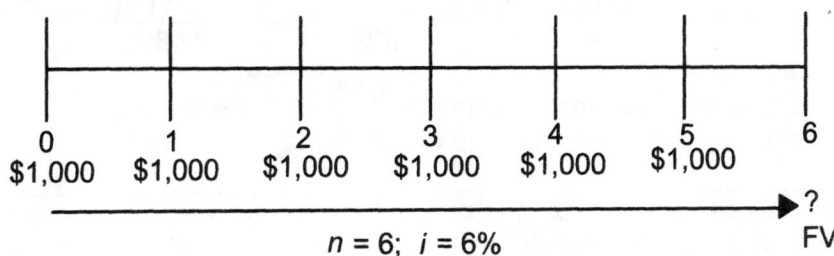

Step 3:   Table 3 with factors for future value of an ordinary annuity (FVF-OA$_{n,i}$) can be used to derive the factor needed here for future value of an annuity due (FVF-AD$_{n,i}$). The process is as follows:

|                            |         |
|----------------------------|---------|
| FVF-OA for $n = 6$, $i = 6\%$   | 6.97532 |
| Multiplied by $1 + i$      | <u>1.06</u> |
| FVF-AD for $n = 6$, $i = 6\%$   | 7.39384 |

Step 4:   Future Value of an Annuity Due = Rent x FVF-AD$_{n,i}$
          Future Value of Annuity Due = $1,000 x 7.39384
          Future Value of Annuity Due = <u>$7,393.84</u>

## ILLUSTRATION 6-4 (Continued)

> **TIP:**   Compare the results of this problem with those of problem 4 above. The solution to problem 4 can be multiplied by $(1 + i)$ to get the answer to number 6.
>           Proof:  $\$6,975.32 \times 1.06 = \$7,393.84$.
>           Although both situations use the same number of equal rents and the same interest rate, the interest is earned on all of the deposits for one period more under the annuity due situation.

7.   **What is the present value of four annual payments of $10,000 each if interest is 10% and the first payment is made today?**

Step 1:   This is a present value of an annuity due problem.
Step 2:   $n = 4$; $i = 10\%$.

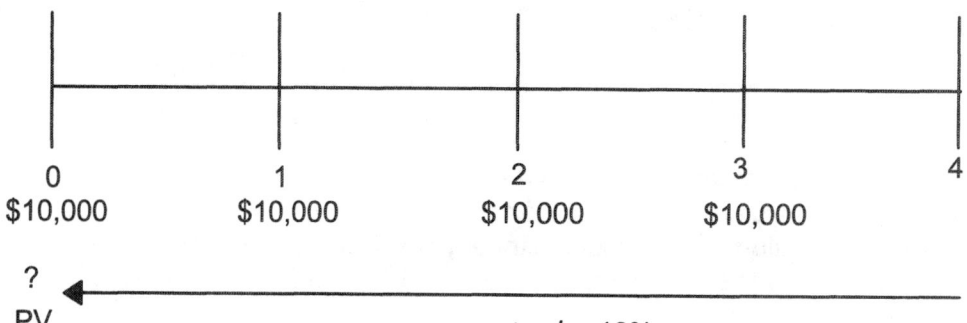

Step 3:   The interest factor from Table 5 is 3.48685.
          This factor can also be derived by using the present value of an ordinary annuity table (Table 4) as follows:

|  |  |
|---|---|
| PVF-OA  for $n = 4$, $i = 10\%$ | 3.16986 |
| Multiplied by $1 + i$ | 1.10 |
| PVF-AD for $n = 4$, $i = 10\%$ | 3.48685 |

Step 4:   Present Value of an Annuity Due = Rent x PVF-AD$_{n,i}$
          Present Value of an Annuity Due = $\$10,000 \times 3.48685$
          Present Value of an Annuity Due = $\underline{\$34,868.50}$

> **TIP:**   Compare the results of this problem with those of problem 5 above. The solution to problem 5 can be multiplied by $(1 + i)$ to get the answer to number 7.
>           Proof:  $\$31,698.60 \times 1.10 = \$34,868.46$
>                   (Difference of $.04 is due to the rounding of the factors.)
>           Although both situations use the same number of equal rents and the same interest rate, the discounting is done on all of the deposits for one period less under the annuity due situation.

## ILLUSTRATION 6-4 (Continued)

8.  **What amount must be deposited at the end of each year in an account paying 8% interest if it is desired to have $10,000 at the end of the fifth year?**

Step 1:  This is a future value of an ordinary annuity problem.
Step 2:  $n = 5$; $i = 8\%$.

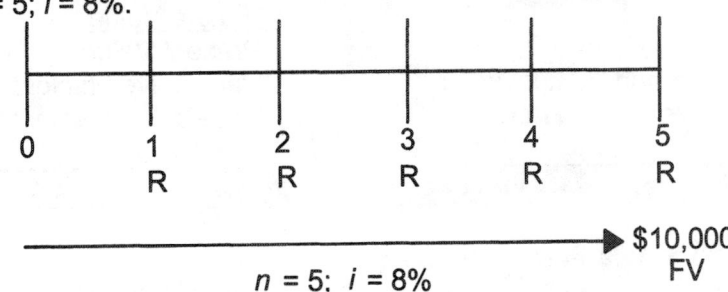

Step 3:  The interest factor from Table 3 is 5.86660.
Step 4:  Future Value of an Ordinary Annuity = Rent x FVF-OA$_{n,i}$
$10,000 = Rent x 5.86660
$10,000 ÷ 5.86660 = Rent
Rent = $1,704.56

| | | |
|---|---|---|
| **TIP:** | You can prove this solution by: | $1,704.56 x 5.86660 = $9,999.97 <br> The difference of $.03 is due to rounding. |

## ILLUSTRATION 6-5
## SUMMARY OF SIX TYPES OF FUTURE VALUE
## AND PRESENT VALUE PROBLEMS (L.O. 5, 6, 7)

1. **Future Value of a Single Sum**
   a. Future Value $\qquad$ = Present Value x $FVF_{n,i}$

   b. $FVF_{n,i}$ $\qquad$ = $\dfrac{\text{Future Value}}{\text{Present Value}}$

        (1) "$i$" unknown and "$n$" known, or $\qquad$ Trace solved factor to Table 1.
        (2) "$n$" unknown and "$i$" known $\qquad$ Trace solved factor to Table 1.

> **TIP:**   The present value amount is sometimes called the **principal.**

2. **Present Value of a Single Sum**
   a. Present Value $\qquad$ = Future Value x $PVF_{n,i}$

   b. $PVF_{n,i}$ $\qquad$ = $\dfrac{\text{Present Value}}{\text{Future Value}}$

        (1) "$i$" unknown and "$n$" known, or $\qquad$ Trace solved factor to Table 2.
        (2) "$n$" unknown and "$i$" known $\qquad$ Trace solved factor to Table 2.

3. **Future Value of an Ordinary Annuity**
   a. Future Value of an Ordinary Annuity $\qquad$ = Rent x $FVF\text{-}OA_{n,i}$

   b. Rent $\qquad$ = $\dfrac{\text{Future Value of an Ordinary Annuity}}{FVF\text{-}OA_{n,i}}$

   c. $FVF\text{-}OA_{n,i}$ $\qquad$ = $\dfrac{\text{Future Value of an Ordinary Annuity}}{\text{Rent}}$

        (1) "$i$" unknown and "$n$" known, or $\qquad$ Trace solved factor to Table 3.
        (2) "$n$" unknown and "$i$" known $\qquad$ Trace solved factor to Table 3.

4. **Present Value of an Ordinary Annuity**
   a. Present Value of an Ordinary Annuity $\qquad$ = Rent x $PVF\text{-}OA_{n,i}$

   b. Rent $\qquad$ = $\dfrac{\text{Present Value of an Ordinary Annuity}}{PVF\text{-}OA_{n,i}}$

   c. $PVF\text{-}OA_{n,i}$ $\qquad$ = $\dfrac{\text{Present Value of an Ordinary Annuity}}{\text{Rent}}$

        (1) "$i$" unknown and "$n$" known, or $\qquad$ Trace solved factor to Table 4.
        (2) "$n$" unknown and "$i$" known $\qquad$ Trace solved factor to Table 4.

## ILLUSTRATION 6-5 (Continued)

5. **Future Value of an Annuity Due**

   a. Future Value of an Annuity Due    $=$ Rent x FVF-AD$_{n,i}$

   b. Rent    $=$ $\dfrac{\text{Future Value of an Annuity Due}}{\text{FVF-AD}_{n,i}}$

> **TIP:** There is no table in this book for Future Value of an Annuity Due, so ordinary annuity factors must be modified as follows:
>
> $$\text{FVF-AD}_{n,i} = \text{FVF-OA}_{n,i} \times (1 + i) \quad \textbf{OR} \quad \text{FVF-AD}_{n,i} = \text{FVF-OA}_{n+1,i} - 1.00000$$

6. **Present Value of an Annuity Due**

   a. Present Value of an Annuity Due    $=$ Rent x PVF-AD$_{n,i}$

   b. Rent    $=$ $\dfrac{\text{Present Value of an Annuity Due}}{\text{PVF-AD}_{n,i}}$

   c. PVF-AD$_{n,i}$    $=$ $\dfrac{\text{Present Value of an Annuity Due}}{\text{Rent}}$

      (1) "$i$" unknown and "$n$" known, or    Trace solved factor to Table 5.
      (2) "$n$" unknown and "$i$" known    Trace solved factor to Table 5.

> **TIP:** Factors for the present value of an annuity due can be derived by adjusting factors from the Table for Present Value of an Ordinary Annuity as follows:
>
> $$\text{PVF-AD}_{n,i} = \text{PVF-OA}_{n,i} \times (1 + i) \quad \textbf{OR} \quad \text{PVF-AD}_{n,i} = \text{PVF-OA}_{n-1,i} + 1.00000$$

---

**Abbreviations:**

| | | |
|---|---|---|
| $i$ | $=$ | Interest Rate |
| $n$ | $=$ | Number of Periods or Rents |
| FVF$_{n,i}$ | $=$ | Future Value of 1 Factor for $n$ periods at $i$ interest |
| PVF$_{n,i}$ | $=$ | Present Value of 1 Factor for $n$ periods at $i$ interest |
| FVF-OA$_{n,i}$ | $=$ | Future Amount of an Ordinary Annuity of 1 Factor for $n$ periods at $i$ interest |
| PVF-OA$_{n,i}$ | $=$ | Present Value of an Ordinary Annuity of 1 Factor for $n$ periods at $i$ interest |
| FVF-AD$_{n,i}$ | $=$ | Future Amount of an Annuity Due of 1 Factor for $n$ periods at $i$ interest |
| PVF-AD$_{n,i}$ | $=$ | Present Value of an Annuity Due of 1 Factor for $n$ periods at $i$ interest |

## EXERCISE 6-1

**Purpose:** (L.O.3) This exercise will test your knowledge of the applicability of the five compound interest tables discussed in this chapter.

## Instructions

For each independent situation below, (1) indicate which table you would need to use in order to locate the appropriate factor to solve for the figure requested, and (2) indicate if you divide (D) or multiply (M) by that factor to solve for the figure requested. Use the appropriate numerals and letters to indicate your answer for each.

|       |                                         |
|-------|-----------------------------------------|
| I.    | Future Value of 1                       |
| II.   | Present Value of 1                      |
| III.  | Future Value of an Ordinary Annuity of 1 |
| IV.   | Present Value of an Ordinary Annuity of 1 |
| V.    | Present Value of an Annuity Due of 1    |

**TIP:** There are two approaches to solving problems involving present value or future value of a single sum; there is only one approach available for solving annuity problems.

(1)    (2)

_____ _____    1.   $1,000 is put on deposit today to earn 6% interest, compounded annually. How much will be on deposit at the end of 8 years?

_____ _____    2.   What amount today is equivalent to receiving $600 at the end of every year for 6 years, assuming interest is compounded annually at the rate of 5%?

_____ _____    3.   If you wish to be able to withdraw the sum of $8,000 at the end of 12 years, how much do you have to deposit today, assuming interest is compounded annually at the rate of 6%?

_____ _____    4.   If $400 is put in a savings account at the end of every year for 5 years, how much will be accumulated in the account if all amounts that remain on deposit earn 6% interest, compounded annually?

_____ _____    5.   What amount today is equivalent to receiving $1,000 ten years from now if interest of 7% is compounded annually?

_____ _____    6.   What amount today is equivalent to receiving $1,000 at the end of each year for ten years if interest of 7% is compounded annually?

_____ _____    7.   How much must be deposited today to allow for the withdrawal of $1,000 at the end of each year for ten years if interest of 7% is compounded annually?

_____ _____    8.   What is the present value of $500 due in 8 years at 6% compounded interest?

_____ _____ 9. What is the future value of an ordinary annuity of $100 per period for 6 years at 7% compounded interest?

_____ _____ 10. How much money must be deposited today to be able to withdraw $700 at the end of 7 years, assuming 7% compounded interest?

_____ _____ 11. How much money must be deposited today to be able to withdraw $700 at the beginning of each of 7 years, assuming 7% compounded interest?

_____ _____ 12. What is the discounted value of $700 due in 7 years at a 7% compounded interest rate?

_____ _____ 13. What is the future value of $700 put on deposit now for 7 years at 7% compounded interest?

_____ _____ 14. What is the future value in seven years of $700 put on deposit at the end of each of 7 years if all amounts on deposit earn 7% compound interest?

_____ _____ 15. How much can be withdrawn at the end of 5 years if $1,000 is deposited now at a 6% compound interest rate?

_____ _____ 16. What amount can be withdrawn at the end of each period for five years if $1,000 is deposited now and all amounts on deposit earn 6% interest compounded annually?

_____ _____ 17. If a debt of $5,000 is to be repaid in five equal beginning-of-year installments, what is the amount of each installment if interest at 7% is charged on the unpaid balance?

_____ _____ 18. What amount must be deposited at the end of each of four years to accumulate a fund of $7,000 at the end of the fourth year, assuming interest at a rate of 6% compounded annually?

## Solution to Exercise 6-1

| | | | | | |
|----|-----|---|------|----|---|
| 1. | I | M | or | II | D |
| 2. | IV | M | | | |
| 3. | II | M | or | I | D |
| 4. | III | M | | | |
| 5. | II | M | or | I | D |
| 6. | IV | M | | | |
| 7. | IV | M | | | |
| 8. | II | M | or | I | D |
| 9. | III | M | | | |
| 10. | II | M | or | I | D |
| 11. | V | M | | | |
| 12. | II | M | or | I | D |
| 13. | I | M | or | II | D |
| 14. | III | M | | | |
| 15. | I | M | or | II | D |
| 16. | IV | D | | | |
| 17. | V | D | | | |
| 18. | III | D | | | |

**Approach and Explanation:** Draw a time diagram and place each fact given in the appropriate position on the diagram. Determine what is to be solved for in the question. Think about the content of each of the five compound interest tables included at the end of this chapter. Review the use of the interest factors as summarized in **Illustration 6-5**. The titles and the contents of the five interest tables are as follows:

1.   **Future Value of 1 Table.** Contains the amount to which $1 will accumulate if deposited now at a specified rate of interest and left for a specified number of periods (Table 1).

2.   **Present Value of 1 Table.** Contains the amount that must be deposited now at a specified rate of interest to equal $1 at the end of a specified number of periods (Table 2).

3.   **Future Value of an Ordinary Annuity of 1 Table.** Contains the amount to which periodic rents of $1 will accumulate if the payments (rents) are invested at the **end** of each period at a specified rate of interest for a specified number of periods (Table 3).

4.   **Present Value of an Ordinary Annuity of 1 Table.** Contains the amount that must be deposited now at a specified rate of interest to permit withdrawals of $1 at the **end** of regular periodic intervals for the specified number of periods (Table 4).

5.   **Present Value of an Annuity Due of 1 Table.** Contains the amount that must be deposited now at a specified rate of interest to permit withdrawals of $1 at the **beginning** of regular periodic intervals for the specified number of periods (Table 5).

# EXERCISE 6-2

**Purpose:**  (L.O.5,6,7) This exercise will illustrate some key concepts such as (1) the more frequently interest is compounded, the more interest will accumulate; (2) the greater the interest rate, the lower the present value will be; and (3) there is more interest reflected in an annuity due situation than in an ordinary annuity situation.

## Instructions

Answer each of the questions below following the steps outlined in **Illustration 6-3**. Interest tables are included at the end of this chapter. Use the appropriate factors where needed.

There are a wide variety of situations in which present value and/or future value concepts must be applied. A few of them are illustrated in the questions that follow.

1.  If $1,000 is put on deposit today to earn 6% interest, how much will be on deposit at the end of 10 years if interest is compounded annually?

2.  If $1,000 is put on deposit today to earn 6% interest, how much will be on deposit at the end of 10 years if interest is compounded semiannually?

3.  In comparing questions 1 and 2, which answer would you expect to be the larger? Why?

4.  What is the value today of $1,000 due 10 years in the future if the time value of money is 6% and interest is compounded once annually?

5.  What is the value today of $1,000 due 10 years in the future if the time value of money is 6% and interest is compounded semiannually?

6.  In comparing questions 4 and 5, which answer would you expect to be the larger? Why?

7.  What is the present value of $1,000 due in 10 years if interest is compounded annually at 10%?

8.  What is the present value of $1,000 due in 10 years if interest is compounded annually at 8%?

9.  In comparing questions 7 and 8, which answer would you expect to be the larger? Why?

10. If $1,000 is deposited at the end of each year for 10 years and all amounts on deposit draw 6% interest compounded annually, how much will be on deposit at the end of 10 years?

11.    If $1,000 is deposited at the beginning of each year for 10 years and all amounts on deposit draw 6% interest compounded annually, how much will be on deposit at the end of 10 years?

12.    In comparing questions 10 and 11, which answer would you expect to be the larger? Why?

## Solution to Exercise 6-2

1.    (1)    This is a future value of a single sum problem.
      (2)    $n = 10$; $i = 6\%$.

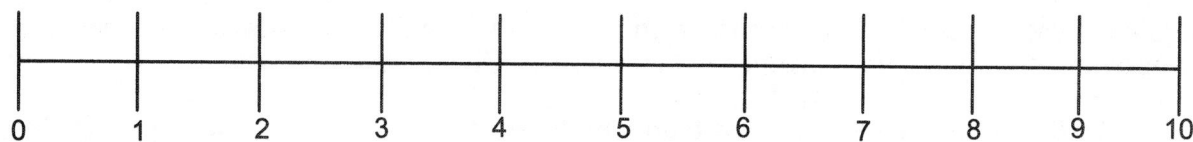

$$n = 10; i = 6\%$$

      (3)    The interest factor from Table 1 is 1.79085.
      (4)    Future Value = Present Value x $\text{FVF}_{n,i}$
             Future Value = $1,000 x 1.79085
             Future Value = $1,790.85

2.    (1)    This is a future value of a single sum problem.
      (2)    $n = 10 \times 2 = 20$; $i = 6\% \div 2 = 3\%$

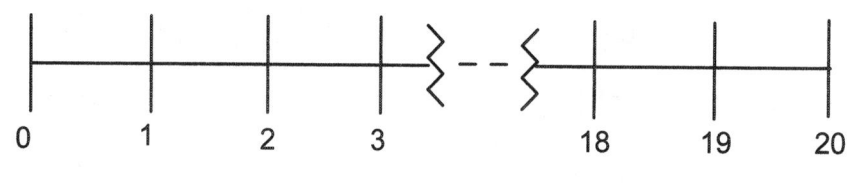

$$n = 20; i = 3\%$$

      (3)    The interest factor from Table 1 is 1.80611.
      (4)    Future Value = Present Value x $\text{FVF}_{n,i}$
             Future Value = $1,000 x 1.80611
             Future Value = $1,806.11

3.  We would expect the answer to question 2 to be a little larger than the answer to question 1 because the interest is compounded more frequently in question 2 which means there will be a larger amount of accumulated interest by the end of year 10 in this scenario.

4.  (1)  This is a present value of a single sum problem.
    (2)  $n = 10$; $i = 6\%$.

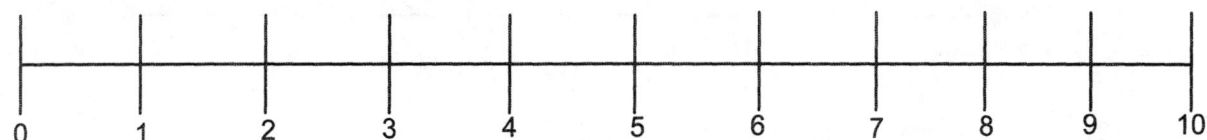

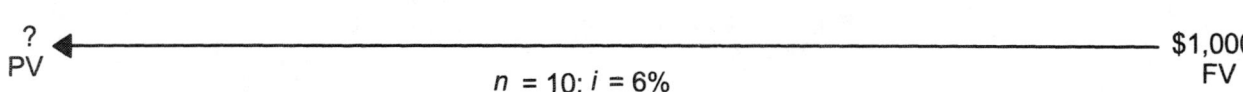

    (3)  The interest factor from Table 2 is .55839.
    (4)  Present Value = Future Value x $PVF_{n,i}$
         Present Value = $1,000 x .55839
         Present Value = <u>$558.39</u>

5.  (1)  This is a present value of single sum problem.
    (2)  $n = 10 \times 2 = 20$; $i = 6\% \div 2 = 3\%$

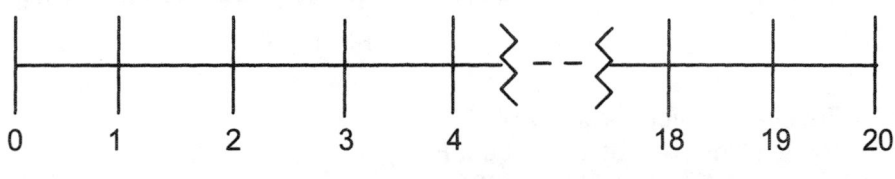

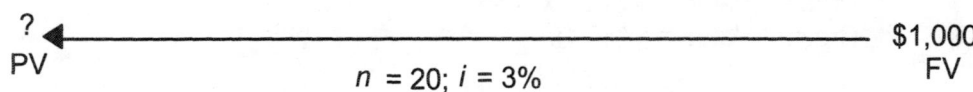

    (3)  The interest factor from Table 2 is .55368.
    (4)  Present Value = Future Value x $PVF_{n,i}$
         Present Value = $1,000 x .55368
         Present Value = <u>$553.68</u>

6.  We would expect the answer to question 4 to be the larger because the more frequently that interest is compounded, the more the total interest will be. The greater the interest, the less the present value. Thus, the answer to question 5 has more interest reflected and a lesser present value figure.

7.    (1)    This is a present value of a single-sum problem.
      (2)    $n = 10$; $i = 10\%$

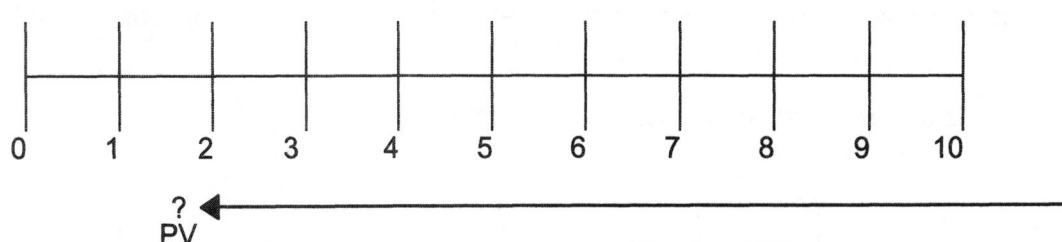

      (3)    The interest factor from Table 2 is .38554.
      (4)    Present Value = Future Value x $PVF_{n,i}$
             Present Value = $1,000 x .38554
             Present Value = <u>$385.54</u>

8.    (1)    This is a present value of a single-sum problem.
      (2)    $n = 10$; $i = 8\%$

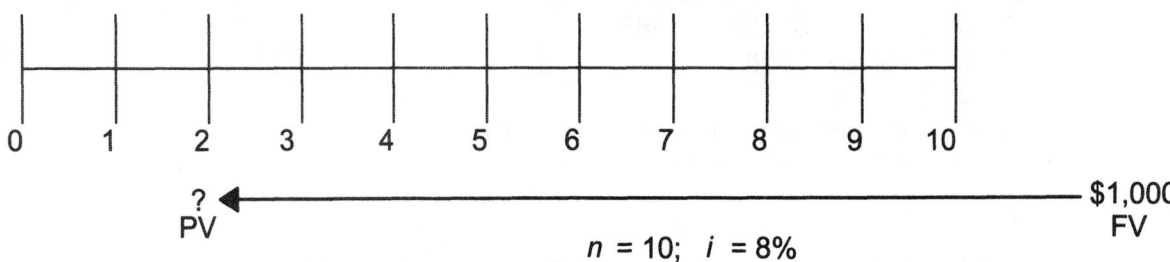

      (3)    The interest factor from Table 2 is .46319.
      (4)    Present Value = Future Value x $PVF_{n,i}$
             Present Value = $1,000 x .46319
             Present Value = <u>$463.19</u>

9.    We would expect the answer to question 8 to be the larger because the smaller the discount rate, the larger the present value. This is the case because the interest amount is smaller. The less the interest, the greater the present value figure.

10.    (1)    This is a future value of an ordinary annuity problem.
       (2)    $n = 10$; $i = 6\%$

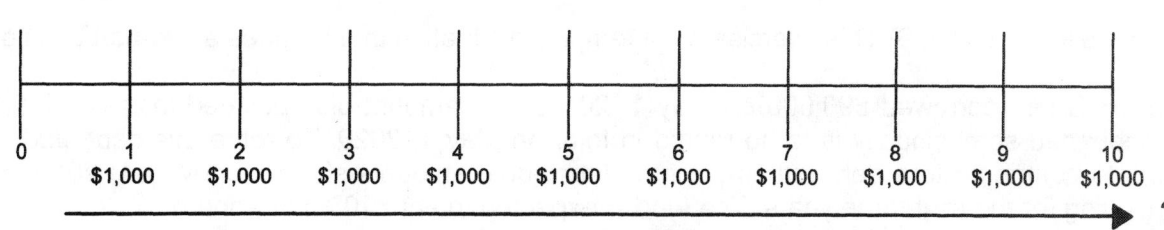

$$n = 10; \quad i = 6\%$$

       (3)    The interest factor from Table 3 is 13.18079.
       (4)    Future Value of an Ordinary Annuity = Rent x FVF-OA$_{n,i}$
              Future Value of an Ordinary Annuity = $1,000 x 13.18079
              Future Value of an Ordinary Annuity = $13,180.79

11.    (1)    This is a future value of an annuity due problem.
       (2)    $n = 10$; $i = 6\%$

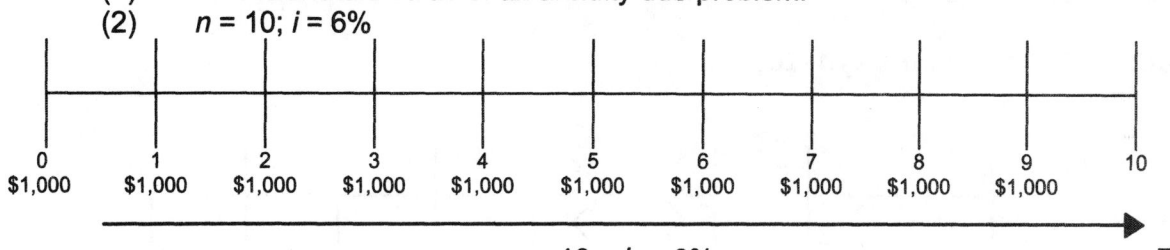

$$n = 10; \quad i = 6\%$$

       (3)    The interest factor can be derived as follows:
              FVF-OA for $n = 10$, $i = 6\%$ (Table 3)          13.18079
              Multiply by $(1 + i)$                          x    1.06
              FVF-AD for $n = 10$, i = 6%                       13.97164
       (4)    Future Value of an Annuity Due = Rent x FVF-AD$_{n,i}$
              Future Value of an Annuity Due = $1,000 x 13.97164
              Future Value of an Annuity Due = $13,971.64

12.    We would expect the answer to question 11 to be the larger because there is one more
       interest period reflected in the annuity due arrangement. The number of rents are the
       same, the interest rate is the same, but the rents begin earlier in the annuity due setup
       so there is one more interest period reflected.

> **TIP:**  In computing the **future amount** of an **ordinary annuity**, the number of compounding periods is
> **one less** than the number of rents. In computing the **future amount** of an **annuity due**, the
> number of compounding periods is the **same** as the number of rents. On the other hand, in
> computing the **present value** of an **ordinary annuity**, the final rent is discounted back the **same**
> number of periods that there are rents. In computing the **present value** of an **annuity due**, there
> is **one less** discount period than there are rents.

## EXERCISE 6-3

**Purpose:**    (L.O.5, 6) This exercise will exemplify a situation that requires a two-part solution.

Judson Green borrowed $90,000 on May 1, 2010. This amount plus accrued interest at 12% compounded semiannually is to be repaid in total on May 1, 2020. To retire this debt, Judson plans to contribute to a debt retirement fund four equal amounts starting on May 1, 2016 and continuing for the next three years. The fund is expected to earn 10% per annum.

## Instructions
How much must be contributed each year by Judson Green to provide a fund sufficient to retire the debt on May 1, 2020?

## Solution to Exercise 6-3

**Amount to be repaid on May 1, 2020:**
Time diagram:

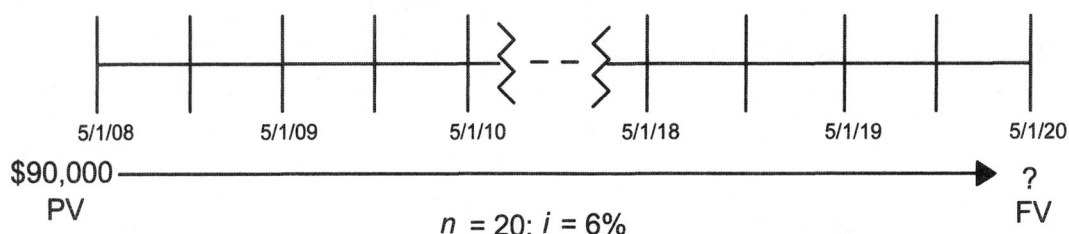

| | | |
|---|---|---|
| Future Value | = | $90,000 x FVF$_{n,i}$ |
| Future Value | = | $90,000 x 3.20714 |
| Future Value | = | $288,642.60 |

**Amount of annual contribution to retirement fund:**
Time diagram:

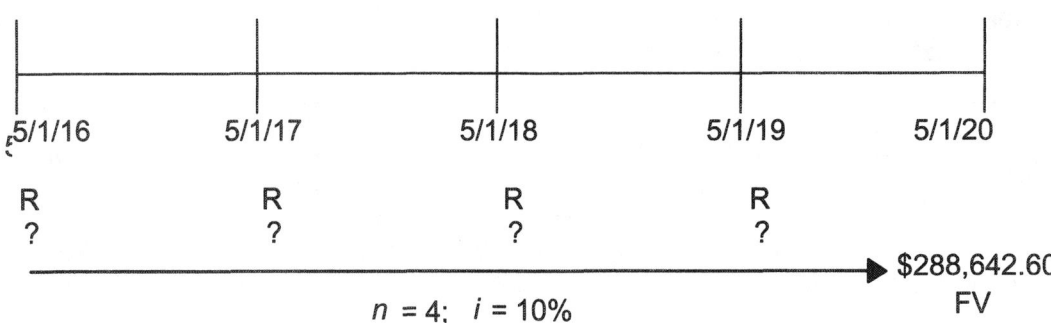

R = rent; FV = future value

Future value of ordinary annuity of 1 for 4 periods at 10%   4.64100
Multiplied by (1 + $i$)                                      x   1.10
Future value of annuity due of 1 for 4 periods at 10%       5.10510
Future value of an annuity due = Rent x FVF-AD$_{n,i}$
$288,642.60 = Rent x 5.10510
$288,642.60 ÷ 5.10510 = Rent
Rent = $56,540.05

**Approach:** First solve for the future value of a single sum. This future amount is $288,642.60. Then solve for the rent reflected in the future value of an annuity due. The rent is $56,540.05. The solution to the first part establishes the future value of an annuity due for which the rent must be determined in the second part of the problem.


# EXERCISE 6-4

**Purpose:**   (L.O. 5, 6, 7) This exercise will illustrate how to solve present value problems that require the computation of the rent in an annuity or the number of periods or the interest rate.


## Instructions

Using the appropriate interest table, provide the solution to each of the following four questions by computing the unknowns.

(a)   Jimmy Gunshanan has $5,000 to invest today at 5% to pay a debt of $7,387. How many years will it take him to accumulate enough to liquidate the debt if interest is compounded once annually?

(b)   Jimmy's friend Nathan has a $6,312.40 debt that he wishes to repay four years from today. He intends to invest $5,000.00 for four years and use the accumulated funds to liquidate the debt. What rate of interest will he need to earn annually in order to accumulate enough to pay the debt if interest is compounded annually?

(c)   Patricia McKiernan wishes to accumulate $35,000 to use for a trip around the world. She plans to gather the designated sum by depositing payments into an account at Sun Bank which pays 4% interest, compounded annually. What is the amount of each payment that Patricia must make at the end of each of six years to accumulate a fund balance of $35,000 by the end of the sixth year?

(d)   Your sister is twenty years old today and she wishes to accumulate $900,000 by her fifty-fifth birthday so she can retire to her summer place on Lake Tahoe. She wishes to accumulate the $900,000 by making annual deposits on her twentieth through her fifty-fourth birthdays. What annual deposit must your sister make if the fund will earn 8% interest compounded annually?

## Solution to Exercise 6-4

(a)    Time diagram:

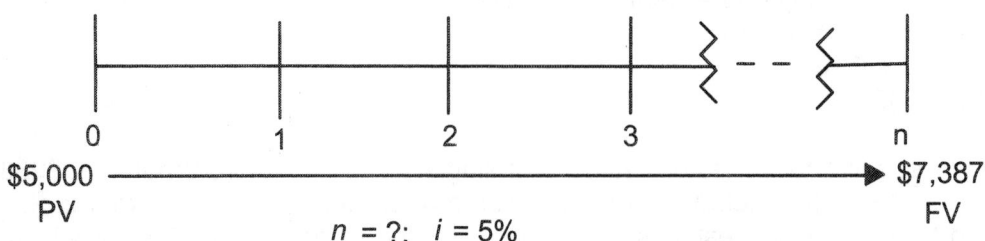

$n = ?$;   $i = 5\%$

*Future Value Approach*

Future value = Present value x $FVF_{n,i}$
$7,387.00 = \$5,000$ x $FVF_{n,i}$
1.4774 = FV factor for $i = 5\%$, $n = ?$
By reference to Table 1, 1.47746 is
   the FV factor for $i = 5\%$, $n = 8$
$n = \underline{8\ years}$

**OR**    *Present Value Approach*

Present value = Future value x $PVF_{n,i}$
$5,000.00 = \$7,387$ x $PVF_{n,i}$
.67686 = PV factor for $i = 5\%$, $n = ?$
By reference to Table 2, .67684 is
   the PV factor for $i = 5\%$, $n = 8$
$n = \underline{8\ years}$

(b)    Time diagram:

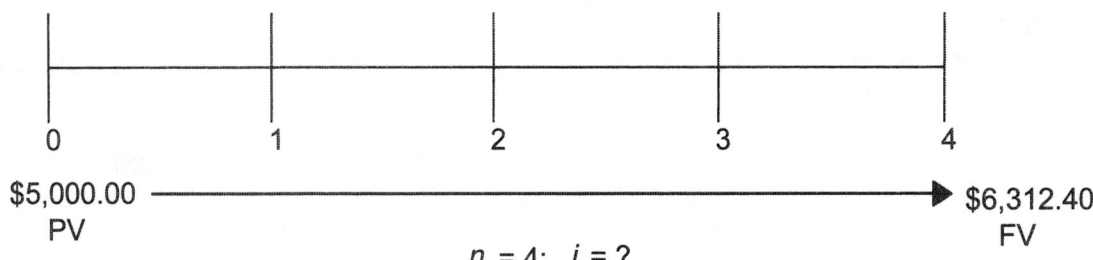

$n = 4$;   $i = ?$

*Future Value Approach*

Future value = Present value x $FVF_{n,i}$
$6,312.40 = \$5,000.00$ x $FVF_{n,i}$
1.26248 = FV factor for $n = 4$, $i = ?$
By reference to Table 1, 1.26248 is
   the FV factor for $n = 4$, $i = 6\%$.
$i = \underline{6\%}$

**OR**    *Present Value Approach*

Present value = Future value x $PVF_{n,i}$
$5,000.00 = \$6,312.40$ x $PVF_{n,i}$
.79209 = PV factor for $n = 4$, $i = ?$
By reference to Table 2, .79209 is the
   PV factor for $n = 4$, $i = 6\%$.
$i = \underline{6\%}$

(c)    Time diagram:

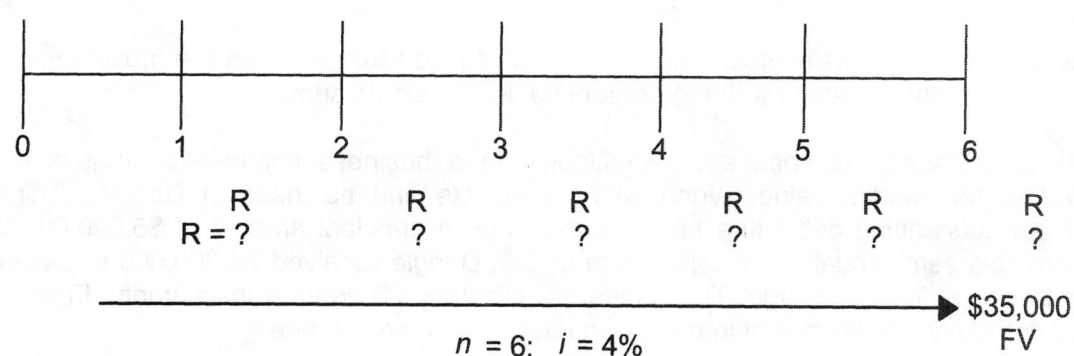

$n = 6; \quad i = 4\%$

Future Value = Rent x FVF-OA$_{n,i}$
$35,000 = Rent x 6.63298
$35,000 ÷ 6.63298 = Rent
$5,276.66 = Rent

(d)    Time diagram:

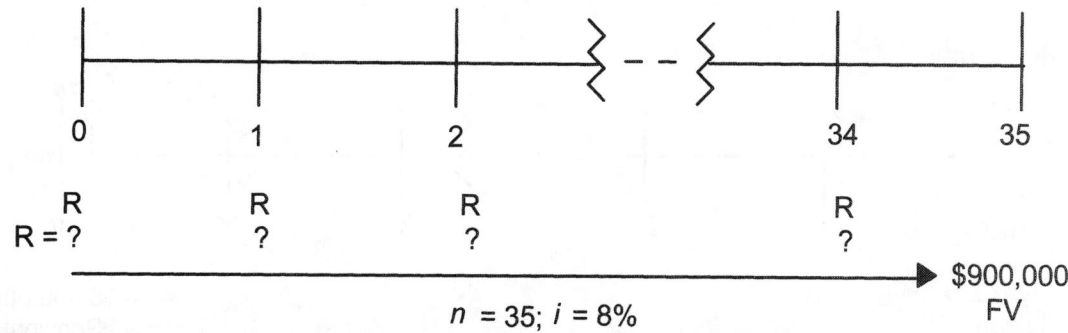

$n = 35; \quad i = 8\%$

| | |
|---|---|
| Future value of an ordinary annuity due of 1 for 35 periods at 8% | 172.31680 |
| Multiplied by (1 + $i$) | x    1.08 |
| Future value of annuity due of 1 for 35 periods at 8% | 186.10214 |

Future value of annuity due = Rent x FVF-AD$n,i$
$900,000 = Rent x 186.10214
$900,000 ÷ 186.10214 = Rent
$4,836.05 = Rent

## EXERCISE 6-5

**Purpose:**    (L.O. 8) This exercise will illustrate a situation that involves the present value of an annuity along with the present value of a single sum.

Your client, E-Trader, Inc., has acquired Doogle in a business combination that is to be accounted at fair market value. Along with the assets and business of Doogle, E-Trader assumed an outstanding debenture bond issue having a principal amount of $5,000,000 with interest payable semiannually at a stated rate of 6%. Doogle received $5,800,000 in proceeds from the issuance five years ago. The bonds are currently 20 years from maturity. Equivalent securities command an 8% rate of interest with interest paid semiannually.

### Instructions
Your client requests your advice regarding the amount to record as the fair value (present value) of the acquired bond issue.

### Solution to Exercise 6-5

Time diagram:

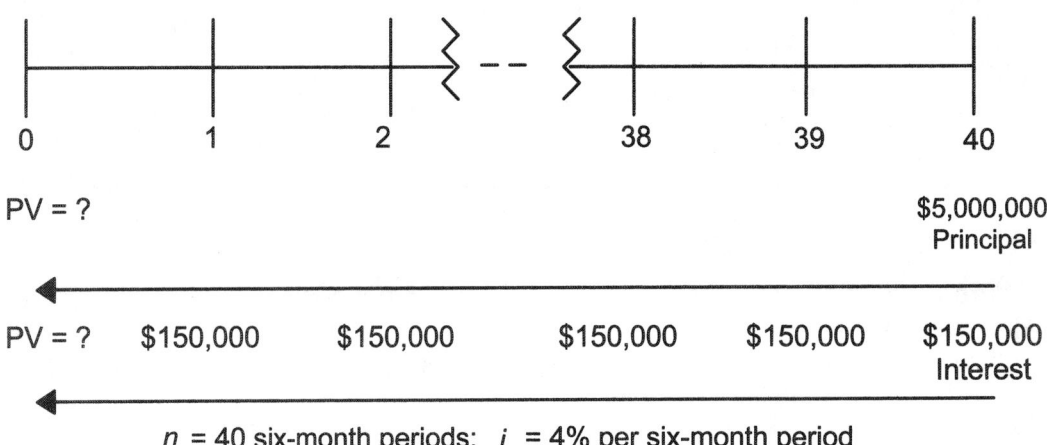

$n$ = 40 six-month periods;  $i$ = 4% per six-month period

| | |
|---|---:|
| Present value of the principal = $5,000,000 x .20829 | $ 1,041,450.00 |
| Present value of the interest payments = $150,000 x 19.79277 | 2,968,915.50 |
| Total present value of bond liability | $ 4,010,365.50 |

**Approach and Explanation:** Draw a time diagram and enter all future cash flows where they belong. The fair value of the bond liability being acquired by E-Trader is determined by discounting all of the future cash flows related to the bond issue back to the present date using the current market rate of interest (4% per six-month interest period). The face amount of the bonds ($5,000,000) is a single sum due in 20 years (40 semiannual periods). The interest payments constitute an ordinary annuity for forty semiannual periods. Each interest payment is computed by multiplying the stated rate (3% per interest period) by the face amount of the bonds ($5,000,000).

## EXERCISE 6-6

**Purpose:**   (L.O. 9) This exercise will apply the expected cash flow approach.

Ozzie Electronics sells high-end plasma TVs and offers a 3-year warranty on all new TVs sold. Ozzie has entered into an agreement with Electronic Service Labs to provide all warranty services on the 95 TVs sold in 2009. The controller for Ozzie estimates the following expected warranty cash outflow associated with the TVs sold in 2009.

|        | Cash Flow Estimate | Probability Assessment |
|--------|--------------------|------------------------|
| 2010   | $20,000            | 20%                    |
|        | 30,000             | 60%                    |
|        | 40,000             | 20%                    |
| 2011   | $25,000            | 30%                    |
|        | 30,000             | 50%                    |
|        | 45,000             | 20%                    |
| 2012   | $30,000            | 20%                    |
|        | 45,000             | 40%                    |
|        | 60,000             | 40%                    |

## Instructions
Determine the fair value of the warranty liability for the sales made in 2009. Use expected cash flow and present value techniques. Use an annual discount rate of 6%.

## Solution to Exercise 6-6

|      | Cash Flow Estimate | X | Probability Assessment = | Expected Cash Flow | | |
|------|--------------------|---|--------------------------|--------------------|---|---|
| 2010 | $20,000            | 20% | $ 4,000                | | | |
|      | 30,000             | 60% | 18,000                 | | | |
|      | 40,000             | 20% | 8,000                  | | X PV Factor, | |
|      |                    |     |                        | | n = 1, I = 6% | Present Value |
|      |                    |     | $30,000                | | .94340 | $28,302.00 |
| 2011 | $25,000            | 30% | $ 7,500                | | | |
|      | 30,000             | 50% | 15,000                 | | | |
|      | 45,000             | 20% | 9,000                  | | X PV Factor, | |
|      |                    |     |                        | | n = 2, I = 6% | Present Value |
|      |                    |     | $31,500                | | .89000 | $28,035.00 |
| 2012 | $30,000            | 20% | $ 6,000                | | | |
|      | 45,000             | 40% | 18,000                 | | | |
|      | 60,000             | 40% | 24,000                 | | X PV Factor, | |
|      |                    |     |                        | | n = 3, I = 6% | Present Value |
|      |                    |     | $48,000                | | .83962 | $40,301.76 |
|      |                    |     | Total Estimated Liability | | | $96,638.76 |

## ILLUSTRATION 6-6
## USING FINANCIAL CALCULATORS

Once you have mastered the underlying concepts in this chapter, you will find it extremely beneficial to learn how to solve time value of money problems by using a financial calculator. A business professional uses a financial calculator rather than the tables used in this chapter because most business applications involve an interest rate or time periods not provided in the interest tables. For example, most real life problems involve interest compounded monthly or daily. Thus a 6% annual rate compounded monthly for 5 years requires our calculations to use a .5% rate (not provided in the tables) for 60 periods (not provided in the tables). The most common keys used to solve time value of money problems are:

| N | I | PV | PMT | FV |
|---|---|----|-----|----|

where

| N | = | number of periods |
|----|---|-------------------|
| I | = | interest rate per period (some calculators use I/YR or i) |
| PV | = | present value (occurs at the beginning of the first period) |
| PMT | = | payment (all payments are equal, and none are skipped) |
| FV | = | future value (occurs at the end of the last period) |

On many calculators, these keys are actual buttons on the face of the calculator, on others, they appear on the display after the user accesses a present value menu.

In solving time value of money problems, you generally know (or are given) three of four variables and will solve for the remaining variable. The fifth key (the key not used) is given a value of zero to ensure that this variable is not used in the computation.

To illustrate the use of a financial calculator, let's assume that you want to know the future value of $10,000 invested to earn 8%, compounded annually for 5 years.

| Inputs: | 5 | 8 | -10,000 | 0 | ? |
|---------|---|---|---------|---|---|
| | N | I | PV | PMT | FV |
| Answer: | | | | | 14,693.30 |

The diagram shows you the information (inputs) to enter into the calculator, N = 5, I = 8, PV = -10,000, and PMT is not used (or PMT = 0) because a series of payments did not occur in the problem. You press FV for the answer and the future value is $14,693.30. This is the same answer you would get using compound interest tables ($10,000 X 1.46933 = $14693.30).

The use of plus and minus signs in time value of money problems with a financial calculator can be confusing. Most financial calculators are programmed so that the positive and negative cash flows in any problem offset each other. In the future value problem above, we identified the $10,000 initial investment as a negative (outflow); the answer 14,693.30 was shown as a positive, reflecting a cash inflow. If the 10,000 were entered as a positive, then the final answer would have been reported as a negative (-14,693.30) If you understand what is required in a problem, you should be able to interpret a positive or negative amount in determining the solution to a problem.

In the problem above, we assumed that compounding  occurs once a year. Some financial calculators have a default setting, which assumes that compounding occurs 12 times a year. You must determine what default period has been programmed into your calculator and change it as necessary to arrive at the proper compounding period.

Most financial calculators store and calculate using 12 decimal places. As a result, because compound interest tables generally have factors only up to 5 decimal places, a slight difference in the final answer can result. In most time value of money problems, the final answer will not include more than two decimal points.

To illustrate the future value of an ordinary annuity, assume that you are asked to determine the future value of five $1,000 deposits made at the end of each of the next 6 years, each of which earns interest at 6%, compounded annually. The setup is as follows:

| Inputs: | 6 | 6 | 0 | -1,000 | ? |
|---|---|---|---|---|---|
| | N | I | PV | PMT | FV |
| Answer: | | | | | 6,975.32 |

In this case, you enter N = 6, I = 6, PV = 0, PMT = -1,000, and then press FV to arrive at the answer 6,975.32. The $1,000 payments are shown as negatives because the deposits represent cash outflows that will accumulate with interest to the amount to be received (cash inflow) at the end of 6 years.

Recall that in any annuity problem you must determine whether the periodic payments occur at the beginning or the end of the period. If the first payment occurs at the beginning of the period, most financial calculators have a key marked "Begin" (or "Due") that you press to switch from the end-of-period payment mode (for an ordinary annuity) to beginning-of-period payment mode (for an annuity due). For most calculators, the word BEGIN is displayed to indicate that the calculator is set for an annuity due problem. (Some calculators use DUE).

With a financial calculator you can solve for any interest rate or for any number of periods in a time value of money problem. For example, assume you are financing a car with a 3-year loan. The loan has a 9.5% nominal annual interest rate, compounded monthly. The price of the car is $6,000, and you want to determine the monthly payments, assuming that the payments start one month after the purchase.

| Inputs: | 36 | 9.5 | 6,000 | ? | 0 |
|---|---|---|---|---|---|
| | N | I | PV | PMT | FV |
| Answer: | | | | -192.20 | |

By entering N = 36 (12 x 3), I = 9.5, PV = 6,000, FV = 0, and then pressing PMT, you can determine that the monthly payments will be $192.20. Note that the payment key is usually programmed for 12 payments per year. Thus, you must change the default (compounding period) if the payments are different than monthly.

# ANALYSIS OF MULTIPLE-CHOICE TYPE QUESTIONS

**QUESTION**
1. (L.O. 3, 7.) A grandfather wishes to set up a fund today that will allow his grandson to withdraw $5,000 from the fund at the beginning of each year for four years to pay for college expenses. The first withdrawal is to occur later today. How should grandpa compute the required investment if the fund is to earn 6% interest compounded annually and the fund is to be exhausted by his last withdrawal?
   a. $5,000 multiplied by the factor for the present value of an annuity due of 1 where $n = 4$, $i = 6\%$.
   b. $5,000 divided by the factor for the present value of an annuity due of 1 where $n = 4$, $i = 6\%$.
   c. $5,000 multiplied by the factor for the future amount of an annuity due of 1 where $n = 4$, $i = 6\%$.
   d. $5,000 divided by the factor for the future amount of an annuity due of 1 where $n = 4$, $i = 6\%$.

**Approach and Explanation:** Follow the steps in solving future value and present value problems:
1. This is a present value of an annuity due problem.
2. Time diagram:

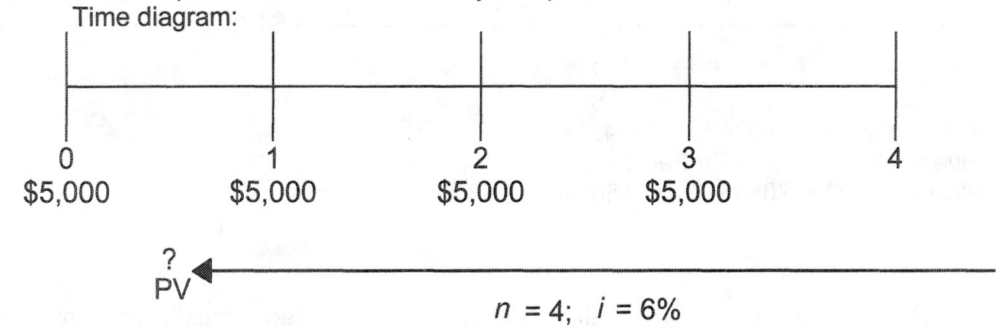

3. The factor for present value of annuity due for $n = 4$, $i = 6\%$ can be found in Table 5; it can also be derived by multiplying the factor for $n = 4$, $i = 6\%$ from the table for present value of an ordinary annuity times $1 + i$.
4. Present Value of an Annuity Due = Rent x Present Value of an Annuity Due Factor.
Therefore, the present value of the annuity due equals $5,000 multiplied by the factor for present value of an annuity due for $n = 4$, $i = 6\%$. (Solution = a.)

**Questions 2 and 3** use the following present value table. Given below are the present value factors for $1.00 discounted at 9% for one to five periods.

| Periods | Present Value of $1<br>$i = 9\%$ |
|---|---|
| 1 | .91743 |
| 2 | .84168 |
| 3 | .77218 |
| 4 | .70843 |
| 5 | .64993 |

**QUESTION**

2.  (L.O.3,5) What amount should be deposited in a bank account today if a balance of $1,000 is desired four years from today and the prevailing interest rate is 9%?
    a.  $1,000 x .91743 x 4
    b.  $1,000 x .70843
    c.  $1,000 ÷ .70843
    d.  $1,000 x (.91743 + .84168 + .77218 + .70843)

**Approach and Explanation:** Follow the steps in solving future value and present value problems:
1.  This is a present value of a single sum problem.
2.  Time diagram:

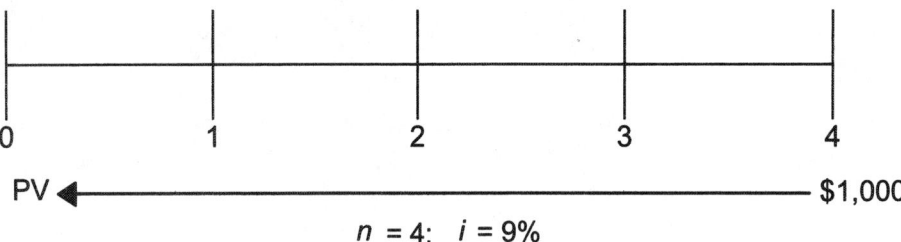

$$n = 4; \quad i = 9\%$$

3.  The present value factor is .70843 for $n = 4$, $i = 9\%$.
4.  Present Value = Future Value x PV Factor
    Present Value = $1,000 x .70843          (Solution = b.)

**QUESTION**

3.  (L.O.3,5) If $1,000 is deposited today to earn 9% interest compounded annually, how much will be on deposit at the end of three years?
    a.  $1,000 x .77218
    b.  $1,000 ÷ .77218
    c.  ($1,000 ÷ .91743) x 3
    d.  ($1,000 ÷ .77218) x 3

**Approach and Explanation:**
1.   This is a future value of a single sum problem.
2.   Time diagram:

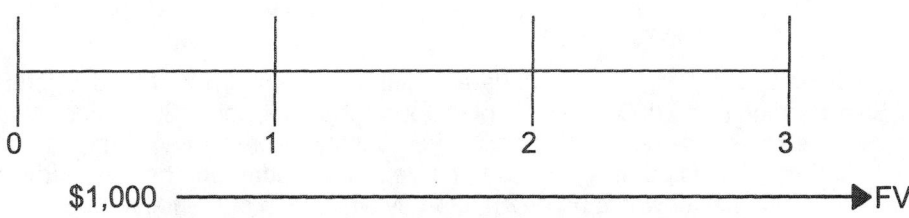

$$n = 3; \quad i = 9\%$$

3.   The future value factor is not given; however, for a single sum, the future value factor is the inverse of the present value factor. Therefore, 1.00000 divided by the present value factor for $n = 3$, $i = 9\%$ equals the future value factor for $n = 3$, $i = 9\%$.
4.   Future Value = Present Value x FV Factor
     Future Value = $1,000 x (1 ÷ .77218)
     Future Value = $1,000 ÷ .77218 (Solution = b.)

> **TIP:**   By looking at the time diagram, you can reason out that the amount on deposit at the end of three years should be greater than $1,000 but less than $1,500 (three years of 9% simple interest would give a balance of $1,270 and the compounding process would yield a little higher figure). In looking at the alternative answers, you can see that selection "a" will yield a result that is less than $1,000; selection "b" will give a result close to $1,300; selection "c" will give a result close to $3,200; and selection "d" will yield a result that is close to $3,900. Therefore, a reasonableness test would show that answer selection "b" must be the correct choice.

**QUESTION**
4.   (L.O.4) In the time diagram below, which concept is being depicted?

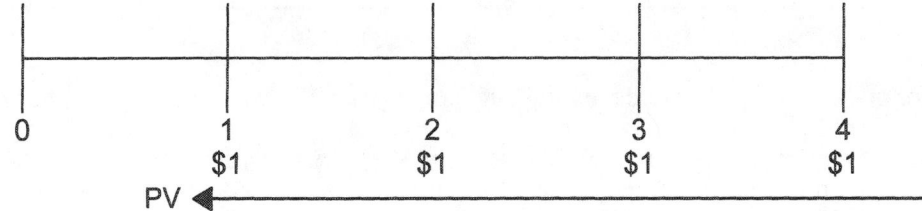

   a.   Present value of an ordinary annuity
   b.   Present value of an annuity due
   c.   Future value of an ordinary annuity
   d.   Future value of an annuity due

**Explanation:** It is an annuity since there is a series of equal periodic payments or receipts. The annuity is an ordinary one because the payments are due at the **end** (not the beginning) of each period. The arrow is drawn so that it is headed back to the present rather than forward to the future. Thus, we have a present value problem. (Solution = a.)

**QUESTION**
5.   (L.O.6) If the interest rate is 10%, the factor for the future value of annuity due of 1 for $n = 5$, $i = 10\%$ is equal to the factor for the future value of an ordinary annuity of 1 for $n = 5$, $i = 10\%$:
   a.   plus 1.10.
   b.   minus 1.10.
   c.   multiplied by 1.10.
   d.   divided by 1.10.

**Explanation:** All amounts involved in an annuity due come in exactly one period earlier than for an ordinary annuity. Therefore, all of the rents and accumulated interest are allowed to generate interest for one more period in the annuity due case. (Solution = c.)

**QUESTION**

6.  (L.O.7) A grandmother is setting up a savings account to help fund her granddaughter's college expenses. She is putting $40,000 in an account today that will earn 6% interest compounded annually. How much may Josey, the granddaughter, withdraw at the beginning of each of four years of college if her first withdrawal is to be one year from today and her last withdrawal is to exhaust the fund? The answer would be determined by which one of the following?

    a.  $40,000 multiplied by the factor for the present value of an ordinary annuity of 1 where $n = 4$, $i = 6\%$.

    b.  $40,000 divided by the factor for the present value of an ordinary annuity of 1 where $n = 4$, $i = 6\%$.

    c.  $40,000 multiplied by the factor for the future amount of an ordinary annuity of 1 where $n = 4$, $i = 6\%$.

    d.  $40,000 divided by the factor for the future amount of an ordinary annuity of 1 where $n = 4$, $i = 6\%$.

**Approach and Explanation:** Follow the steps in solving future value and present value problems.

1.  This is a present value of an ordinary annuity problem although by the wording of the question it could easily be confused with an annuity due situation. There are four rents and the first one is to be received a year from today.

2.  Time diagram:

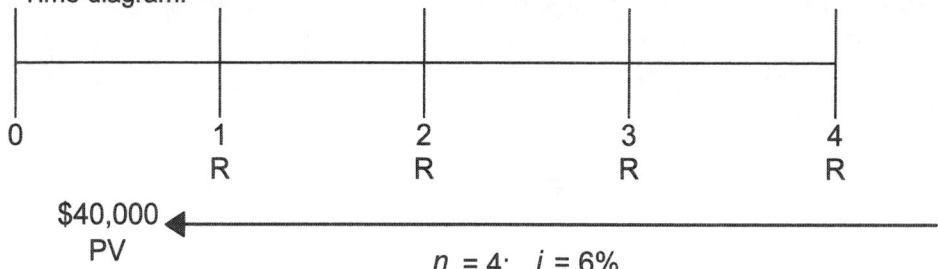

$$n = 4; \quad i = 6\%$$

3.  The factor for present value of an ordinary annuity for $n = 4$, $i = 6\%$ would be obtained from Table 4.

4.  Present Value of an Ordinary Annuity = Rent x Present Value of an Ordinary Annuity Factor. The Rent would be determined by dividing both sides of the equation by the factor. Therefore, the rent would equal the $40,000 divided by the factor for the present value of an ordinary annuity of 1. (Solution = b.)

**QUESTION**

7.  (L.O. 4) On December 1, 2010, Michael Hess Company sold some machinery to Shawn Keling Company. The two companies entered into an installment sales contract at a predetermined interest rate. The contract required four equal annual payments with the first payment due on December 1, 2010, the date of the sale. What present value concept is appropriate for this situation?

    a.  Future amount of an annuity of 1 for four periods

    b.  Future amount of 1 for four periods

    c.  Present value of an ordinary annuity of 1 for four periods

    d.  Present value of an annuity due of 1 for four periods.

**Explanation:** There is a series of equal payments due at the first of each period (year) because the first payment is due at the date of the sale (December 1, 2010); hence, this is an annuity due. The relevant amount to solve for would be the present value of the annuity; this present value would be involved in the determination of the sale (or purchase) price of the machinery. (Solution = d.)

**QUESTION**

8.  (L.O.4) On May 1, 2010, a company purchased a new machine that it does not have to pay for until May 1, 2012. The total payment on May 1, 2012 will include both principal and accumulated interest. Assuming interest is computed at a 10% rate compounded annually, the total payment due will be the price of the machine multiplied by what time value of money factor?
    a.  Future value of 1
    b.  Future value of an ordinary annuity of 1
    c.  Present value of 1
    d.  Present value of an ordinary annuity of 1

**Explanation:** The total payment due will be the price today (present value) plus the interest that will accumulate in two years. In computing the future value of a given amount today, the given amount is multiplied by a future value of 1 factor. (Solution = a.)

**QUESTION**

9.  (L.O.3) A series of equal receipts at equal intervals of time when each receipt is received at the beginning of each time period is called an:
    a.  ordinary annuity.
    b.  annuity in arrears.
    c.  annuity due.
    d.  unearned receipt.

**Explanation:** A series of equal receipts or payments at equal intervals is called an annuity. An ordinary annuity is an annuity where the rents (receipts or payments) occur at the **end** of each period; another name for an **ordinary annuity** is an **annuity in arrears**. An annuity due is one where the first rent occurs at the **beginning** of the first period; another name for an **annuity due** is an **annuity in advance**. (Solution = c.)

**QUESTION**

10.  (L.O. 5) Which of the following statements is **true**?
    a.  The higher the discount rate, the higher the present value.
    b.  The process of accumulating interest on interest is referred to as discounting.
    c.  If money is worth 10% compounded annually, $1,100 due one year from today is equivalent to $1,000 today.
    d.  If a single sum is due on December 31, 2013, the present value of that sum decreases as the date draws closer to December 31, 2013.

**Explanation:** Selection "a" is false because the higher the discount rate the lower the present value. Selection "b" is false because the process of accumulating interest on interest is referred to as compounding; discounting refers to the process of computing present value. Selection "d" is false because the present value of a single sum increases over time due to the time value of money (accumulation of interest). Selection "c" is correct because 10% of $1,000 is $100 interest; $1,000 today plus interest of $100 for one year means $1,100 one year from today is equivalent to $1,000 today if money is worth 10%. (Solution = c.)

**QUESTION**

11. (L.O. 8) Jake Co. has outstanding a 7% 10-year bond issue with a face value of $200,000. The bond was originally sold to yield a 6% annual interest rate. Jake uses the effective interest method. On December 31, 2009, the carrying amount of the bond was $210,000. What amount of unamortized premium should Jake report in its December 31, 2010 balance sheet?
    a.   $9,000.
    b.   $8,600.
    c.   $7,900.
    d.   $2,100.

**Explanation:** The carrying value at the beginning of the period ($210,000) is multiplied by the yield (effective) rate (6%) to determine interest expense for the period ($210,000 x 6% = $12,600). The face value ($200,000) is multiplied by the stated rate (7%) to determine the cash amount of interest for the period ($200,000 x 7% = $14,000). The difference between the interest expense of $12,600 and the amount of interest to be paid in cash of $14,000 is the amount of premium amortization for the period of $1,400. The unamortized premium is therefore $10,000 minus $1,400 = $8,600. (Solution = b.)

**QUESTION**

12. (L.O. 9) The interest rate to be used in performing an expected cash flow application is the
    a.   pure rate of return.
    b.   expected inflation rate.
    c.   risk-free rate.
    d.   credit risk rate of interest.

**Explanation:** The **pure rate of interest** (2% - 4%) is the amount a lender would charge if there are no possibilities of default and no expectation of inflation. The **expected inflation rate** is the estimated rate to compensate for loss of purchasing power in an inflationary economy. The **credit risk rate of interest** is a rate reflecting an enterprise's financial stability and profitability. The **risk-free rate of return** is defined as the pure rate of return plus the expected inflation rate. The FASB notes that the expected cash flow framework adjusts for credit risk because it incorporates the probability of receipt or payment into the computation of expected cash flows. Therefore, the rate used to discount the expected cash flows should consider only the pure rate of interest and the inflation rate. (Solution = c.)

## Table 1  FUTURE VALUE OF 1 (FUTURE VALUE OF A SINGLE SUM)

| (n) Periods | 2% | 2-1/2% | 3% | 4% | 5% | 6% |
|---|---|---|---|---|---|---|
| | | | $FVF_{n,i} = (1 + i)^n$ | | | |
| 1 | 1.02000 | 1.02500 | 1.03000 | 1.04000 | 1.05000 | 1.06000 |
| 2 | 1.04040 | 1.05063 | 1.06090 | 1.08160 | 1.10250 | 1.12360 |
| 3 | 1.06121 | 1.07689 | 1.09273 | 1.12486 | 1.15763 | 1.19102 |
| 4 | 1.08243 | 1.10381 | 1.12551 | 1.16986 | 1.21551 | 1.26248 |
| 5 | 1.10408 | 1.13141 | 1.15927 | 1.21665 | 1.27628 | 1.33823 |
| 6 | 1.12616 | 1.15969 | 1.19405 | 1.26532 | 1.34010 | 1.41852 |
| 7 | 1.14869 | 1.18869 | 1.22987 | 1.31593 | 1.40710 | 1.50363 |
| 8 | 1.17166 | 1.21840 | 1.26677 | 1.36857 | 1.47746 | 1.59385 |
| 9 | 1.19509 | 1.24886 | 1.30477 | 1.42331 | 1.55133 | 1.68948 |
| 10 | 1.21899 | 1.28008 | 1.34392 | 1.48024 | 1.62889 | 1.79085 |
| 11 | 1.24337 | 1.31209 | 1.38423 | 1.53945 | 1.71034 | 1.89830 |
| 12 | 1.26824 | 1.34489 | 1.42576 | 1.60103 | 1.79586 | 2.01220 |
| 13 | 1.29361 | 1.37851 | 1.46853 | 1.66507 | 1.88565 | 2.13293 |
| 14 | 1.31948 | 1.41297 | 1.51259 | 1.73168 | 1.97993 | 2.26090 |
| 15 | 1.34587 | 1.44830 | 1.55797 | 1.80094 | 2.07893 | 2.39656 |
| 16 | 1.37279 | 1.48451 | 1.60471 | 1.87298 | 2.18287 | 2.54035 |
| 17 | 1.40024 | 1.52162 | 1.65285 | 1.94790 | 2.29202 | 2.69277 |
| 18 | 1.42825 | 1.55966 | 1.70243 | 2.02582 | 2.40662 | 2.85434 |
| 19 | 1.45681 | 1.59865 | 1.75351 | 2.10685 | 2.52695 | 3.02560 |
| 20 | 1.48595 | 1.63862 | 1.80611 | 2.19112 | 2.65330 | 3.20714 |
| 21 | 1.51567 | 1.67958 | 1.86029 | 2.27877 | 2.78596 | 3.39956 |
| 22 | 1.54598 | 1.72157 | 1.91610 | 2.36992 | 2.92526 | 3.60354 |
| 23 | 1.57690 | 1.76461 | 1.97359 | 2.46472 | 3.07152 | 3.81975 |
| 24 | 1.60844 | 1.80873 | 2.03279 | 2.56330 | 3.22510 | 4.04893 |
| 25 | 1.64061 | 1.85394 | 2.09378 | 2.66584 | 3.38635 | 4.29187 |
| 26 | 1.67342 | 1.90029 | 2.15659 | 2.77247 | 3.55567 | 4.54938 |
| 27 | 1.70689 | 1.94780 | 2.22129 | 2.88337 | 3.73346 | 4.82235 |
| 28 | 1.74102 | 1.99650 | 2.28793 | 2.99870 | 3.92013 | 5.11169 |
| 29 | 1.77584 | 2.04641 | 2.35657 | 3.11865 | 4.11614 | 5.41839 |
| 30 | 1.81136 | 2.09757 | 2.42726 | 3.24340 | 4.32194 | 5.74349 |
| 31 | 1.84759 | 2.15001 | 2.50008 | 3.37313 | 4.53804 | 6.08810 |
| 32 | 1.88454 | 2.20376 | 2.57508 | 3.50806 | 4.76494 | 6.45339 |
| 33 | 1.92223 | 2.25885 | 2.65234 | 3.64838 | 5.00319 | 6.84059 |
| 34 | 1.96068 | 2.31532 | 2.73191 | 3.79432 | 5.25335 | 7.25103 |
| 35 | 1.99989 | 2.37321 | 2.81386 | 3.94609 | 5.51602 | 7.68609 |
| 36 | 2.03989 | 2.43254 | 2.89828 | 4.10393 | 5.79182 | 8.14725 |
| 37 | 2.08069 | 2.49335 | 2.98523 | 4.26809 | 6.08141 | 8.63609 |
| 38 | 2.12230 | 2.55568 | 3.07478 | 4.43881 | 6.38548 | 9.15425 |
| 39 | 2.16474 | 2.61957 | 3.16703 | 4.61637 | 6.70475 | 9.70351 |
| 40 | 2.20804 | 2.68506 | 3.26204 | 4.80102 | 7.03999 | 10.28572 |

| 8% | 9% | 10% | 11% | 12% | 15% | (n) Periods |
|---|---|---|---|---|---|---|
| 1.08000 | 1.09000 | 1.10000 | 1.11000 | 1.12000 | 1.15000 | 1 |
| 1.16640 | 1.18810 | 1.21000 | 1.23210 | 1.25440 | 1.32250 | 2 |
| 1.25971 | 1.29503 | 1.33100 | 1.36763 | 1.40493 | 1.52088 | 3 |
| 1.36049 | 1.41158 | 1.46410 | 1.51807 | 1.57352 | 1.74901 | 4 |
| 1.46933 | 1.53862 | 1.61051 | 1.68506 | 1.76234 | 2.01136 | 5 |
| 1.58687 | 1.67710 | 1.77156 | 1.87041 | 1.97382 | 2.31306 | 6 |
| 1.71382 | 1.82804 | 1.94872 | 2.07616 | 2.21068 | 2.66002 | 7 |
| 1.85093 | 1.99256 | 2.14359 | 2.30454 | 2.47596 | 3.05902 | 8 |
| 1.99900 | 2.17189 | 2.35795 | 2.55803 | 2.77308 | 3.51788 | 9 |
| 2.15892 | 2.36736 | 2.59374 | 2.83942 | 3.10585 | 4.04556 | 10 |
| 2.33164 | 2.58043 | 2.85312 | 3.15176 | 3.47855 | 4.65239 | 11 |
| 2.51817 | 2.81267 | 3.13843 | 3.49845 | 3.89598 | 5.35025 | 12 |
| 2.71962 | 3.06581 | 3.45227 | 3.88328 | 4.36349 | 6.15279 | 13 |
| 2.93719 | 3.34173 | 3.79750 | 4.31044 | 4.88711 | 7.07571 | 14 |
| 3.17217 | 3.64248 | 4.17725 | 4.78459 | 5.47357 | 8.13706 | 15 |
| 3.42594 | 3.97031 | 4.59497 | 5.31089 | 6.13039 | 9.35762 | 16 |
| 3.70002 | 4.32763 | 5.05447 | 5.89509 | 6.86604 | 10.76126 | 17 |
| 3.99602 | 4.71712 | 5.55992 | 6.54355 | 7.68997 | 12.37545 | 18 |
| 4.31570 | 5.14166 | 6.11591 | 7.26334 | 8.61276 | 14.23177 | 19 |
| 4.66096 | 5.60441 | 6.72750 | 8.06231 | 9.64629 | 16.36654 | 20 |
| 5.03383 | 6.10881 | 7.40025 | 8.94917 | 10.80385 | 18.82152 | 21 |
| 5.43654 | 6.65860 | 8.14028 | 9.93357 | 12.10031 | 21.64475 | 22 |
| 5.87146 | 7.25787 | 8.95430 | 11.02627 | 13.55235 | 24.89146 | 23 |
| 6.34118 | 7.91108 | 9.84973 | 12.23916 | 15.17863 | 28.62518 | 24 |
| 6.84847 | 8.62308 | 10.83471 | 13.58546 | 17.00000 | 32.91895 | 25 |
| 7.39635 | 9.39916 | 11.91818 | 15.07986 | 19.04007 | 37.85680 | 26 |
| 7.98806 | 10.24508 | 13.10999 | 16.73865 | 21.32488 | 43.53532 | 27 |
| 8.62711 | 11.16714 | 14.42099 | 18.57990 | 23.88387 | 50.06561 | 28 |
| 9.31727 | 12.17218 | 15.86309 | 20.62369 | 26.74993 | 57.57545 | 29 |
| 10.06266 | 13.26768 | 17.44940 | 22.89230 | 29.95992 | 66.21177 | 30 |
| 10.86767 | 14.46177 | 19.19434 | 25.41045 | 33.55511 | 76.14354 | 31 |
| 11.73708 | 15.76333 | 21.11378 | 28.20560 | 37.58173 | 87.56507 | 32 |
| 12.67605 | 17.18203 | 23.22515 | 31.30821 | 42.09153 | 100.69983 | 33 |
| 13.69013 | 18.72841 | 25.54767 | 34.75212 | 47.14252 | 115.80480 | 34 |
| 14.78534 | 20.41397 | 28.10244 | 38.57485 | 52.79962 | 133.17552 | 35 |
| 15.96817 | 22.25123 | 30.91268 | 42.81808 | 59.13557 | 153.15185 | 36 |
| 17.24563 | 24.25384 | 34.00395 | 47.52807 | 66.23184 | 176.12463 | 37 |
| 18.62528 | 26.43668 | 37.40434 | 52.75616 | 74.17966 | 202.54332 | 38 |
| 20.11530 | 28.81598 | 41.14479 | 58.55934 | 83.08122 | 232.92482 | 39 |
| 21.72452 | 31.40942 | 45.25926 | 65.00087 | 93.05097 | 267.86355 | 40 |

## Table 2  PRESENT VALUE OF 1 (PRESENT VALUE OF A SINGLE SUM)

$$PVF_{n,i} = \frac{1}{(1 + i)^n} = (1 + i)^{-n}$$

| (n) Periods | 2% | 2-1/2% | 3% | 4% | 5% | 6% |
|---|---|---|---|---|---|---|
| 1 | .98039 | .97561 | .97087 | .96154 | .95238 | .94340 |
| 2 | .96117 | .95181 | .94260 | .92456 | .90703 | .89000 |
| 3 | .94232 | .92860 | .91514 | .88900 | .86384 | .83962 |
| 4 | .92385 | .90595 | .88949 | .85480 | .82270 | .79209 |
| 5 | .90573 | .88385 | .86261 | .82193 | .78353 | .74726 |
| 6 | .88797 | .86230 | .83748 | .79031 | .74622 | .70496 |
| 7 | .87056 | .84127 | .81309 | .75992 | .71068 | .66506 |
| 8 | .85349 | .82075 | .78941 | .73069 | .67684 | .62741 |
| 9 | .83676 | .80073 | .76642 | .70259 | .64461 | .59190 |
| 10 | .82035 | .78120 | .74409 | .67556 | .61391 | .55839 |
| 11 | .80426 | .76214 | .72242 | .64958 | .58468 | .52679 |
| 12 | .78849 | .74356 | .70138 | .62460 | .55684 | .49697 |
| 13 | .77303 | .72542 | .68095 | .60057 | .53032 | .46884 |
| 14 | .75788 | .70773 | .66112 | .57748 | .50507 | .44230 |
| 15 | .74301 | .69047 | .64186 | .55526 | .48102 | .41727 |
| 16 | .72845 | .67362 | .62317 | .53391 | .45811 | .39365 |
| 17 | .71416 | .65720 | .60502 | .51337 | .43630 | .37136 |
| 18 | .70016 | .64117 | .58739 | .49363 | .41552 | .35034 |
| 19 | .68643 | .62553 | .57029 | .47464 | .39573 | .33051 |
| 20 | .67297 | .61027 | .55368 | .45639 | .37689 | .31180 |
| 21 | .65978 | .59539 | .53755 | .43883 | .35894 | .29416 |
| 22 | .64684 | .58086 | .52189 | .42196 | .34185 | .27751 |
| 23 | .63416 | .56670 | .50669 | .40573 | .32557 | .26180 |
| 24 | .62172 | .55288 | .49193 | .39012 | .31007 | .24698 |
| 25 | .60593 | .53939 | .47761 | .37512 | .29530 | .23300 |
| 26 | .59758 | .52623 | .46369 | .36069 | .28124 | .21981 |
| 27 | .58586 | .51340 | .45019 | .34682 | .26785 | .20737 |
| 28 | .57437 | .50088 | .43708 | .33348 | .25509 | .19563 |
| 29 | .56311 | .48866 | .42435 | .32065 | .24295 | .18456 |
| 30 | .55207 | .47674 | .41199 | .30832 | .23138 | .17411 |
| 31 | .54125 | .46511 | .39999 | .29646 | .22036 | .16425 |
| 32 | .53063 | .45377 | .38834 | .28506 | .20987 | .15496 |
| 33 | .52023 | .44270 | .37703 | .27409 | .19987 | .14619 |
| 34 | .51003 | .43191 | .36604 | .26355 | .19035 | .13791 |
| 35 | .50003 | .42137 | .35538 | .25342 | .18129 | .13011 |
| 36 | .49022 | .41109 | .34503 | .24367 | .17266 | .12274 |
| 37 | .48061 | .40107 | .33498 | .23430 | .16444 | .11579 |
| 38 | .47119 | .39128 | .32523 | .22529 | .15661 | .10924 |
| 39 | .46195 | .38174 | .31575 | .21662 | .14915 | .10306 |
| 40 | .45289 | .37243 | .30656 | .20829 | .14205 | .09722 |

| 8% | 9% | 10% | 11% | 12% | 15% | (n) Periods |
|---|---|---|---|---|---|---|
| .92593 | .91743 | .90909 | .90090 | .89286 | .86957 | 1 |
| .85734 | .84168 | .82645 | .81162 | .79719 | .75614 | 2 |
| .79383 | .77218 | .75132 | .73119 | .71178 | .65752 | 3 |
| .73503 | .70843 | .68301 | .65873 | .63552 | .57175 | 4 |
| .68058 | .64993 | .62092 | .59345 | .56743 | .49718 | 5 |
| .63017 | .59627 | .56447 | .53464 | .50663 | .43233 | 6 |
| .58349 | .54703 | .51316 | .48166 | .45235 | .37594 | 7 |
| .54027 | .50187 | .46651 | .43393 | .40388 | .32690 | 8 |
| .50025 | .46043 | .42410 | .39092 | .36061 | .28426 | 9 |
| .46319 | .42241 | .38554 | .35218 | .32197 | .24719 | 10 |
| .42888 | .38753 | .35049 | .31728 | .28748 | .21494 | 11 |
| .39711 | .35554 | .31863 | .28584 | .25668 | .18691 | 12 |
| .36770 | .32618 | .28966 | .25751 | .22917 | .16253 | 13 |
| .34046 | .29925 | .26333 | .23199 | .20462 | .14133 | 14 |
| .31524 | .27454 | .23939 | .20900 | .18270 | .12289 | 15 |
| .29189 | .25187 | .21763 | .18829 | .16312 | .10687 | 16 |
| .27027 | .23107 | .19785 | .16963 | .14564 | .09293 | 17 |
| .25025 | .21199 | .17986 | .15282 | .13004 | .08081 | 18 |
| .23171 | .19449 | .16351 | .13768 | .11611 | .07027 | 19 |
| .21455 | .17843 | .14864 | .12403 | .10367 | .06110 | 20 |
| .19866 | .16370 | .13513 | .11174 | .09256 | .05313 | 21 |
| .18394 | .15018 | .12285 | .10067 | .08264 | .04620 | 22 |
| .17032 | .13778 | .11168 | .09069 | .07379 | .04017 | 23 |
| .15770 | .12641 | .10153 | .08170 | .06588 | .03493 | 24 |
| .14602 | .11597 | .09230 | .07361 | .05882 | .03038 | 25 |
| .13520 | .10639 | .08391 | .06631 | .05252 | .02642 | 26 |
| .12519 | .09761 | .07628 | .05974 | .04689 | .02297 | 27 |
| .11591 | .08955 | .06934 | .05382 | .04187 | .01997 | 28 |
| .10733 | .08216 | .06304 | .04849 | .03738 | .01737 | 29 |
| .09938 | .07537 | .05731 | .04368 | .03338 | .01510 | 30 |
| .09202 | .06915 | .05210 | .03935 | .02980 | .01313 | 31 |
| .08520 | .06344 | .04736 | .03545 | .02661 | .01142 | 32 |
| .07889 | .05820 | .04306 | .03194 | .02376 | .00993 | 33 |
| .07305 | .05340 | .03914 | .02878 | .02121 | .00864 | 34 |
| .06763 | .04899 | .03558 | .02592 | .01894 | .00751 | 35 |
| .06262 | .04494 | .03235 | .02335 | .01691 | .00653 | 36 |
| .05799 | .04123 | .02941 | .02104 | .01510 | .00568 | 37 |
| .05369 | .03783 | .02674 | .01896 | .01348 | .00494 | 38 |
| .04971 | .03470 | .02430 | .01708 | .01204 | .00429 | 39 |
| .04603 | .03184 | .02210 | .01538 | .01075 | .00373 | 40 |

## Table 3  FUTURE VALUE OF AN ORDINARY ANNUITY OF 1

$$FVF\text{-}OA_{n,i} = \frac{(1+i)^n - 1}{i}$$

| (n) Periods | 2% | 2-1/2% | 3% | 4% | 5% | 6% |
|---|---|---|---|---|---|---|
| 1 | 1.00000 | 1.00000 | 1.00000 | 1.00000 | 1.00000 | 1.00000 |
| 2 | 2.02000 | 2.02500 | 2.03000 | 2.04000 | 2.05000 | 2.06000 |
| 3 | 3.06040 | 3.07563 | 3.09090 | 3.12160 | 3.15250 | 3.18360 |
| 4 | 4.12161 | 4.15252 | 4.18363 | 4.24646 | 4.31013 | 4.37462 |
| 5 | 5.20404 | 5.25633 | 5.30914 | 5.41632 | 5.52563 | 5.63709 |
| 6 | 6.30812 | 6.38774 | 6.46841 | 6.63298 | 6.80191 | 6.97532 |
| 7 | 7.43428 | 7.54743 | 7.66246 | 7.89829 | 8.14201 | 8.39384 |
| 8 | 8.58297 | 8.73612 | 8.89234 | 9.21423 | 9.54911 | 9.89747 |
| 9 | 9.75463 | 9.95452 | 10.15911 | 10.58280 | 11.02656 | 11.49132 |
| 10 | 10.94972 | 11.20338 | 11.46338 | 12.00611 | 12.57789 | 13.18079 |
| 11 | 12.16872 | 12.48347 | 12.80780 | 13.48635 | 14.20679 | 14.97164 |
| 12 | 13.41209 | 13.79555 | 14.19203 | 15.02581 | 15.91713 | 16.86994 |
| 13 | 14.68033 | 15.14044 | 15.61779 | 16.62684 | 17.71298 | 18.88214 |
| 14 | 15.97394 | 16.51895 | 17.08632 | 18.29191 | 19.59863 | 21.01507 |
| 15 | 17.29342 | 17.93193 | 18.59891 | 20.02359 | 21.57856 | 23.27597 |
| 16 | 18.63929 | 19.38022 | 20.15688 | 21.82453 | 23.65749 | 25.67253 |
| 17 | 20.01207 | 20.86473 | 21.76159 | 23.69751 | 25.84037 | 28.21288 |
| 18 | 21.41231 | 22.38635 | 23.41444 | 25.64541 | 28.13238 | 30.90565 |
| 19 | 22.84056 | 23.94601 | 25.11687 | 27.67123 | 30.53900 | 33.75999 |
| 20 | 24.29737 | 25.54466 | 26.87037 | 29.77808 | 33.06595 | 36.78559 |
| 21 | 25.78332 | 27.18327 | 28.67649 | 31.96920 | 35.71925 | 39.99273 |
| 22 | 27.29898 | 28.86286 | 30.53678 | 34.24797 | 38.50521 | 43.39229 |
| 23 | 28.84496 | 30.58443 | 32.45288 | 36.61789 | 41.43048 | 46.99583 |
| 24 | 30.42186 | 32.34904 | 34.42647 | 39.08260 | 44.50200 | 50.81558 |
| 25 | 32.03030 | 34.15776 | 36.45926 | 41.64591 | 47.72710 | 54.86451 |
| 26 | 33.67091 | 36.01171 | 38.55304 | 44.31174 | 51.11345 | 59.15638 |
| 27 | 35.34432 | 37.91200 | 40.70963 | 47.08421 | 54.66913 | 63.70577 |
| 28 | 37.05121 | 39.85980 | 42.93092 | 49.96758 | 58.40258 | 68.52811 |
| 29 | 38.79223 | 41.85630 | 45.21885 | 52.96629 | 62.32271 | 73.63980 |
| 30 | 40.56808 | 43.90270 | 47.57542 | 56.08494 | 66.43885 | 79.05819 |
| 31 | 42.37944 | 46.00027 | 50.00268 | 59.32834 | 70.76079 | 84.80168 |
| 32 | 44.22703 | 48.15028 | 52.50276 | 62.70147 | 75.29883 | 90.88978 |
| 33 | 46.11157 | 50.35403 | 55.07784 | 66.20953 | 80.06377 | 97.34316 |
| 34 | 48.03380 | 52.61289 | 57.73018 | 69.85791 | 85.06696 | 104.18376 |
| 35 | 49.99448 | 54.92821 | 60.46208 | 73.65222 | 90.32031 | 111.43478 |
| 36 | 51.99437 | 57.30141 | 63.27594 | 77.59831 | 95.83632 | 119.12087 |
| 37 | 54.03425 | 59.73395 | 66.17422 | 81.70225 | 101.62814 | 127.26812 |
| 38 | 56.11494 | 62.22730 | 69.15945 | 85.97034 | 107.70955 | 135.90421 |
| 39 | 58.23724 | 64.78298 | 72.23423 | 90.40915 | 114.09502 | 145.05846 |
| 40 | 60.40198 | 67.40255 | 75.40126 | 95.02552 | 120.79977 | 154.76197 |

| 8% | 9% | 10% | 11% | 12% | 15% | (n) Periods |
|---|---|---|---|---|---|---|
| 1.00000 | 1.00000 | 1.00000 | 1.00000 | 1.00000 | 1.00000 | 1 |
| 2.08000 | 2.09000 | 2.10000 | 2.11000 | 2.12000 | 2.15000 | 2 |
| 3.24640 | 3.27810 | 3.31000 | 3.34210 | 3.37440 | 3.47250 | 3 |
| 4.50611 | 4.57313 | 4.64100 | 4.70973 | 4.77933 | 4.99338 | 4 |
| 5.86660 | 5.98471 | 6.10510 | 6.22780 | 6.35285 | 6.74238 | 5 |
| 7.33592 | 7.52334 | 7.71561 | 7.91286 | 8.11519 | 8.75374 | 6 |
| 8.92280 | 9.20044 | 9.48717 | 9.78327 | 10.08901 | 11.06680 | 7 |
| 10.63663 | 11.02847 | 11.43589 | 11.85943 | 12.29969 | 13.72682 | 8 |
| 12.48756 | 13.02104 | 13.57948 | 14.16397 | 14.77566 | 16.78584 | 9 |
| 14.48656 | 15.19293 | 15.93743 | 16.72201 | 17.54874 | 20.30372 | 10 |
| 16.64549 | 17.56029 | 18.53117 | 19.56143 | 20.65458 | 24.34928 | 11 |
| 18.97713 | 20.14072 | 21.38428 | 22.71319 | 24.13313 | 29.00167 | 12 |
| 21.49530 | 22.95339 | 24.52271 | 26.21164 | 28.02911 | 34.35192 | 13 |
| 24.21492 | 26.01919 | 27.97498 | 30.09492 | 32.39260 | 40.50471 | 14 |
| 27.15211 | 29.36092 | 31.77248 | 34.40536 | 37.27972 | 47.58041 | 15 |
| 30.32428 | 33.00340 | 35.94973 | 39.18995 | 42.75328 | 55.71747 | 16 |
| 33.75023 | 36.97371 | 40.54470 | 44.50084 | 48.88367 | 65.07509 | 17 |
| 37.45024 | 41.30134 | 45.59917 | 50.39593 | 55.74972 | 75.83636 | 18 |
| 41.44626 | 46.01846 | 51.15909 | 56.93949 | 63.43968 | 88.21181 | 19 |
| 45.76196 | 51.16012 | 57.27500 | 64.20283 | 72.05244 | 102.44358 | 20 |
| 50.42292 | 56.76453 | 64.00250 | 72.26514 | 81.69874 | 118.81012 | 21 |
| 55.45676 | 62.87334 | 71.40275 | 81.21431 | 92.50258 | 137.63164 | 22 |
| 60.89330 | 69.53194 | 79.54302 | 91.14788 | 104.60289 | 159.27638 | 23 |
| 66.76476 | 76.78981 | 88.49733 | 102.17415 | 118.15524 | 184.16784 | 24 |
| 73.10594 | 84.70090 | 98.34706 | 114.41331 | 133.33387 | 212.79302 | 25 |
| 79.95442 | 93.32398 | 109.18177 | 127.99877 | 150.33393 | 245.71197 | 26 |
| 87.35077 | 102.72314 | 121.09994 | 143.07864 | 169.37401 | 283.56877 | 27 |
| 95.33883 | 112.96822 | 134.20994 | 159.81729 | 190.69889 | 327.10408 | 28 |
| 103.96594 | 124.13536 | 148.63093 | 178.39719 | 214.58275 | 377.16969 | 29 |
| 113.28231 | 136.30754 | 164.49402 | 199.02088 | 241.33268 | 434.74515 | 30 |
| 123.34587 | 149.57522 | 181.94343 | 221.91317 | 271.29261 | 500.95692 | 31 |
| 134.21354 | 164.03699 | 201.13777 | 247.32362 | 304.84772 | 577.10046 | 32 |
| 145.95062 | 179.80032 | 222.25154 | 275.52922 | 342.42945 | 644.66553 | 33 |
| 158.62667 | 196.98234 | 245.47670 | 306.83744 | 384.52098 | 765.36535 | 34 |
| 172.31680 | 215.71076 | 271.02437 | .341.58955 | 431.66350 | 881.17016 | 35 |
| 187.10215 | 236.12472 | 299.12681 | 380.16441 | 484.46312 | 1014.34568 | 36 |
| 203.07032 | 258.37595 | 330.03949 | 422.98249 | 543.59869 | 1167.49753 | 37 |
| 220.31595 | 282.62978 | 364.04343 | 470.51056 | 609.83053 | 1343.62216 | 38 |
| 238.94122 | 309.06646 | 401.44778 | 523.26673 | 684.01020 | 1546.16549 | 39 |
| 259.05652 | 337.88245 | 442.59256 | 581.82607 | 767.09142 | 1779.09031 | 40 |

## Table 4  PRESENT VALUE OF AN ORDINARY ANNUITY OF 1

$$\text{PVF-OA}_{n,i} = \frac{1 - \dfrac{1}{(1+i)^n}}{i}$$

| (n) Periods | 2% | 2-1/2% | 3% | 4% | 5% | 6% |
|---|---|---|---|---|---|---|
| 1 | .98039 | .97561 | .97087 | .96154 | .95238 | .94340 |
| 2 | 1.94156 | 1.92742 | 1.91347 | 1.88609 | 1.85941 | 1.83339 |
| 3 | 2.88388 | 2.85602 | 2.82861 | 2.77509 | 2.72325 | 2.67301 |
| 4 | 3.80773 | 3.76197 | 3.71710 | 3.62990 | 3.54595 | 3.46511 |
| 5 | 4.71346 | 4.64583 | 4.57971 | 4.45182 | 4.32948 | 4.21236 |
| 6 | 5.60143 | 5.50813 | 5.41719 | 5.24214 | 5.07569 | 4.91732 |
| 7 | 6.47199 | 6.34939 | 6.23028 | 6.00205 | 5.78637 | 5.58238 |
| 8 | 7.32548 | 7.17014 | 7.01969 | 6.73274 | 6.46321 | 6.20979 |
| 9 | 8.16224 | 7.97087 | 7.78611 | 7.43533 | 7.10782 | 6.80169 |
| 10 | 8.98259 | 8.75206 | 8.53020 | 8.11090 | 7.72173 | 7.36009 |
| 11 | 9.78685 | 9.51421 | 9.25262 | 8.76048 | 8.30641 | 7.88687 |
| 12 | 10.57534 | 10.25776 | 9.95400 | 9.38507 | 8.86325 | 8.38384 |
| 13 | 11.34837 | 10.98319 | 10.63496 | 9.98565 | 9.39357 | 8.85268 |
| 14 | 12.10625 | 11.69091 | 11.29607 | 10.56312 | 9.89864 | 9.29498 |
| 15 | 12.84926 | 12.38138 | 11.93794 | 11.11839 | 10.37966 | 9.71225 |
| 16 | 13.57771 | 13.05500 | 12.56110 | 11.65230 | 10.83777 | 10.10590 |
| 17 | 14.29187 | 13.71220 | 13.16612 | 12.16567 | 11.27407 | 10.47726 |
| 18 | 14.99203 | 14.35336 | 13.75351 | 12.65930 | 11.68959 | 10.82760 |
| 19 | 15.67846 | 14.97889 | 14.32380 | 13.13394 | 12.08532 | 11.15812 |
| 20 | 16.35143 | 15.58916 | 14.87747 | 13.59033 | 12.46221 | 11.46992 |
| 21 | 17.01121 | 16.18455 | 15.41502 | 14.02916 | 12.82115 | 11.76408 |
| 22 | 17.65805 | 16.76541 | 15.93692 | 14.45112 | 13.16300 | 12.04158 |
| 23 | 18.29220 | 17.33211 | 16.44361 | 14.85684 | 13.48857 | 12.30338 |
| 24 | 18.91393 | 17.88499 | 16.93554 | 15.24696 | 13.79864 | 12.55036 |
| 25 | 19.52346 | 18.42438 | 17.41315 | 15.62208 | 14.09394 | 12.78336 |
| 26 | 20.12104 | 18.95061 | 17.87684 | 15.98277 | 14.37519 | 13.00317 |
| 27 | 20.70690 | 19.46401 | 18.32703 | 16.32959 | 14.64303 | 13.21053 |
| 28 | 21.28127 | 19.96489 | 18.76411 | 16.66306 | 14.89813 | 13.40616 |
| 29 | 21.84438 | 20.45355 | 19.18845 | 16.98371 | 15.14107 | 13.59072 |
| 30 | 22.39646 | 20.93029 | 19.60044 | 17.29203 | 15.37245 | 13.76483 |
| 31 | 22.93770 | 21.39541 | 20.00043 | 17.58849 | 15.59281 | 13.92909 |
| 32 | 23.46833 | 21.84918 | 20.38877 | 17.87355 | 15.80268 | 14.08404 |
| 33 | 23.98856 | 22.29188 | 20.76579 | 18.14765 | 16.00255 | 14.23023 |
| 34 | 24.49859 | 22.72379 | 21.13184 | 18.41120 | 16.19290 | 14.36814 |
| 35 | 24.99862 | 23.14516 | 21.48722 | 18.66461 | 16.37419 | 14.49825 |
| 36 | 25.48884 | 23.55625 | 21.83225 | 18.90828 | 16.54685 | 14.62099 |
| 37 | 25.96945 | 23.95732 | 22.16724 | 19.14258 | 16.71129 | 14.73678 |
| 38 | 26.44064 | 24.34860 | 22.49246 | 19.36786 | 16.86789 | 14.84602 |
| 39 | 26.90259 | 24.73034 | 22.80822 | 19.58448 | 17.01704 | 14.94907 |
| 40 | 27.35548 | 25.10278 | 23.11477 | 19.79277 | 17.15909 | 15.04630 |

| 8% | 9% | 10% | 11% | 12% | 15% | (n) Periods |
|---|---|---|---|---|---|---|
| .92593 | .91743 | .90909 | .90090 | .89286 | .86957 | 1 |
| 1.78326 | 1.75911 | 1.73554 | 1.71252 | 1.69005 | 1.62571 | 2 |
| 2.57710 | 2.53130 | 2.48685 | 2.44371 | 2.40183 | 2.28323 | 3 |
| 3.31213 | 3.23972 | 3.16986 | 3.10245 | 3.03735 | 2.85498 | 4 |
| 3.99271 | 3.88965 | 3.79079 | 3.69590 | 3.60478 | 3.35216 | 5 |
| 4.62288 | 4.48592 | 4.35526 | 4.23054 | 4.11141 | 3.78448 | 6 |
| 5.20637 | 5.03295 | 4.86842 | 4.71220 | 4.56376 | 4.16042 | 7 |
| 5.74664 | 5.53482 | 5.33493 | 5.14612 | 4.96764 | 4.48732 | 8 |
| 6.24689 | 5.99525 | 5.75902 | 5.53705 | 5.32825 | 4.77158 | 9 |
| 6.71008 | 6.41766 | 6.14457 | 5.88923 | 5.65022 | 5.01877 | 10 |
| 7.13896 | 6.80519 | 6.49506 | 6.20652 | 5.93770 | 5.23371 | 11 |
| 7.53608 | 7.16073 | 6.81369 | 6.49236 | 6.19437 | 5.42062 | 12 |
| 7.90378 | 7.48690 | 7.10336 | 6.74987 | 6.42355 | 5.58315 | 13 |
| 8.24424 | 7.78615 | 7.36669 | 6.98187 | 6.62817 | 5.72448 | 14 |
| 8.55948 | 8.06069 | 7.60608 | 7.19087 | 6.81086 | 5.84737 | 15 |
| 8.85137 | 8.31256 | 7.82371 | 7.37916 | 6.97399 | 5.95424 | 16 |
| 9.12164 | 8.54363 | 8.02155 | 7.54879 | 7.11963 | 6.04716 | 17 |
| 9.37189 | 8.75563 | 8.20141 | 7.70162 | 7.24967 | 6.12797 | 18 |
| 9.60360 | 8.95012 | 8.36492 | 7.83929 | 7.36578 | 6.19823 | 19 |
| 9.81815 | 9.12855 | 8.51356 | 7.96333 | 7.46944 | 6.25933 | 20 |
| 10.01680 | 9.29224 | 8.64869 | 8.07507 | 7.56200 | 6.31246 | 21 |
| 10.20074 | 9.44243 | 8.77154 | 8.17574 | 7.64465 | 6.35866 | 22 |
| 10.37106 | 9.58021 | 8.88322 | 8.26643 | 7.71843 | 6.39884 | 23 |
| 10.52876 | 9.70661 | 8.98474 | 8.34814 | 7.78432 | 6.43377 | 24 |
| 10.67478 | 9.82258 | 9.07704 | 8.42174 | 7.84314 | 6.46415 | 25 |
| 10.80998 | 9.92897 | 9.16095 | 8.48806 | 7.89566 | 6.49056 | 26 |
| 10.93516 | 10.02658 | 9.23722 | 8.54780 | 7.94255 | 6.51353 | 27 |
| 11.05108 | 10.11613 | 9.30657 | 8.60162 | 7.98442 | 6.53351 | 28 |
| 11.15841 | 10.19828 | 9.36961 | 8.65011 | 8.02181 | 6.55088 | 29 |
| 11.25778 | 10.27365 | 9.42691 | 8.69379 | 8.05518 | 6.56598 | 30 |
| 11.34980 | 10.34280 | 9.47901 | 8.73315 | 8.08499 | 6.57911 | 31 |
| 11.43500 | 10.40624 | 9.52638 | 8.76860 | 8.11159 | 6.59053 | 32 |
| 11.51389 | 10.46444 | 9.56943 | 8.80054 | 8.13535 | 6.60046 | 33 |
| 11.58693 | 10.51784 | 9.60858 | 8.82932 | 8.15656 | 6.60910 | 34 |
| 11.65457 | 10.56682 | 9.64416 | 8.85524 | 8.17550 | 6.61661 | 35 |
| 11.71719 | 10.61176 | 9.67651 | 8.87859 | 8.19241 | 6.62314 | 36 |
| 11.77518 | 10.65299 | 9.70592 | 8.89963 | 8.20751 | 6.62882 | 37 |
| 11.82887 | 10.69082 | 9.73265 | 8.91859 | 8.22099 | 6.63375 | 38 |
| 11.87858 | 10.72552 | 9.75697 | 8.93567 | 8.23303 | 6.63805 | 39 |
| 11.92461 | 10.75736 | 9.77905 | 8.95105 | 8.24378 | 6.64178 | 40 |

## Table 5  PRESENT VALUE OF AN ANNUITY DUE OF 1

$$PVF\text{-}AD_{n,i} = 1 + \dfrac{1 - \dfrac{1}{(1+i)^{n-1}}}{i}$$

| (n) Periods | 2% | 2-1/2% | 3% | 4% | 5% | 6% |
|---|---|---|---|---|---|---|
| 1 | 1.00000 | 1.00000 | 1.00000 | 1.00000 | 1.00000 | 1.00000 |
| 2 | 1.98039 | 1.97561 | 1.97087 | 1.96154 | 1.95238 | 1.94340 |
| 3 | 2.94156 | 2.92742 | 2.91347 | 2.88609 | 2.85941 | 2.83339 |
| 4 | 3.88388 | 3.85602 | 3.82861 | 3.77509 | 3.72325 | 3.67301 |
| 5 | 4.80773 | 4.76197 | 4.71710 | 4.62990 | 4.54595 | 4.46511 |
| 6 | 5.71346 | 5.64583 | 5.57971 | 5.45182 | 5.32948 | 5.21236 |
| 7 | 6.60143 | 6.50813 | 6.41719 | 6.24214 | 6.07569 | 5.91732 |
| 8 | 7.47199 | 7.34939 | 7.23028 | 7.00205 | 6.78637 | 6.58238 |
| 9 | 8.32548 | 8.17014 | 8.01969 | 7.73274 | 7.46321 | 7.20979 |
| 10 | 9.16224 | 8.97087 | 8.78611 | 8.43533 | 8.10782 | 7.80169 |
| 11 | 9.98259 | 9.75206 | 9.53020 | 9.11090 | 8.72173 | 8.36009 |
| 12 | 10.78685 | 10.51421 | 10.25262 | 9.76048 | 9.30641 | 8.88687 |
| 13 | 11.57534 | 11.25776 | 10.95400 | 10.38507 | 9.86325 | 9.38384 |
| 14 | 12.34837 | 11.98319 | 11.63496 | 10.98565 | 10.39357 | 9.85268 |
| 15 | 13.10625 | 12.69091 | 12.29607 | 11.56312 | 10.89864 | 10.29498 |
| 16 | 13.84926 | 13.38138 | 12.93794 | 12.11839 | 11.37966 | 10.71225 |
| 17 | 14.57771 | 14.05500 | 13.56110 | 12.65230 | 11.83777 | 11.10590 |
| 18 | 15.29187 | 14.71220 | 14.16612 | 13.16567 | 12.27407 | 11.47726 |
| 19 | 15.99203 | 15.35336 | 14.75351 | 13.65930 | 12.68959 | 11.82760 |
| 20 | 16.67846 | 15.97889 | 15.32380 | 14.13394 | 13.08532 | 12.15812 |
| 21 | 17.35143 | 16.58916 | 15.87747 | 14.59033 | 13.46221 | 12.46992 |
| 22 | 18.01121 | 17.18455 | 16.41502 | 15.02916 | 13.82115 | 12.76408 |
| 23 | 18.65805 | 17.76541 | 16.93692 | 15.45112 | 14.16300 | 13.04158 |
| 24 | 19.29220 | 18.33211 | 17.44361 | 15.85684 | 14.48857 | 13.30338 |
| 25 | 19.91393 | 18.88499 | 17.93554 | 16.24696 | 14.79864 | 13.55036 |
| 26 | 20.52346 | 19.42438 | 18.41315 | 16.62208 | 15.09394 | 13.78336 |
| 27 | 21.12104 | 19.95061 | 18.87684 | 16.98277 | 15.37519 | 14.00317 |
| 28 | 21.70690 | 20.46401 | 19.32703 | 17.32959 | 15.64303 | 14.21053 |
| 29 | 22.28127 | 20.96489 | 19.76411 | 17.66306 | 15.89813 | 14.40616 |
| 30 | 22.84438 | 21.45355 | 20.18845 | 17.98371 | 16.14107 | 14.59072 |
| 31 | 23.39646 | 21.93029 | 20.60044 | 18.29203 | 16.37245 | 14.76483 |
| 32 | 23.93770 | 22.39541 | 21.00043 | 18.58849 | 16.59281 | 14.92909 |
| 33 | 24.46833 | 22.84918 | 21.38877 | 18.87355 | 16.80268 | 15.08404 |
| 34 | 24.98856 | 23.29188 | 21.76579 | 19.14765 | 17.00255 | 15.23023 |
| 35 | 25.49859 | 23.72379 | 22.13184 | 19.41120 | 17.19290 | 15.36814 |
| 36 | 25.99862 | 24.14516 | 22.48722 | 19.66461 | 17.37419 | 15.49825 |
| 37 | 26.48884 | 24.55625 | 22.83225 | 19.90828 | 17.54685 | 15.62099 |
| 38 | 26.96945 | 24.95732 | 23.16724 | 20.14258 | 17.71129 | 15.73678 |
| 39 | 27.44064 | 25.34860 | 23.49246 | 20.36786 | 17.86789 | 15.84602 |
| 40 | 27.90259 | 25.73034 | 23.80822 | 20.58448 | 18.01704 | 15.94907 |

| 8% | 9% | 10% | 11% | 12% | 15% | (n) Periods |
|---|---|---|---|---|---|---|
| 1.00000 | 1.00000 | 1.00000 | 1.00000 | 1.00000 | 1.00000 | 1 |
| 1.92593 | 1.91743 | 1.90909 | 1.90090 | 1.89286 | 1.86957 | 2 |
| 2.78326 | 2.75911 | 2.73554 | 2.71252 | 2.69005 | 2.62571 | 3 |
| 3.57710 | 3.53130 | 3.48685 | 3.44371 | 3.40183 | 3.28323 | 4 |
| 4.31213 | 4.23972 | 4.16986 | 4.10245 | 4.03735 | 3.85498 | 5 |
| 4.99271 | 4.88965 | 4.79079 | 4.69590 | 4.60478 | 4.35216 | 6 |
| 5.62288 | 5.48592 | 5.35526 | 5.23054 | 5.11141 | 4.78448 | 7 |
| 6.20637 | 6.03295 | 5.86842 | 5.71220 | 5.56376 | 5.16042 | 8 |
| 6.74664 | 6.53482 | 6.33493 | 6.14612 | 5.96764 | 5.48732 | 9 |
| 7.24689 | 6.99525 | 6.75902 | 6.53705 | 6.32825 | 5.77158 | 10 |
| 7.71008 | 7.41766 | 7.14457 | 6.88923 | 6.65022 | 6.01877 | 11 |
| 8.13896 | 7.80519 | 7.49506 | 7.20652 | 6.93770 | 6.23371 | 12 |
| 8.53608 | 8.16073 | 7.18369 | 7.49236 | 7.19437 | 6.42062 | 13 |
| 8.90378 | 8.48690 | 8.10336 | 7.74987 | 7.42355 | 6.58315 | 14 |
| 9.24424 | 8.78615 | 8.36669 | 7.98187 | 7.62817 | 6.72448 | 15 |
| 9.55948 | 9.06069 | 8.60608 | 8.19087 | 7.81086 | 6.84737 | 16 |
| 9.85137 | 9.31256 | 8.82371 | 8.37916 | 7.97399 | 6.95424 | 17 |
| 10.12164 | 9.54363 | 9.02155 | 8.54879 | 8.11963 | 7.04716 | 18 |
| 10.37189 | 9.75563 | 9.20141 | 8.70162 | 8.24967 | 7.12797 | 19 |
| 10.60360 | 9.95012 | 9.36492 | 8.83929 | 8.36578 | 7.19823 | 20 |
| 10.81815 | 10.12855 | 9.51356 | 8.96333 | 8.46944 | 7.25933 | 21 |
| 11.01680 | 10.29224 | 9.64869 | 9.07507 | 8.56200 | 7.31246 | 22 |
| 11.20074 | 10.44243 | 9.77154 | 9.17574 | 8.64465 | 7.35866 | 23 |
| 11.37106 | 10.58021 | 9.88322 | 9.26643 | 8.71843 | 7.39884 | 24 |
| 11.52876 | 10.70661 | 9.98474 | 9.34814 | 8.78432 | 7.43377 | 25 |
| 11.67478 | 10.82258 | 10.07704 | 9.42174 | 8.84314 | 7.46415 | 26 |
| 11.80998 | 10.92897 | 10.16095 | 9.48806 | 8.89566 | 7.49056 | 27 |
| 11.93518 | 11.02658 | 10.23722 | 9.54780 | 8.94255 | 7.51353 | 28 |
| 12.05108 | 11.11613 | 10.30657 | 9.60162 | 8.98442 | 7.53351 | 29 |
| 12.15841 | 11.19828 | 10.36961 | 9.65011 | 9.02181 | 7.55088 | 30 |
| 12.25778 | 11.27365 | 10.42691 | 9.69379 | 9.05518 | 7.56598 | 31 |
| 12.34980 | 11.34280 | 10.47901 | 9.73315 | 9.08499 | 7.57911 | 32 |
| 12.43500 | 11.40624 | 10.52638 | 9.76860 | 9.11159 | 7.59053 | 33 |
| 12.51389 | 11.46444 | 10.56943 | 9.80054 | 9.13535 | 7.60046 | 34 |
| 12.58693 | 11.51784 | 10.60858 | 9.82932 | 9.15656 | 7.60910 | 35 |
| 12.65457 | 11.56682 | 10.64416 | 9.85524 | 9.17550 | 7.61661 | 36 |
| 12.71719 | 11.61176 | 10.67651 | 9.87859 | 9.19241 | 7.62314 | 37 |
| 12.77518 | 11.65299 | 10.70592 | 9.89963 | 9.20751 | 7.62882 | 38 |
| 12.82887 | 11.69082 | 10.73265 | 9.91859 | 9.22099 | 7.63375 | 39 |
| 12.87858 | 11.72552 | 10.75697 | 9.93567 | 9.23303 | 7.63805 | 40 |

# CHAPTER 7

# CASH AND RECEIVABLES

## OVERVIEW

In previous chapters, you learned the basic formats for general purpose financial statements. In this chapter you begin your in-depth study of accounting for items appearing on the balance sheet: (1) what is to be included in an item classification, (2) rules for determining the dollar amount to be reported, (3) disclosure requirements, (4) special accounting procedures which may be required and, (5) related internal control procedures. In this chapter, you will learn what is to be included under the cash caption on the balance sheet. Also, the methods of accounting for accounts receivable and notes receivable are discussed. Some key internal controls which should be employed for business activities involving cash are discussed in the appendix to this chapter.

Many businesses grant credit to customers. They know that, when making sales "on account," a risk exists because some accounts will never be collected. However, the cost of these bad debts is more than offset by the profit from the extra sales made due to the attraction of granting credit. The collections department may make many attempts to collect an account before "writing-off" a bad debtor. Frequently, an account is deemed to be uncollectible a year or more after the date of the credit sale. In this chapter, we will discuss the allowance method of accounting for bad debts. The allowance method permits the accountant to estimate the amount of bad debt expense that should be matched with current revenues rather than waiting to book expense at the time of an actual write-off.

## SUMMARY OF LEARNING OBJECTIVES

1.  **Identify items considered cash.** To be reported as "cash," an asset must be readily available for the payment of current obligations and free from contractual restrictions that limit its use in satisfying debts. Cash consists of coin, currency, and available funds on deposit at the bank. Negotiable instruments such as money orders, certified checks, cashier's checks, personal checks, and bank drafts are also viewed as cash. Savings accounts are usually classified as cash.

2.  **Indicate how cash and related items are reported.** Companies report cash as a current asset in the balance sheet. The reporting of other related items are: (1) **Restricted cash:** The SEC recommends that companies state separately legally restricted deposits held as compensating balances against short-term borrowing among the "cash and cash equivalent items" in Current Assets. Restricted deposits held against long-term borrowing arrangements should be separately classified as noncurrent assets in either the Investments or Other Assets sections. (2) **Bank overdrafts:** Companies should report overdrafts separately in the Current Liabilities section of the balance sheet. These items are sometimes included with accounts payable; in this case, unless they are immaterial in amount, the amount of overdrafts should be disclosed in the related notes. (3) **Cash equivalents:** Companies often report this item together with cash as "cash and cash equivalents."

3. **Define receivables and identify the different types of receivables.** Receivables are claims held against customers and others for money, goods, or services. The receivables are classified into three types: (1) current or noncurrent, (2) trade or nontrade, and (3) accounts receivable or notes receivable.

4. **Explain accounting issues related to the recognition of accounts receivable.** Two issues that may complicate the measurement of accounts receivable are: (1) the availability of discounts (trade and cash discounts) and (2) the length of time between the sale and the payment due dates (the interest element). Ideally, companies should measure receivables in terms of their present value—that is, the discounted value of the cash to be received in the future. The profession specifically excludes from the present value considerations receivables arising from normal business transactions that are due in customary trade terms within approximately one year.

5. **Explain accounting issues related to the valuation of accounts receivable.** Companies value and report short-term receivables at net realizable value—the net amount expected to be received in cash, which is not necessarily the amount legally receivable. Determining net realizable value requires estimating uncollectible receivables.

6. **Explain accounting issues related to the recognition of notes receivable.** Companies record short-term notes at face value and long-term notes receivable at the present value of the cash they expect to collect. When the interest stated on an interest-bearing note is equal to the effective (market) rate of interest, the note is recorded at face value. When the stated rate differs from the effective rate and the note is exchanged for something other than cash, a company records either a discount or premium.

7. **Explain accounting issues related to the valuation of notes receivable.** Like accounts receivable, short-term notes receivable are recorded and reported at their net realizable value. The same is true of long-term receivables. Special issues relate to uncollectibles and impairments.

8. **Explain accounting issues related to disposition of accounts and notes receivable.** To accelerate the receipt of cash from receivables, the owner may transfer the receivables to another company for cash. The transfer of receivables to a third party for cash may be accomplished in one of two ways: (1) **Secured borrowing:** A creditor often requires that the debtor designate or pledge receivables as security for a loan. (2) **Sales (factoring) of receivables:** Factors are finance companies or banks that buy receivables from businesses and then collect the remittances directly from the customers. In many cases, transferors may have some continuing involvement with the receivables sold. Companies use a financial components approach to record this type of transaction.

9. **Explain how to report and analyze receivables.** Companies should report receivables with appropriate offset of valuation accounts against receivables, classify receivables as current or noncurrent, identify pledged or designated receivables, and identify concentrations of risks arising from receivables. Analysts assess receivables based on receivables turnover and the days outstanding.

*10. **Explain common techniques employed to control cash.** The common techniques employed to control cash are: (1) **Using bank accounts:** a company can vary the number and location of banks and the types of accounts to obtain desired control objectives. (2) **The imprest petty cash system:** It may be impractical to require small amounts of various expenses to be paid by check, yet some control over them is important. (3) **Physical protection of cash balances:** Adequate control of receipts and disbursements is a part of the protection of cash balances.
        *This material is covered in Appendix 7A in the text.

Every effort should be made to minimize the cash on hand in the office. (4) **Reconciliation of bank balances:** Cash on deposit is not available for count and is proved by preparing a bank reconciliation.

**\*\*11. Describe the accounting for a loan impairment.** A creditor bases an impairment loan loss on the difference between the present value of the future cash flows (using the historical effective interest rate) and the carrying amount of the note.

       \*\*This material is covered in Appendix B in the text.

# TIPS ON CHAPTER TOPICS

**TIP:** Trade accounts receivable result from the sale of products or services to customers. Nontrade accounts receivable (amounts that are due from nontrade customers who do not buy goods or services in the normal course of the company's main business activity) should be listed separately from the trade accounts receivable balance on the balance sheet.

**TIP:** In the event that a customer's account has a credit balance on the balance sheet date, it should be classified as a current liability and not offset against other accounts receivable with debit balances.

**TIP:** The net realizable value of accounts receivable is the amount of the receivables expected to be ultimately converted to cash.

**TIP:** Whenever you want to analyze the effect of (1) recording bad debt expense, (2) writing off an individual customer's account receivable, and/or (3) the collection of an account receivable that was previously written off, write down the related journal entry(ies) and analyze each debit and credit separately. (See **Illustration 7-1** for examples.)

**TIP:** Given a $1,000 receivable to be collected three years from today, that receivable has a value today (present value) that is less than $1,000 due to the time value of money (i.e. interest). The present value of the $1,000 due in three years is the amount of money that, if invested today at a specified interest rate, would grow to be $1,000 at the end of a three-year period. The higher the interest rate, the lower the present value. Present value concepts are used in this chapter in accounting for notes receivable. If you need to review these concepts and applications, consult **Chapter 6** of your book.

**TIP:** There are two methods of accounting for bad debts; they are:
1. **Direct Write-Off Method:** No entry is made until a specific account has definitely been established as uncollectible. Then the loss is recorded by crediting Accounts Receivable and debiting Bad Debt Expense.
2. **Allowance Method:** An estimate is made of the expected uncollectible accounts from all sales made on account or from the total of outstanding receivables. This estimate is entered as an expense and an indirect reduction in accounts receivable (via an increase in the allowance account) in the period in which the sale is recorded.

The direct write-off method is not a generally accepted method for an entity having a material amount of bad debts because it fails to properly match bad debt expense with the related revenue (in the period the credit sale was recognized) and it overstates Accounts Receivable as to their net realizable value.

> **TIP:** A note receivable is considered to be **impaired** when it is probable that the creditor will be unable to collect all amounts due (both principal and interest) according to the contractual terms of the loan. In that case, the present value of the expected future cash flows is determined by discounting those flows at the historical effective rate. This present value amount is deducted from the carrying amount of the receivable to measure the loss.

## EXERCISE 7-1

**Purpose:** (L.O. 1)  This exercise will review the items which are included in the "Cash" caption on a balance sheet.

In auditing the balance sheet at December 31, 2010 for the Maxwell Vermillion Company, you find the following:

|     |                                                                                                                                              | Cash | Not in Cash |
| --- | -------------------------------------------------------------------------------------------------------------------------------------------- | ---- | ----------- |
| (a) | Coins and currency for change funds.                                                                                                         |      |             |
| (b) | Coins and currency which are from the current day's receipts which have not yet been deposited in the bank.                                   |      |             |
| (c) | Petty cash.                                                                                                                                  |      |             |
| (d) | General checking account at First Union Bank.                                                                                                |      |             |
| (e) | General checking account at Sun Trust Bank.                                                                                                  |      |             |
| (f) | Unused stamps.                                                                                                                               |      |             |
| (g) | Deposit in transit.                                                                                                                          |      |             |
| (h) | Customer's NSF check (returned with bank statement).                                                                                         |      |             |
| (i) | Postdated checks from customers.                                                                                                             |      |             |
| (j) | Certificate of deposit--60 day CD purchased on December 1, 2010.                                                                             |      |             |
| (k) | Certificate of deposit—matures in 6 months.                                                                                                  |      |             |
| (l) | 100 shares of General Motors stock (intention is to sell in one year or less).                                                               |      |             |
| (m) | Cash to be used to retire long-term debt.                                                                                                    |      |             |
| (n) | Travel advances made to executives for business purposes.                                                                                    |      |             |
| (o) | Cash advance to executive for personal reasons.                                                                                              |      |             |
| (p) | Money market fund that provides checking account privileges.                                                                                 |      |             |
| (q) | Commercial paper with maturity of 270 days.                                                                                                  |      |             |
| (r) | Treasury bills with 182-day maturity.                                                                                                        |      |             |
| (s) | Treasury Bills with a 91-day maturity.                                                                                                       |      |             |
| (t) | Commercial paper with original maturity of 30 days.                                                                                          |      |             |
| (u) | Money on deposit in Bank of America, held as compensating balances against a short-term bank obligation and other short-term borrowing arrangements. |      |             |
| (v) | Money on deposit in Wells Fargo Bank, held as compensating balances against a long-term loan from the bank and other long-term borrowing arrangements. |      |             |
| (w) | Cash fund restricted for the payment of an existing obligation classified as a current liability.                                            |      |             |
| (x) | Bank overdraft.                                                                                                                              |      |             |
| (y) | Money market savings certificate with original maturity of 48 months, intended to be held until maturity.                                    |      |             |

## Instructions

Select the items from the list above that should be included in the "Cash" caption on the balance sheet as of December 31, 2010. For any item not included in "Cash", indicate the proper classification.

## Solution to Exercise 7-1

Items to be **included** as "Cash" on the balance sheet include:

(a)  Coins and currency for change funds.

(b)  Coins and currency which are from the current day's receipts which have not yet been deposited in the bank   this is said to be "cash on hand" or could be considered a "deposit in transit" in preparing a bank reconciliation (see Appendix 7A).

(c)  Petty cash   included in "Cash" because this fund is used to meet current operating expenses and to liquidate current liabilities.

(d)  General checking account at First Union Bank   the amount included should be the "adjusted cash balance" per a bank reconciliation (see Appendix 7A).

(e)  General checking account at Sun Trust Bank   the amount included should be the "adjusted cash balance" per a bank reconciliation (see Appendix 7A).

(g)  Deposit in transit   this amount is already reflected in the "balance per books" and will be reflected in the "adjusted cash balance" per the bank reconciliation (see Appendix 7A).

(p)  Money market fund that provides checking account privileges.

Items to be **excluded** from "Cash" include:

(f)  Unused stamps   report as a Prepaid Expense (such as Office Supplies on Hand).

(h)  Customer's NSF check   classify in Accounts Receivable.

(i)  Postdated checks from customers   classify in Accounts Receivable.

(j)  Certificate of deposit--60 day--original maturity date was 3 months or less   classify as cash equivalents (which are often combined with "Cash").

(k)  Certificate of deposit--original maturity date not 3 months or less   classify as Short-term Investment.

(l)  100 shares of General Motors Stock   classify as Short-term Investment because there is a lack of intent to hold for a long-term purpose and is readily marketable.

(m)  Cash to be used to retire long-term debt   classify as Long-term Investment (assuming the related debt is classified as long-term).

(n)  Travel advances made to executives for business purposes   classify in Prepaid Expenses.

(o)  Cash advance to executive for personal reasons   classify as a receivable (will later be collected from employee or deducted from employee's paycheck).

(q)  Commercial paper   report as a Short-term Investment.

(r)  Treasury bills with 182-day maturity   report as a Short-term Investment.

(s)  Treasury bills with a 91-day maturity—classify as cash equivalents (which are often combined with "Cash").

(t)  Commercial paper with original maturity of 30 days—classify as cash equivalents (which are often combined with "Cash").

(u)   Deposit maintained as compensating balances against short-term borrowing arrangement—separate from other cash and classify with cash and cash equivalents in current assets.

(v)   Deposit maintained as compensating balances against long-term borrowing arrangement—report as noncurrent asset either in the Investments or Other Assets section of the balance sheet.

(w)   Restricted funds for payment of obligation classified as current liability—classify in Current Assets but report separately from regular cash items.

(x)   Bank overdraft—classify in Current Liabilities. (This answer assumes there is no right of offset.)

(y)   Money market savings certificates with original maturity of 48 months, intended to be held until maturity—report as long-term Investment.

> **TIP:**   Items (j), (s) and (t) are cash equivalents. Most entities include cash equivalents with cash; others report them as temporary (short-term) investments (immediately following cash in the current asset section of the balance sheet).

**Explanation:**  Cash, the most liquid of assets, is the standard medium of exchange and the basis for measuring and accounting for all other items.  To be included in the Cash caption under current assets, the cash must be readily available for current obligations, and it must be free of from any contractual restriction that limits its use in satisfying debts.  Cash in a fund that is restricted for some long-term purpose (such as for future plant expansion) is classified as a long-term investment.

Cash consists of coin, currency, and available funds on deposit at the bank.  Negotiable instruments such as money orders, certified checks, cashier's checks, personal checks, and bank drafts are also viewed as cash.  Savings accounts are usually classified as cash, although the bank has the legal right to demand notice before withdrawal.  But, because prior notice is rarely demanded by banks, savings accounts are considered cash.

Money market funds, money market savings certificates, certificates of deposit (CDs), and similar types of deposits and "short-term paper" that provide small investors with an opportunity to earn high rates of interest are more appropriately classified as temporary investments than as cash.  The reason is that these securities usually contain restrictions or penalties on their conversion to cash.  Money market funds that provide checking account privileges, however, are usually classified as cash.

> **TIP:**   Cash is often combined with cash equivalents and reported by the caption "cash and cash equivalents." **Cash equivalents** are short-term highly liquid investments that are both (a) readily convertible to known amounts of cash, and (b) so near their maturity that they present insignificant risk of changes in interest rates. Generally only investments with original maturities of (three) months or less qualify under these definitions. Examples of cash equivalents are Treasury bills, commercial paper, and money market funds.

TIP:    An entity that has cash in an amount that exceeds its immediate needs will usually temporarily invest the excess cash. A variety of "short-term paper" is available for investment. For example, **certificates of deposit** (CDs) represent formal evidence of indebtedness, issued by a bank, subject to withdrawal under the specific terms of the instrument. Issued in $10,000 and $100,000 denominations, they generally mature in 30 to 360 days and generally pay interest at the short-term interest rate in effect at the date of issuance. Some banks have CDs that have a 3- or 5-year term. In **money market funds**, a variation of the mutual fund, the yield is determined by the mix of Treasury bills, and commercial paper making up the fund's portfolio. Most money market funds require an initial minimum investment of $5,000; many allow withdrawal by check or wire transfer. **Treasury bills** are U.S. government obligations generally having 91- and 182-day maturities; they are sold in $10,000 denominations at weekly government auctions. **Commercial paper** is a short-term note (30 to 270 days) issued by corporations with good credit ratings. Issued in $5,000 and $10,000 denominations, these notes generally yield a higher rate than Treasury bills.

TIP:    Banks and other lending institutions often require customers to whom they lend money to maintain minimum cash balances in checking or savings accounts. These minimum balances, called **compensating balances,** are defined by the SEC as: "that portion of any demand deposit (or any time deposit or certificate of deposit) maintained by a corporation which constitutes support for existing borrowing arrangements of the corporation with a lending institution. The SEC recommends that **legally restricted deposits** held as compensating balances against **short-term** borrowing arrangements be stated separately among the "cash and cash equivalent items" in current assets. Restricted deposits held as compensating balances against **long-term** borrowing arrangements should be separately classified as noncurrent assets in either Investments or Other Assets sections, using a caption such as "Cash on Deposit Maintained as Compensating Balance."

# EXERCISE 7-2

**Purpose:** (L.O. 2) This exercise will require you to properly classify items qualifying as "cash" and to properly report a bank overdraft.

The Skogsberg Corporation had the following items at a balance sheet date:

| | |
|---|---|
| Checking account at Sun Trust Bank | $ 12,400 |
| Checking account at Bank of America | 10,500 |
| Checking account at First Union Bank | (3,000) |
| Checking account at Republic Bank | 5,100 |
| Postdated check from customer | 600 |
| Savings account at Sun Trust Bank | 32,000 |
| Money market fund at Sun Trust (with checking privileges) | 40,000 |
| Deposit at telephone company (required for service) | 1,000 |
| NSF check received from customer (reflected as a positive amount in a bank balance above) | 210 |
| Change fund | 450 |
| Cash from customer not yet deposited in bank | 1,750 |

## Instructions:

(a)    Compute the amount to be reported with the "Cash" caption in current assets at the balance sheet date.

(b)    Indicate the proper reporting for items that are **not** included in your answer to part (a).

## SOLUTION TO EXERCISE 7-2

(a)

| | |
|---|---:|
| Checking account at Sun Trust Bank | $ 12,400 |
| Checking account at Bank of America | 10,500 |
| Checking account at Republic Bank | 5,100 |
| Savings account at Sun Trust Bank | 32,000 |
| Money market fund at Sun Trust | 40,000 |
| NSF check from customer | (210) |
| Change fund | 450 |
| Receipts to be deposited (Cash on Hand) | 1,750 |
| Total Cash | $101,990 |

(b)    (1)    The overdraft of $3,000 at First Union Bank is classified as a current liability. The only time a bank overdraft is used to offset positive balances in other bank accounts (that is, reflected in the Cash caption) is when the overdraft occurs in an account that is in the same bank as other accounts with positive balances that equal or exceed the amount of overdraft (that is, when a legal right of offset is assumed to exist).

(2)    The postdated check from customer for $600 is classified as a receivable in current assets.

(3)    The $1,000 deposit at the telephone company is classified as an other asset (if the deposit is to remain beyond one year from the balance sheet date) or as a separate item in current assets usually listed after prepaid expenses (if the deposit is to be returned or applied to the telephone bill within the next year).

(4)    The NSF check from a customer for $210 should be reclassified to the receivables section of current assets.

# ILLUSTRATION 7-1
# ENTRIES FOR THE ALLOWANCE METHOD (L.O. 5)

| Journal Entry | | | Effect on Net Income | Effect on Working Capital | Effect on Allowance Account | Effect on Net Receivables |
|---|---|---|---|---|---|---|
| **Entry to record bad debt expense, $1,000** | | | Decrease | | | |
| Bad Debt Expense | 1,000 | | $1,000 | No effect | No effect | No effect |
| Allowance for Doubtful Accounts | | 1,000 | No effect | Decrease $1,000 | Increase $1,000 | Decrease $1,000 |
| Net effect of entry | | | Decrease $1,000 | Decrease $1,000 | Increase $1,000 | Decrease $1,000 |
| **Entry to write-off a customer's account, $200** | | | | Increase $200 | Decrease $200 | Increase $200 |
| Allowance for Doubtful Accounts | 200 | | No effect | | No effect | |
| Accounts Receivable | | 200 | No effect | Decrease $200 | | Decrease $200 |
| Net effect of entry | | | No effect | No effect | Decrease $200 | No effect |
| **Entries to record collection of account receivable previously written off, $120** | | | | Increase $120 | | Increase $120 |
| Accounts Receivable | 120 | | No effect | | No effect | |
| Allowance for Doubtful Accounts | | 120 | No effect | Decrease $120 | Increase $120 | Decrease $120 |
| Cash | 120 | | No effect | Increase $120 | No effect | No effect |
| Accounts Receivable | | 120 | No effect | Decrease $120 | No effect | Decrease $120 |
| Net effect of entries | | | No effect | No effect | Increase $120 | Decrease $120 |

**TIP:** Be careful to distinguish the entry to write-off a customer account from the entry to record bad debt expense. The journal entry to record the estimated bad debt expense for a period and to adjust the corresponding allowance for doubtful accounts involves a debit to Bad Debt Expense and a credit to Allowance for Doubtful Accounts. The entry to write off an individual customer's account (an actual bad debt) involves a debit to Allowance for Doubtful Accounts and a credit to Accounts Receivable.

**TIP:** Two entries are necessary to record the recovery of an account that was previously written off:
1.    An entry to record the reinstatement of the account receivable (debit Accounts Receivable and credit Allowance for Doubtful Accounts). This is simply a reverse of the write-off entry.
2.    An entry to record the collection of the receivable (debit Cash and credit Accounts Receivable).

**TIP:** Allowance for Doubtful Accounts is often called Allowance for Uncollectible Accounts. (Both of these account titles start with "Allowance for" which typically indicates a contra type balance sheet account.) Reserve for Bad Debts is a frequently used but objectionable title for the allowance account.

**TIP:** Bad Dept Expense is often called Uncollectible Accounts Expense **or** Doubtful Accounts Expense. Provision for Bad Debts is another name for the Bad Debt Expense account.

## ILLUSTRATION 7-1 (Continued)

**TIP:** Notice that the entry to record bad debts reduces current assets and reduces net income. The entry to record the write-off of an individual account has **no** net effect on the amount of current assets nor does it affect income. It merely reduces Accounts Receivable and the Allowance for Doubtful Accounts account (which is a contra item) so the entry has no net effect on the net realizable value of accounts receivable. Thus, it is the entry to record the bad debt expense that impacts **both** the income statement and the balance sheet.

**TIP:** The normal balance of the Allowance for Doubtful Accounts is a credit. Therefore, a debit balance in this account indicates an abnormal balance. It is not uncommon to have a debit balance in the allowance account before adjusting entries are prepared because individual accounts may be written off at various times during a period and the entry to adjust the allowance account is prepared at the end of the period before financial statements are prepared. After adjustment, the allowance account should have a credit balance.

**TIP:** When it is time to prepare the adjusting entry for bad debts (at the end of an accounting period), the existing balance in the Allowance for Doubtful Accounts account (that is, the balance before adjustment) is **NOT** considered in determining the amount of the adjusting entry **IF** the percentage-of-sales approach is used. However, the balance in the allowance account before adjustment **IS** used in determining the amount of the adjusting entry when the aging analysis approach (one method of estimating the net realizable value of existing receivables) is used to implement the allowance method of accounting for bad debts. The application of these two guidelines is illustrated by the **Solution to Exercise 7-3** (entries 1 and 2).

**TIP:** When using the allowance method and estimating bad debt expense as a percentage of credit sales for the period, the amount of bad debt expense is simply calculated and recorded; a by-product of this approach is the increasing of the allowance account. When using the allowance method and estimating the net realizable value of accounts receivable (such as by an aging analysis), the amount of uncollectible accounts calculated represents the new ending balance of the allowance account. The adjusting entry records the amount necessary to increase (or decrease) the current allowance account balance to equal the newly computed one. A by-product of this approach is the increasing of bad debt expense for the period.

**TIP:** Sales Discounts Forfeited is classified as an "Other Revenue" item on the income statement.

**TIP:** Theoretically, the net method is better in that the receivable is stated closer to its realizable value, and the net sales figure measures the revenue earned from the sale. As a practical matter, however, the net method is seldom used because it requires additional analysis and bookkeeping. For example, the net method requires adjusting entries to record sales discounts forfeited on accounts receivable that have passed the discount period.

**TIP:** An estimate of uncollectible accounts must be made for long-term receivables in the same manner as is done for short-term trade accounts receivable (that is, use the allowance method to account for bad debts).

**TIP:** Specific long-term receivables such as loans that are identified as impaired must receive an impairment evaluation. An **impairment loss** is calculated by the difference between the investment in the loan (generally the principal plus accrued interest) and the expected future cash flows discounted at the loan's historical effective interest rate. When using the historical effective interest rate, the value of the investment will change only if some of the legally contracted cash flows are reduced. A company recognizes a loss in this case because the future cash flows have changed. The company ignores interest rate changes caused by current economic events that affect the fair value of the loan. An impairment loss is recorded by a debt to Bad Debt Expense and a credit to Allowance for Doubtful Accounts.

## CASE 7-1

**Purpose:** (L.O. 5)  This exercise will identify the two approaches of applying the allowance method of accounting for uncollectible accounts receivable.

Howell's Department Store offers a store credit card for the convenience of its customers. Even though the store follows up on delinquent accounts, past experience indicates that a predictable amount of credit sales will ultimately result in uncollectible accounts. Because bad debts are a material amount, Howell uses the allowance method of accounting for uncollectible accounts.

### Instructions
(a)    Describe the two methods available for determining the amount of the adjusting entry to record bad debts expense and to adjust the allowance account.  Also discuss the emphasis of each method.
(b)    Explain why the direct write-off method is not a generally accepted accounting method for Howell's Department Store.

### Solution Case 7-1

(a)    When using the allowance method of accounting for bad debts, there are two methods available for determining the amount of the adjusting entry to record bad debts expense and to adjust the allowance account.  They are:
   (1)    **The percentage of sales basis:**  This method focuses on estimating bad debts expense.  The average percentage relationship between actual bad debt losses and net credit sales (or total credit sales) of the period is used to determine the amount of expense for the period.  This method focuses on the matching of current bad debts expense with revenues of the current period and thus emphasizes the income statement.  The amount of bad debts expense is simply calculated and recorded **without** regard to the existing balance in the allowance account; a by-product of this approach is the increase in the allowance account.

   (2)    **The percentage of receivables basis:** This method focuses on estimating the cash (net) realizable value of the current receivables and thus emphasizes the balance sheet. It only incidentally measures bad debts expense; the expense reported may not be the best figure to match with the amount of credit sales of the current period. The existing balance in the allowance account (that is, the balance before adjustment) is a factor in determining the required adjusting entry because this method focuses on increasing the allowance balance to an appropriate figure. If this method is to be used, the **aging** technique is preferable to the use of a simple

percentage times total accounts receivable. An aging analysis takes into consideration the age of a receivable. The older the age, the lower the probability of collection.

---

**TIP**:     Very often, an entity may use the percentage-of-sales method to account for bad debts for interim periods and then use the aging method to adjust the allowance account at year-end for annual reporting purposes.

---

(b)     Under the direct write-off method, bad debt losses are not estimated and no allowance account is used. No entry regarding bad debts is made until a specific account has definitely been established as uncollectible. Then the loss is recorded by a debit to Bad Debts Expense and a credit to Accounts Receivable. (Under the direct write-off method, if an account previously written off is recovered in the future, the amount collected is debited to cash and credited to a revenue account titled Uncollectible Accounts Recovered.)

When the direct write-off method is used, Accounts Receivable will be reported at its gross amount and bad debts expense is often recorded in a period different from the period in which the revenue was recorded. Thus, no attempt is made to match bad debts expense to sales revenues in the income statement or to show the cash (net) realizable value of the accounts receivable in the balance sheet. Consequently, unless bad debt losses are insignificant, the direct write-off method is **not** acceptable for financial reporting purposes. Howell's bad debts are material (significant) in amount. The direct write-off method is, however, used for tax purposes.

# EXERCISE 7-3

**Purpose:** (L.O. 5, 8) This exercise will require you to record: (1) the adjusting entry to recognize bad debt expense and adjust the Allowance for Doubtful Accounts account, and (2) the transfer of accounts receivable with recourse.

The trial balance before adjustment at December 31, 2010 for the G & H Wood Company shows the following balances:

|  | Dr. | Cr. |
|---|---|---|
| Accounts Receivable | $ 90,000 | |
| Allowance for Doubtful Accounts | 2,120 | |
| Sales (all on credit) | | $ 500,000 |
| Sales Returns and Allowances | 7,600 | |

## Instructions

Using the data above, give the journal entries required to record each of the following cases (each situation is **independent**):

1.  The company estimates bad debts to be 1.5% of net credit sales.
2.  G & H Wood Company performs an aging analysis at December 31, 2010 which indicates an estimate of $6,000 of uncollectible accounts.
3.  The company wants to maintain the Allowance for Doubtful Accounts at 4% of gross accounts receivable.
4.  To obtain additional cash, G & H Wood Company factors, without recourse, $20,000 of accounts receivable with Fleetwood Finance. The finance charge is 10% of the amount factored.

## Solution to Exercise 7-3

1.  Bad Debt Expense [($500,000 - $7,600) x 1.5%]...................... 7,386
          Allowance for Doubtful Accounts.................................... 7,386

    **Explanation:** The percentage of net credit sales approach to applying the allowance method of accounting for bad debts focuses on determining an appropriate expense figure. The existing balance in the allowance account is **not** relevant in the computation.

2.  Bad Debt Expense .................................................................. 8,120
          Allowance for Doubtful Accounts
          ($6,000 + $2,120)...................................................... 8,120

    **Explanation:** An aging analysis provides the best estimate of the net realizable value of accounts receivable. By using the results of the aging to adjust the allowance account, the amount reported for net receivables on the balance sheet is the net realizable value of accounts receivable. It is important to notice that the balance of the allowance account before adjustment is a determinant in the adjustment required. The following T-account reflects the facts used to determine the necessary adjustment:

                        Allowance for Doubtful Accounts

| Unadjusted balance | 2,120 | Adjustment needed | 8,120 |
|---|---|---|---|
| | | Desired balance at 12/31/10 | 6,000 |

3.   Bad Debt Expense ................................................................   5,720
        Allowance for Doubtful Accounts
           [($90,000 x 4%) + $2,120] ..........................................   5,720

**Explanation:** This entry is to adjust the allowance account. A by-product of the entry is the recognition of uncollectible accounts expense. Because an appropriate balance for the valuation account is determined to be a percentage of the receivable balance at the balance sheet date, the existing balance ($2,120 debit) in the allowance account **must** be considered in computing the necessary adjustment.

4.   Cash . . ...............................................................................   18,000
        Loss on Sale of Receivables ($20,000 x 10%) .........................   2,000
           Accounts Receivable .................................................   20,000

**Explanation:** The factoring of accounts receivable without recourse is accounted for as a sale of accounts receivable; hence, the receivables are removed from the accounts, cash is recorded, and a loss is recognized for the excess of the face value of the receivables over the proceeds received.

# EXERCISE 7-4

**Purpose:**   (L.O. 6) This exercise will illustrate the accounting for a situation involving the exchange of a noncash asset or service for a promissory note where the fair value of the asset or service is known.

General Host's annual accounting period ends on December 31. On July 1, 2010, General Host Company sold land having a fair market value of $700,000 in exchange for a four-year noninterest-bearing promissory note in the face amount of $1,101,460. The land is carried on General Host Company's books at a cost of $620,000.

## Instructions
(a)   Prepare the journal entry that should be recorded by General Host company for the sale of the land in exchange for the note.
(b)   Prepare the amortization schedule for the note receivable accepted in the transaction.
(c)   Prepare the necessary journal entries at December 31, 2010 and December 31, 2011 that relate to the note receivable.

## Solution to Exercise 7-4

(a)  Timeline:

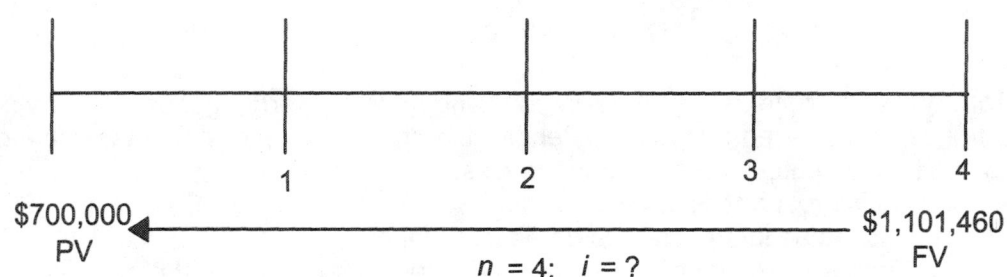

|          |        | 1      |        | 2      |        | 3      |        | 4      |
|----------|--------|--------|--------|--------|--------|--------|--------|--------|

$700,000  $1,101,460
PV                                   FV
$n = 4;\ i = ?$

7/1/10   Notes Receivable ............................................   1,101,460.00
Discount on Notes Receivable...................                           401,460.00
Land........................................................              620,000.00
Gain on Sale of Land
($700,000 - $620,000) ..........................                          80,000.00

The exchange price is equal to the fair market value of the property (which is $700,000). The interest rate implicit in this price is therefore calculated by:
  $700,000 = $1,101,460 x PV Factor
  $700,000 ÷ $1,101,460 = .63552
  By reference to Table 2 (Present Value of 1 Table) in **Appendix to Chapter 6**, .63552 is the PV factor for $n = 4$, $i = 12\%$.

(b)   **Amortization Schedule for Note**

| Date | 0% Stated Interest | 12% Effective Interest | Amortization of Discount | PV Balance |
|------|--------------------|------------------------|--------------------------|------------|
| 7/01/10 |        |                 |               | $ 700,000.00 |
| 6/30/11 | $0     | $ 84,000.00[a]  | $ 84,000.00   | 784,000.00 |
| 6/30/12 | 0      | 94,080.00       | 94,080.00     | 878,080.00 |
| 6/30/13 | 0      | 105,369.60      | 105,369.60    | 983,449.60 |
| 6/30/14 | 0      | 118,010.40[1]   | 118,010.40    | 1,101,460.00 |
| Totals  | $0     | $401,460.00     | $ 401,460.00  |            |

[a]$700,000.00 x 12% = $84,000.00.
[1]Includes rounding error of $3.55.

TIP:   In most exercises, we round to the nearest dollar. When working assignments dealing with interest, it is helpful to round to the nearest penny. That way you can more readily determine if any "plug" figure at the end of an amortization schedule is due to a rounding error (rounding difference) or an error of greater consequence.

(c)   12/31/10   Discount on Notes Receivable ............................   42,000.00
Interest Revenue ...........................................                   42,000.00
(1/2 x $84,000 = $42,000)

| 12/31/11 | Discount on Notes Receivable ............................ | 89,040.00 | |
|---|---|---|---|
| | Interest Revenue ............................................ | | 89,040.00 |

(1/2 x $84,000 = $42,000;
1/2 x $94,080 = $47,040;
$42,000 + $47,040 = $89,040)

**Explanation:** When a note is received in exchange for property, goods, or services in a bargained transaction entered into at arms length, the stated interest rate is assumed to be fair and is thus used to compute interest revenue unless:

1.   No interest rate is stated, or
2.   The stated interest rate is unreasonable, or
3.   The face amount of the note is materially different from the current cash sales price for the same or similar items or from the current market value of the debt instrument.

In these circumstances, the present value of the note is measured by the fair value of the property, goods, or services. General Host received a note in exchange for land, and the fair value of the land was known to be $700,000; thus, the fair value of the land was used to establish the present value of the note and the rate implicit in the note was then computed to be 12%. (See **Exercise 7-5** for an example of a situation where the fair value of the property, goods, or services exchanged for a note is not known.)

# EXERCISE 7-5

**Purpose:**   (L.O. 6) This exercise will illustrate the accounting for a situation involving the exchange of a noncash asset or service for a promissory note where the fair value of the asset or service is **not** known.

Fairmont Company's annual accounting period ends on December 31. On July 1, 2010, Fairmont Company rendered services in exchange for a 3%, 8-year promissory note having a face value of $300,000 with interest payable annually.  Fairmont Company recently had to pay 8% interest for money that it borrowed from Arizona National Bank.  The customer in this transaction has a credit rating that requires them to borrow money at 12% interest.

## Instructions

(a)   Prepare the journal entry that should be recorded by Fairmont Company for the sale of the services in exchange for the note.
(b)   Prepare the amortization schedule for the note receivable accepted in the transaction.
(c)   Prepare the necessary journal entries at December 31, 2010, June 30, 2011, and December 31, 2011 that relate to the note receivable.  Assume the customer makes the scheduled interest payments on time.  Also, assume amortization is recorded only at year-end. Fairmont does not use reversing entries.

## Solution to Exercise 7-5

(a) Timeline:

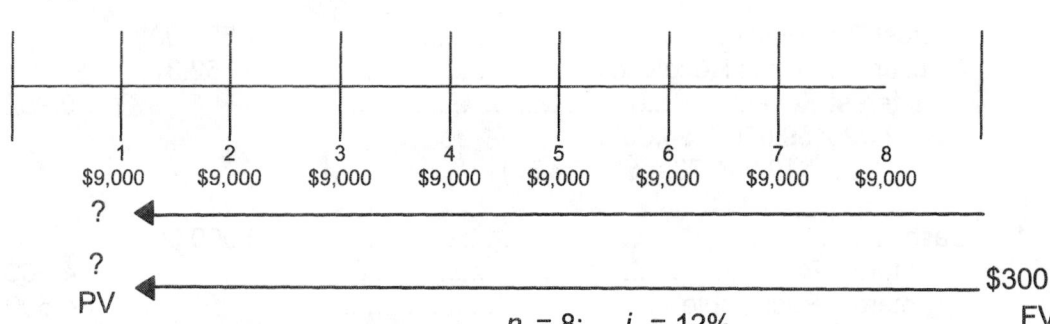

$n = 8;$  $i = 12\%$

| 7/1/10 | Notes Receivable | 300,000.00 | |
| | Discount on Notes Receivable | | 134,127.24 |
| | Service Revenue | | 165,872.76 |

Use the market rate of interest to compute the present value of the note which is then used to establish the exchange price in the transaction. The market rate of interest should be the rate the borrower normally would have to pay to borrow money for similar activities.

Computation of the present value of the note:

| | | |
|---|---|---|
| Maturity value | | $300,000.00 |
| Present value of $300,000 due in 8 years | | |
| at 12% ($300,000 x .40388) | $121,164.00 | |
| Present value of $9,000 payable annually | | |
| for 8 years at 12% ($9,000 x 4.96764) | 44,708.76 | |
| Present value of the note and interest | | (165,872.76) |
| Discount on note receivable | | $134,127.24 |

(b) **Amortization Schedule for Note**

| Date | 3% Stated Interest | 12% Effective Interest | Amortization of Discount | PV Balance |
|---|---|---|---|---|
| 7/01/10 | | | | $ 165,872.76 |
| 6/30/11 | $ 9,000.00[a] | $ 19,904.73[b] | $ 10,904.73[c] | 176,777.49[d] |
| 6/30/12 | 9,000.00 | 21,213.30 | 12,213.30 | 188,990.79 |
| 6/30/13 | 9,000.00 | 22,678.89 | 13,678.89 | 202,669.68 |
| 6/30/14 | 9,000.00 | 24,320.36 | 15,320.36 | 217,990.04 |
| 6/30/15 | 9,000.00 | 26,158.80 | 17,158.80 | 235,148.84 |
| 6/30/16 | 9,000.00 | 28,217.86 | 19,217.86 | 254,366.70 |
| 6/30/17 | 9,000.00 | 30,524.00 | 21,524.00 | 275,890.70 |
| 6/30/18 | 9,000.00 | 33,109.30[1] | 24,109.30 | 300,000.00 |
| Totals | $72,000.00 | $206,127.24 | $ 134,127.24 | |

[a]$300,000.00 face value x 3% stated interest rate = $9,000.00 stated interest.
[b]$165,872.76 present value x 12% effective interest rate = $19,904.73 effective interest.
[c]$19,904.73 effective interest - $9,000.00 stated interest = $10,904.73 discount amortization.

---

d$165,872.76 PV balance 7/01/10 + $10,904.73 discount amortization for 12 months = $176,777.49 PV balance 6/30/11.
1Includes rounding error of $2.42.

| | | | | | |
|---|---|---|---|---|---|
| (c) | 12/31/10 | Interest Receivable............................................ | 4,500.00 | |
| | | Discount on Notes Receivable ............................ | 5,452.37 | |
| | |    Interest Revenue ........................................... | | 9,952.37 |
| | |      (1/2 x $9,000 = $4,500; | | |
| | |      1/2 x $19,904.73 = $9,952.37) | | |
| | | | | |
| | 6/30/11 | Cash ............................................................... | 9,000.00 | |
| | |    Interest Revenue ........................................... | | 4,500.00 |
| | |    Interest Receivable........................................ | | 4,500.00 |
| | | | | |
| | 12/31/11 | Interest Receivable............................................ | 4,500.00a | |
| | | Discount on Notes Receivable ............................ | 11,559.01b | |
| | |    Interest Revenue ........................................... | | 16,059.01c |

a1/2 x $9,000.00 = $4,500.00 interest receivable at 12/31/11.
b1/2 x $19,904.73 = $9,952.36 interest earned 1/1/11 thru 6/30/11;
   1/2 x $21,213.30 = $10,606.65 interest earned 7/1/11 thru 12/31/11;
   $9,952.36 + $10,606.65 = $20,559.01 total interest earned in 2011;
   $20,559.01 effective interest for 2011 - $9,000.00 stated interest for
   2005 = $11,559.01 discount amortization for 2011.
c$20,559.01 total interest for 2011 - $4,500.00 balance in Interest
   Revenue account before adjustment = $16,059.01 interest to record
   at 12/31/11.

**Explanation:** When a note is received in exchange for property, goods, or services in a bargained transaction entered into at arms length, the stated interest rate is assumed to be fair and is thus used to compute interest revenue unless:

   1.      No interest rate is stated, or
   2.      The stated interest rate is unreasonable, or
   3.      The face amount of the note is materially different from the current cash sales price for the same or similar items or from the current market value of the debt instrument.

In these circumstances, the present value of the note is measured by the fair value of the property, goods, or services. If the fair value of the property, goods, or services is not readily determinable, the market value of the note is used to establish the present value of the note. If the note has no ready market, the present value of the note is approximated by discounting all of the related future cash receipts (for interest and principal) on the note at the market rate of interest. This rate is referred to as an imputed rate and should be equal to the borrower's incremental borrowing rate (that is, the rate of interest the maker of the note would currently have to pay if it borrowed money from another source for this same purpose) Fairmont received a note in exchange for services. No information was given about the fair value of the services or the market value of the note. Thus, the borrower's incremental borrowing rate of 12% was used to impute interest and determine the note's present value.

# ILLUSTRATION 7-2
# FAIR VALUE MEASUREMENT OF NOTES RECEIVABLE (L.O. 7)

Like accounts receivable, companies record and report **short-term notes receivable** at their net realizable value. This involves estimating the amount of uncollectibles by using either a percentage of sales revenue or an analysis of the receivables.

Because the value of **long-term notes receivables** can change significantly over time from its original cost, the FASB allows a company to choose the **fair value** option for receivables whereby the receivables are reported at fair value and the related unrealized **holding gain or loss** (which is the net change in fair value of the receivable from one period to another, exclusive of interest revenue recognized but not recorded) is reported as part of net income. As a result, the company reports the receivable on the balance sheet at fair value each reporting date and it reports the change in fair value each period as part of net income for the period.

The company must be consistent with its method of choice for long-term receivables. That is, if it elects the fair value option (at the time the financial instrument is originally recognized) then it must continue with that method for that receivable. However, if it does not elect the fair value option for a given financial instrument at the date of recognition, it may not use this option on that specific instrument in subsequent periods.

For example, assume Noreniel Company has notes receivable with a carrying amount of $700,000 at December 31, 2010. The company has elected to use the fair value measurement for these receivables. This is the first valuation for these receivables. The fair value of these receivables is $780,000 at December 31, 2010 and $735,000 at December 31, 2011. Having elected to use the fair value option, Noreniel Company must value these receivables at fair value in all subsequent periods in which it holds these receivables. Thus, the following journal entries would be recorded:

At December 31, 2010
| | | |
|---|---|---|
| Fair Value Adjustment – Notes Receivable | 80,000 | |
| Unrealized holding Gain or Loss – Income | | 80,000 |
| ($780,000 - $700,000 = $80,000) | | |

At December 31, 2011
| | | |
|---|---|---|
| Unrealized Holding Gain or Loss – Income | 45,000 | |
| Fair Value Adjustment – Notes Receivable | | 45,000 |
| ($780,000 - $735,000= $45,000) | | |

Thus the asset would be reported at $780,000 on December 31, 2010 and $735,000 at December 31, 2011. An unrealized holding gain would increase the net income figure for the year ending December 31, 2010 and an unrealized holding loss would decrease net income reported for the year ending December 31, 2011.

**TIP:** One of the main reasons a note receivable may have a fair value that is significantly different than its carrying amount (adjusted historical cost) is the fact that the current relevant interest rate often differs from the stated interest rate in the note (which was the current rate at the date the note originated.)

## ILLUSTRATION 7-3
## ACCOUNTING FOR TRANSFERS OF RECEIVABLES (L.O. 8)

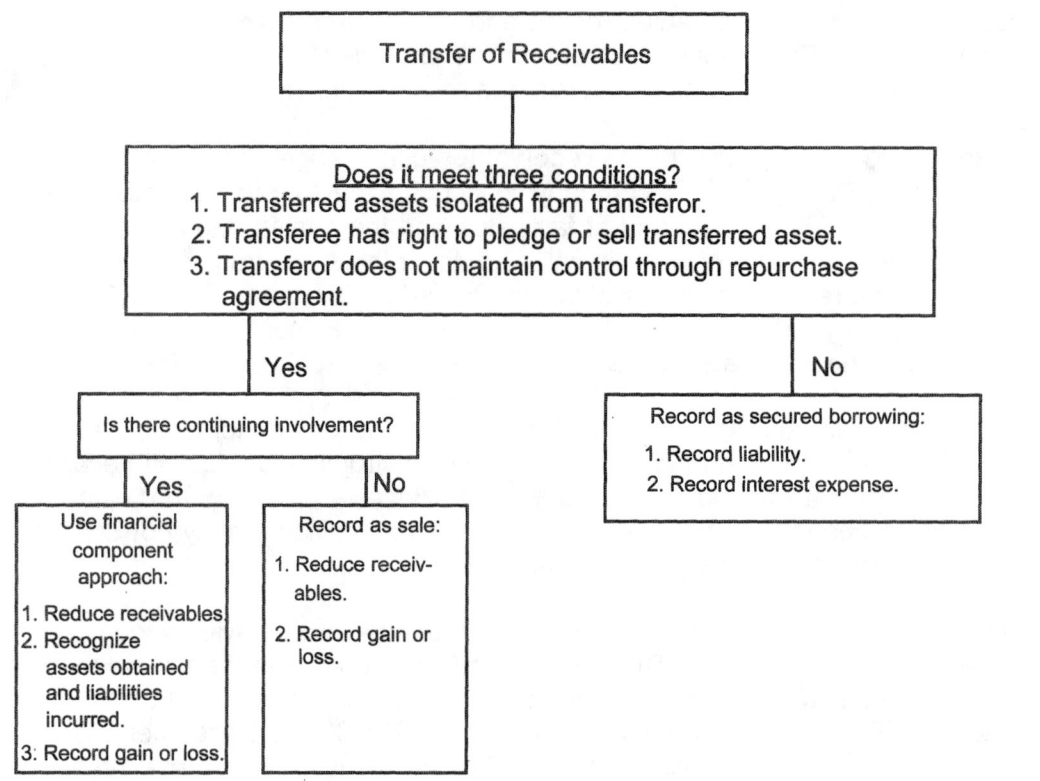

| TIP: | If there is continuing involvement in a sale transaction, the assets obtained and liabilities incurred must be recorded at fair value. |

## EXERCISE 7-6

**Purpose:**   (L.O.8) This exercise will help you to compare two possible ways of structuring a sale of accounts receivable (1) without recourse, or (2) with recourse.

Jedd Hale Corporation factors $90,000 of accounts receivable with Klein-Seay Financing, Inc. Klein-Seay Financing will collect the receivables. The receivable records are transferred to Klein-Seay Financing on August 15, 2010. Klein-Seay Financing assesses a finance charge of 4% of the amount of accounts receivable and also retains an amount equal to 6% of accounts receivable to cover probable adjustments.

## Instructions

(a)   Explain the conditions that must be met for a transfer of receivables with recourse to be accounted for as a sale.
(b)   Explain when the financial components approach is used in accounting for a transfer of accounts receivable.
(c)   Prepare the journal entry for both Jedd Hale Corporation and Klein-Seay Financing to record the transfer of accounts receivable on August 15, 2010 assuming the receivables are sold without recourse.
(d)   Prepare the journal entry for both Jedd Hale Corporation and Klein-Seay Financing to record the transfer of accounts receivable on August 15, 2010 assuming the receivables are sold with recourse and the conditions required for sale accounting are met. Further, assume the recourse obligation has a fair value of $2,000.

## Solution to Exercise 7-6

(a)   The FASB concluded that a sale occurs only if the seller surrenders control of the receivables to the buyer. The following three conditions must be met before a sale can be recorded:
  1.   The transferred asset has been isolated from the transferor (put beyond reach of the transferor and its creditors).
  2.   The transferees have obtained the right to pledge or exchange either the transferred assets or beneficial interests in the transferred assets.
  3.   The transferor does not maintain effective control over the transferred assets through an agreement to repurchase or redeem them before their maturity.

  If the three conditions are met, a sale occurs. Otherwise, the transferor should record the transfer as a secured borrowing. If sale accounting is appropriate, it is still necessary to consider assets obtained and liabilities incurred in the transaction. If there is continuing involvement in a sale transaction, the assets obtained and liabilities incurred must be recorded at fair value.

(b)   A **financial components approach** is used to account for a transfer of accounts receivable with recourse whenever the transfer arrangement meets the conditions necessary for the transfer to be accounted for as a sale (see answer (a) above). If receivables are sold (factored) with recourse, the seller guarantees payment to the purchaser in the event the debtor fails to pay. Under the financial components approach, each party to the sale recognizes the assets and liabilities that it controls after the sale and no longer recognizes the assets and liabilities that were sold or extinguished.

(c)    Sale of receivables without recourse:

| **Jedd Hale Corp.** | | | **Klein-Seay Financing** | | |
|---|---|---|---|---|---|
| Cash | 81,000 | | Accounts Receivable | 90,000 | |
| Due from Factor | 5,400* | | Due to Jedd Hale | | 5,400 |
| Loss on Sale of Re- | | | Financing Revenue | | 3,600 |
| ceivables | 3,600** | | Cash | | 81,000 |
| Accounts Receivable | | 90,000 | | | |

*$90,000 X 6% = $5,400
**$90,000 X 4% = $3,600

**TIP:**    The factor's profit will be the difference between the financing revenue of $3,600 and the amount of any uncollectible receivables.

(d)    Sale of receivables with recourse:

| **Jedd Hale Corp.** | | | **Klein-Seay Financing** | | |
|---|---|---|---|---|---|
| Cash | 81,000 | | Accounts Receivable | 90,000 | |
| Due from Factor | 5,400 | | Due to Jedd Hale | | 5,400 |
| Loss on Sale of Re- | | | Financing Revenue | | 3,600 |
| ceivables | 5,600* | | Cash | | 81,000 |
| Accounts Receivable | | 90,000 | | | |
| Recourse Liability | | 2,000 | | | |

| | |
|---|---|
| *Cash received | $81,000 |
| Due from factor | 5,400 |
| Subtotal | 86,400 |
| Resource obligation | (2,000) |
| Net proceeds expected | $84,400 |
| | |
| Carrying (book) value | $90,000 |
| Net proceeds | (84,400) |
| Loss on sale of receivables | $ 5,600 |

**TIP:**    In this case, a liability of $2,000 is recorded by Jedd Hale to indicate the probable payment to Klein-Seay Financing for uncollectible receivables. If all the receivables are collected, Jedd Hale would eliminate its recourse liability and increase net income. Klein-Seay Financing's profit is the financing revenue of $3,600 because it will have no bad debts related to these receivables.

# EXERCISE 7-7

**Purpose:**   (L.O. 8) This exercise will illustrate the computations and entries involved in accounting for the transfer of receivables that is treated as a secured borrowing transaction.

Nijjar Winery transfers $350,000 of its accounts receivable to Monrovia Bank as collateral for a $250,000 note on September 1, 2010. Nijjar will continue to collect the accounts receivable; the account debtors are not notified of the arrangement. Monrovia Bank assesses a finance charge of 1% of the accounts receivable and interest on the note of 12%. Settlement by Nijjar Winery to the bank is made monthly for all cash collected on the receivables.

## Instructions
Prepare the journal entries for both Nijjar Winery and Monrovia Bank to record the following:
(a)   Transfer of accounts receivable and issuance of the note on September 1, 2010.
(b)   Collection in September of $220,000 of the transferred accounts receivable less cash discounts of $3,000. In addition, sales returns of $7,000 were processed.
(c)   Remittance by Nijjar of September collections plus accrued interest to the bank on October 1.
(d)   Collection in October of the balance of the transferred accounts receivable less $1,000 written off as uncollectible.
(e)   Remittance by Nijjar of the balance due of $33,000 ($250,000 - $217,000) on the note plus interest on November 1.

## Solution to Exercise 7-7

(a)

| **Nijjar Winery** | | | **Monrovia Bank** | | |
|---|---|---|---|---|---|
| Cash | 246,500 | | Notes Receivable | 250,000 | |
| Finance Charge | 3,500* | | Finance Revenue | | 3,500* |
| Notes Payable | | 250,000 | Cash | | 246,500 |

   *1% X $350,000 = $3,500

(b)

| | | | (No Entry) | |
|---|---|---|---|---|
| Cash | 217,000 | | | |
| Sales Discounts | 3,000 | | | |
| Sales Returns | 7,000 | | | |
| Accounts Receivable | | 227,000* | | |

   *$220,000 + $7,000 = $227,000

(c)

| Nijjar Winery | | | Monrovia Bank | | |
|---|---|---|---|---|---|
| Interest Expense | 2,500* | | Cash | 219,500 | |
| Notes Payable | 217,000 | | Interest Revenue | | 2,500* |
| Cash | | 219,500 | Notes Receivable | | 217,000 |

*$250,000 X .12 X. 1/12 = $2,500

(d)

| | | | | |
|---|---|---|---|---|
| Cash | 122,000 | | (No Entry) | |
| Allowance for Doubtful | | | | |
| Accounts | 1,000 | | | |
| Accounts Receivable | | 123,000* | | |

*$350,000 - $227,000 = $123,000

(e)

| | | | | | |
|---|---|---|---|---|---|
| Interest Expense | 330* | | Cash | 33,330 | |
| Notes Payable | 33,000 | | Interest Revenue | | 330* |
| Cash | | 33,330 | Notes Receivable | | 33,000 |

*$33,000 X .12 X 1/12

---

**TIP:** Receivables are often used as collateral in a borrowing transaction. A creditor often requires that the debtor designate or pledge receivables as security for the loan. The debtor continues to collect the accounts receivable; the account debtors are not notified of the arrangement. If the loan is not paid when due, the creditor has the right to convert the collateral to cash   that is, to collect the receivables. (If the receivables are transferred to the transferee for custodial purposes, the custodial arrangement is often referred to as a **pledge**.) **Factors** are finance companies or banks that buy receivables from businesses for a fee and then collect remittances directly from the customers. This exercise **(Exercise 7-7)** illustrates a borrowing transaction whereas **Exercise 7-6** illustrates a sales transaction.

**TIP:** A recent phenomenon in the sale (transfer) of receivables is **securitization**. **Securitization** takes a pool of assets such as credit card receivables, mortgage receivables, or car loan receivables, and sells shares in these pools of interest and principal payments. How does this differ from factoring? Factoring usually involves the sale to only one company, fees are high, the quality of receivables is low, and the seller afterward does not service the receivables. In a securitization, many investors are involved, margins are tight, the receivables are of higher quality, and the seller usually continues to service the receivables. In either a factoring or a securitization transaction, a company sells receivables on either a **without recourse** or a **with recourse** **basis.**

# *ILLUSTRATION 7-4
# TWO FORMATS FOR BANK RECONCILIATIONS (L.O. 10)

**First One:**

    Balance per bank

        Add positive items per books not on bank's records.

        Deduct negative items per books not on bank's records.

        Add or deduct, whichever is applicable, bank error in recording receipts or disbursements.

    Correct cash balance

    Balance per books

        Add positive items per bank not on books.

        Deduct negative items per bank not on books.

        Add or deduct, whichever is applicable, depositor error in recording receipts or disbursements.

    Correct cash balance

**Second One:**

    Balance per bank

        Add positive items per books not on bank's records.

        Deduct negative items per books not on bank's records.

        Add or deduct, whichever is applicable, bank error in recording receipts or disbursements.

        Deduct positive items per bank not on books.

        Add negative items per bank not on books.

        Add or deduct, whichever is applicable, depositor error in recording receipts or disbursements.

    Balance per books

**Examples of reconciling items:**

    Positive item per books not on bank's records:

        Deposit in transit

    Negative item per books not on bank's records:

        Outstanding check

    Positive item per bank not on books:

        Note collected by bank

        Interest paid by bank to depositor on account balance

    Negative item per bank not on books:

        Bank service charge

        Customer's NSF check returned by bank

        Note paid by bank

        Automatic payments made by bank for depositor

    Error by bank:

        In recording receipt

        In recording disbursement

    Error by depositor:

        In recording receipt

        In recording disbursement

## ILLUSTRATION 7-4 (Continued)

**TIP:** The objective of a bank reconciliation is to explain all reasons why the bank balance differs from the book balance and to identify errors and omissions in the bank's records and in the book records. In the context of a bank reconciliation, "per bank" refers to the records of the bank pertaining to the depositor's account and "per books" refers to the depositor's records of the same bank account.

**TIP:** If you have a checking account, look at the back of your bank statement. A bank often includes a form to assist you in reconciling your bank account. Very often that form reconciles the cash balance per bank to the cash balance per books rather than reconciling both the bank cash balance and the book cash balance to the correct (adjusted) cash balance.

**TIP:** A depositor's checking account is a liability on the bank's books, so a bank debit memo decreases the depositor's cash balance and a bank credit memo increases the depositor's cash balance. On the bank statement, debits appear as a result of checks that have cleared during the month or bank debit memos for items such as bank service charges (BSC). Credits on the bank statement represent deposits or bank credit memos.

**TIP:** The "Balance per bank" caption on a bank reconciliation is often replaced with "Balance per bank statement," and "Balance per books" is often titled "Balance per ledger."

**TIP:** The "Correct cash balance" caption on a bank reconciliation is often replaced with "Adjusted cash balance." The adjusted cash balance as determined by the bank reconciliation will be the amount used to report for cash on the balance sheet. (The Cash account in the general ledger often includes cash on hand and cash in the bank, although separate ledger accounts such as Cash in Bank and Cash on Hand may be used. The balance of this account and any other unrestricted cash accounts, such as the Petty Cash account, are added together to report cash on the balance sheet.)

**TIP:** Some items in a bank reconciliation will require adjustments either on the depositor's books or in the bank's records, while the others will not. When the balance per bank to correct cash balance format is used in preparing a single-column bank reconciliation, all of the reconciling items appearing in the lower half of the reconciliation (balance per books to correct cash balance) require adjustment on the depositor's books. All of the reconciling items appearing in the upper half of the reconciliation **except** for deposits in transit and outstanding checks require adjustment on the bank's books.

**TIP:** Unless otherwise indicated, an NSF check is assumed to be a customer's NSF check; that is, an NSF check is considered to be from a customer of the depositor, rather than a depositor's NSF check.

**TIP:** Beginning cash balance **per bank** plus total receipts for the month **per bank** minus total disbursements for the month **per bank** equals ending cash balance **per bank.** Total deposits or receipts per bank for a month include all deposits made by the depositor during the month plus any bank credit memos (such as for interest credited by the bank or a customer's note receivable collected by the bank). Total checks paid or disbursements per bank for a month include all the depositor's checks which cleared the banking system during the month plus any bank debit memos originating during the month (such as for bank service charges or a customer's NSF check).

**TIP:** Beginning cash balance **per books** plus total receipts for the month **per books** minus total disbursements for the month **per books** equals ending cash balance **per books.**

# *EXERCISE 7-8

**Purpose:**    (L.O. 10) This exercise will help you review situations that give rise to reconciling items on a bank reconciliation and identify those which require adjusting entries on the depositor's books.

A sketch of the bank reconciliation at July 31, 2010 for the Ace Electric Company and a list of possible reconciling items appear below.

**Ace Electric Co.**
**BANK RECONCILIATION**
**July 31, 2010**

| | | |
|---|---:|---:|
| Balance per bank statement, July 31 | | $X,XXX |
| A. Add: | $XXX | |
| | XXX | X,XXX |
| | | X,XXX |
| B. Deduct: | | X,XXX |
| Correct cash balance, July 31 | | $X,XXX |
| | | |
| Balance per books, July 31 | | $ X,XXX |
| C. Add: | $XXX | |
| | XXX | X,XXX |
| | | X,XXX |
| D. Deduct: | XXX | |
| | XXX | |
| | XXX | |
| | XXX | X,XXX |
| Correct cash balance, July 31 | | $X,XXX |

_____    1.    Deposits of July 30 amounting to $1,482 have not reached the bank as of July 31.

_____    2.    A customer's check for $40 that was deposited on July 20 was returned NSF by the bank; return has not been recorded by Ace.

_____    3.    Bank service charge for July amounts to $3.

_____    4.    Included with the bank statement was check No. 422 for $702 as payment of an account payable. In comparing the check with the cash disbursement records, it was discovered that the check was incorrectly entered in the cash disbursements journal for $720.

_____    5.    Outstanding checks at July 31 amount to $1,927.

_____    6.    The bank improperly charged a check of the Ace Plumbing Co. for $25 to Ace Electric Co.'s account.

_____    7.    The bank charged $8 during July for printing checks.

_____ 8.   During July, the bank collected a customer's note receivable for the Ace Electric Co.; face amount $1,000, interest $20, and the bank charged a $2 collection fee. This transaction has not been recorded by Ace.

_____ 9.   A check written by Ace in June for $180 cleared the bank during July.

_____ 10.  Deposits of June 30 for $1,200 were recorded by the company on June 30 but were not recorded by the bank until July 2.

## Instructions

(a)   Indicate how each of the 10 items listed above would be handled on the bank reconciliation by placing the proper code letter (A, B, C, D) in the space provided. The applicable code letters appear in the sketch of the bank reconciliation. Use the code "NR" for any item which is not a reconciling item on July 31.

(b)   Assume that the July 31 balance per bank statement was $4,332. Complete the bank reconciliation using the items given and answer the questions that follow:

1.  What is the adjusted (correct) cash balance at July 31? $_____

2.  What is the balance per books **before** adjustment at July 31?

3.  What reconciling items require an adjusting entry on Ace Electric Company's books? (Identify by item numbers.)

4.  What item(s) requires a special entry on the bank's records to correct an error(s)?

## Solution to Exercise 7-8

(a)   1.   A        6.   A
      2.   D        7.   D
      3.   D        8.   C, C, D
      4.   C        9.   NR
      5.   B        10.  NR

| TIP: | Items 9 and 10 would have been reconciling items of cash balances on the June 30 bank reconciliation (the prior month). |
|---|---|

(b)   1.   $3,912* ($4,332 + $1,482 + $25 - $1,927 = $3,912)
      2.   $2,927* [X + $18 + $1,020 - $40 - $3 - $8 - $2 = $3,912 (answer to question 1)]
           X = $2,927
      3.   2; 3; 4; 7; 8
      4.   6

*See the completed bank reconciliation on the following page.

**Approach to part (b) 2:** You can compute the correct cash balance by completing the top half of the bank reconciliation (balance per bank to correct cash balance). The correct cash balance can then be entered on the last line of the bottom half of the reconciliation and used along with certain reconciling items to "work backwards" to compute the $2,927 cash balance per books before adjustment.

## Ace Electric Co.
## BANK RECONCILIATION
## July 31, 2010

| | | |
|---|---:|---:|
| Balance per bank statement, July 31 | | $ 4,332 |
| Add: Deposits in transit on July 31 | $1,482 | |
|     Check improperly charged by bank | 25 | 1,507 |
| | | 5,839 |
| Deduct: Checks outstanding as of July 31 | | 1,927 |
| Correct cash balance at July 31 | | $3,912 |
| | | |
| Balance per books, July 31 | | $2,927 |
| Add: Error in recording check No. 422 | $ 18 | |
|     Collection of customer's note receivable and | | |
|       interest by bank | 1,020 | 1,038 |
| | | 3,965 |
| Deduct: Customer's NSF check | 40 | |
|     Bank service charge for July | 3 | |
|     Cost of printing checks | 8 | |
|     Bank collection fee | 2 | 53 |
| Correct cash balance at July 31 | | $3,912 |

**TIP:** The required adjusting entries on the depositor's books would be:

| | | |
|---|---:|---:|
| Cash | 18 | |
|     Accounts Payable | | 18 |
|       (To correct error in recording check No. 422) | | |
| | | |
| Cash | 1,020 | |
|     Note Receivable | | 1,000 |
|     Interest Revenue | | 20 |
|       (To record collection of note receivable by bank) | | |
| | | |
| Accounts Receivable | 40 | |
|     Cash | | 40 |
|       (To record customer's NSF check) | | |
| | | |
| Miscellaneous Expense | 13 | |
|     Cash | | 13 |
|       (To record bank service charges: | | |
|       [$3 + $8 + $2 = $13]) | | |

**TIP:** The above entries can be combined into one compound entry.

**TIP:** Keep in mind that deposits in transit and outstanding checks are reconciling items but do **not** require adjusting entries on either the bank's books or the depositor's books.

**TIP:** Note that a transportation error (reversing the order of numbers such as $702 and $720) will cause a difference divisible by 9.

## *EXERCISE 7-9

**Purpose:**   (L.O. 10) This exercise reviews the journal entries involved with establishing and maintaining a petty cash fund.

The Kirmani Corporation makes most expenditures by check. The following transactions relate to an imprest fund established by the Kirmani Corporation to handle small expenditures on an expedient basis.

**Transactions**

| | | |
|---|---|---|
| May | 4 | Wrote a $100 check to establish the petty cash fund. |
| | 6 | Paid taxi $2 to deliver papers to a branch office. |
| | 6 | Purchased stamps, $13. |
| | 8 | Paid $15 for advertising posters. |
| | 12 | Paid $6 for mail received with "postage due." |
| | 12 | Paid $8 for coffee supplies. |
| | 13 | Paid $17 for office supplies. |
| | 14 | Paid bus charges of $18 to ship goods to a customer. |
| | 15 | Counted the remaining coins and currency in the fund, $20. Wrote a check to replenish the fund. |

## Instructions

(a)    Record the transactions in general journal form.

(b)    Answer the questions that follow:

1.   How much coin and currency should have been in the petty cash box at the end of the day on May 12?                                                     $_____ .

2.   How much coin and currency should have been in the petty cash box on May 15 before replenishment?                                                     $_____

3.   What was the balance in the Petty Cash ledger account on May 12?   $_____

4.   What was the balance in the Petty Cash ledger account at the end of the day, May 15?                                                     $_____

**TIP:**    In order to answer the last two questions, it would be helpful to post the journal entries to a T-account for Petty Cash.

## Solution to Exercise 7-9

(a) May 4    Petty Cash................................................................... 100

         Cash ....................................................................        100

           (To establish a petty cash fund)

May 15   Miscellaneous Expense ($2 + $8) ............................. 10

         Postage Expense ($13 + $6).................................... 19

         Advertising Expense.................................................. 15

         Office Supplies ......................................................... 17

         Transportation-out .................................................... 18

         Cash Over and Short................................................. 1

           Cash ....................................................................        80

           (To replenish the petty cash fund)

(b) 1. There should have been $56 in coin and currency in the fund at the end of the day on May 12. ($100 - $2 - $13 - $15 - $6 - $8 = $56)

2. There should have been $21 in coin and currency in the fund on May 15 before replenishment. ($100 - $2 - $13 - $15 - $6 - $8 - $17 - $18 = $21)

> **TIP:** Because only $20 was found in the fund at that date, there was a shortage of $1, which must be recorded by a debit to the Cash Over and Short account.

3. $100
4. $100

> **TIP:** The balance of the Petty Cash account changes **only** when the fund is established or the size of the fund is increased or decreased. The Petty Cash account balance is **not** affected by expenditures from the fund nor replenishments. (No journal entry is made at the time an expenditure is made. Expenditures from the fund are accounted for at the date of replenishment.)

> **TIP:** Petty Cash is not normally reported separately on the balance sheet. The balance of the Petty Cash account is generally lumped together with all other cash items when a balance sheet is prepared.

# ANALYSIS OF MULTIPLE-CHOICE TYPE QUESTIONS

**QUESTION**
1.  (L.O. 1) Which of the following items should **not** be included in the Cash caption on the balance sheet?
    a.   Coins and currency in the cash register
    .b.   Checks from other parties presently in the cash register
    c.   Amounts on deposit in checking account at the bank
    d.   Postage stamps on hand

**Explanation:** Cash on hand, cash in banks, and petty cash are often combined and reported simply as Cash. Undeposited checks from other parties is a component of cash on hand. Postage stamps on hand are classified as a prepaid expense. (Solution = d.)

**QUESTION**
2.  (L.O. 2) The SEC recommends that legally restricted deposits held at a bank as compensating balances against long-term borrowing arrangements should be:
    a.   used to reduce the amount reported as long-term debt on the balance sheet.
    b.   reported separately among the "cash and cash equivalent items" in Current Assets on the balance sheet.
    c.   separately classified as noncurrent assets in either the Investments or Other Assets sections of the balance sheet.
    d.   used to reduce the amount reported as short-term debt on the balance sheet.

**Explanation:** The SEC recommends that legally restricted deposits held as compensating balances against short-term borrowing arrangements be stated separately among the "cash and cash equivalent items" in Current Assets. Restricted deposits held as compensating balances against long-term borrowing arrangements should be separately classified as noncurrent assets in either the Investments or Other Assets sections, using a caption such as "Cash on Deposit Maintained as Compensating Balance." To use the asset balance to directly reduce a debt (answer selections "a" and "d" would be "offsetting assets against liabilities" which violates a rule against offsetting or setoff. Only in rare circumstances is it permissable to offset assets and liabilities.) (Solution = c.)

**QUESTION**
3.  (L.O. 4) Trade discounts are
    a.   not recorded in the accounts; rather they are a means of computing a price.
    b.   used to avoid frequent changes in catalogues.
    c.   used to quote different prices for different quantities purchased.
    d.   used to hide the true invoice price from competitors.
    e.   all of the above.

**Explanation:** Customers are often quoted prices on the basis of list or catalogue prices that may be subject to a trade or quantity discount.  Such trade discounts are used to avoid the need for frequent changes in catalogues, to quote different prices for different quantities purchased, or to hide the true invoice price from competitors.  Trade discounts are not recorded in the accounts.  They are used to compute the sales (or purchase) price of an item which is recorded in the accounts.  Thus an item with a list price of $800 subject to a trade discount of 30% has a selling (or purchase) price of $560 which is recorded in the accounts.  (Solution = e.)

**TIP:**   A chain discount occurs when a list price is subject to several trade discounts.  When a chain discount is offered, the amount of each trade discount is determined by multiplying (1) the list price of the merchandise **less** the amount of prior trade discounts by (2) the trade discount percentage.

**QUESTION**
4.  (L.O. 5) Gatorland recorded uncollectible accounts expense of $30,000 and wrote off accounts receivable of $25,000 during the year. The net effect of these two transactions on working capital was a decrease of:
    a.  $55,000.
    b.  $30,000.
    c.  $25,000.
    d.  $5,000.

**Approach and Explanation:** Reconstruct both entries referred to in the question. Then analyze each debit and each credit separately as to its effect on working capital (total current assets minus total current liabilities). (Refer to **Illustration 7-1**.)

|  |  |  | Effect on<br>Working Capital |
|---|---|---|---|
| Uncollectible Accounts Expense | 30,000 |  | None |
|    Allow. for Uncollectible Accounts |  | 30,000 | Decrease 30,000 |
|  |  |  |  |
| Allowance for Uncollectible Accounts | 25,000 |  | Increase 25,000 |
|    Accounts Receivable |  | 25,000 | Decrease 25,000 |
|       Net Effect |  |  | Decrease 30,000 |
|  |  |  | (Solution = b.) |

**QUESTION**
5.  (L.O. 5) Chelser Corporation performed an analysis and an aging of its accounts receivable at December 31, 2010, which disclosed the following:

| | |
|---|---|
| Accounts receivable balance | $ 100,000 |
| Allowance for uncollectible accounts balance | 5,000 |
| Accounts deemed uncollectible | 7,400 |

The net realizable value of the accounts receivable at December 31 is:
    a.  $87,600.
    b.  $92,600.
    c.  $95,000.
    d.  $97,600.

**Approach and Explanation:** Read the last sentence of the question: "The net realizable value of the accounts receivable at December 31 is..." Underline "net realizable value of accounts receivable." Write down the definition of net realizable value of accounts receivable—amount of accounts receivable ultimately expected to be converted into cash. Read the details of the question. If an aging shows $7,400 of the $100,000 accounts are deemed uncollectible, then the remaining $92,600 are expected to be converted into cash. (Because the balance of the allowance account does not agree with the amount of uncollectibles per the aging, the allowance for uncollectible accounts balance must be the unadjusted balance or the percentage of sales method is being used to determine the amount to record as bad debt expense.) (Solution = b.)

**QUESTION**

6.    (L.O. 5) The following data are available for 2010:

| | |
|---|---:|
| Sales, cash | $ 200,000 |
| Sales, credit | 500,000 |
| Accounts Receivable, January 1 | 80,000 |
| Accounts Receivable, December 31 | 72,000 |
| Allowance for Doubtful Accounts, January 1 | 4,000 |
| Accounts written off during 2010 | 4,600 |

The journal entry to record bad debt expense for the period and to adjust the allowance account is to be based on an estimate of 1% of credit sales. The entry to record the uncollectible accounts expense for 2010 would include a debit to the Bad Debt Expense account for:

a.    $7,200.
b.    $5,600.
c.    $4,400.
d.    $5,000.

**Approach and Explanation:** Think about the emphasis of the entry when the percentage-of-sales basis is used. This method emphasizes the income statement. Therefore, 1% times credit sales equals bad debt expense ($500,000 x 1% = $5,000). The balance of the allowance account before adjustment does **not** affect this computation or entry. (Solution = d.)

**QUESTION**

7.    (L.O. 5) The following data are available for 2010:

| | |
|---|---:|
| Sales, cash | $ 200,000 |
| Sales, credit | 500,000 |
| Accounts Receivable, January 1 | 80,000 |
| Accounts Receivable, December 31 | 72,000 |
| Allowance for Doubtful Accounts, January 1 | 4,000 |
| Accounts written off during 2010 | 4,600 |

The journal entry to record bad debt expense for the period and to adjust the allowance account is to be based on an aging analysis of accounts receivable. The aging analysis of accounts receivable at December 31, 2010, reveals that $5,200 of existing accounts receivable are estimated to be uncollectible. The entry to record the uncollectible accounts expense for 2010 will involve a debit to the Bad Debt Expense account for:

a.    $9,800.
b.    $5,800.
c.    $5,200.
d.    $4,600.

**Approach and Explanation:** An aging analysis is performed to determine the best figure to represent the cash (net) realizable value of the accounts receivable in the balance sheet. Thus, $5,200 is the desired balance for the allowance account at the reporting date. Determine the existing balance in the allowance account and the adjusting entry needed to arrive at the desired ending balance.

| Allowance for Doubtful Accounts | | | | |
|---|---|---|---|---|
| Write-offs, 2010 | 4,600 | Balance, 1/1/10 | 4,000 | **Entry** |
| Balance before adjustment | 600 | Adjustment needed | X | **Needed.** |
| | | Desired balance at 12/31/10 | 5,200 | |

Solving for X:    X - $600    = $5,200
                        X    = $5,200 + $600
                        X    = $5,800 (Solution = b.)

## QUESTION

8. (L.O. 5) The following data are available for 2010:

| | |
|---|---:|
| Allowance for Doubtful Accounts, January 1 | $ 41,000 |
| Writeoffs of accounts receivable during the year | 35,000 |
| Net credit sales for the year | 1,300,000 |

Bad debts are estimated to be 3% of net credit sales. The balance of the allowance account after adjustment should be:

a. $4,000.
b. $39,000.
c. $45,000.
d. $80,000.

**Approach and Explanation:** Draw a T-account. Enter the data given and solve for the amount requested.

Allowance for Doubtful Accounts

| | | | |
|---|---|---|---|
| | | 41,000 | Beginning Balance |
| Writeoffs | 35,000 | 39,000 | Expense = 3% X $1,300,000 |
| | | 45,000 | Ending Balance |

(Solution = c.)

## QUESTION

9. (L.O. 6) On January 1, 2010, West Park Co. exchanged equipment for a $480,000 zero-interest-bearing note due on January 1, 2013 from Chamberlain's Health Products. Chamberlain's incremental borrowing rate at January 1, 2010 was 10%. The present value of $1 discounted at 10% for three periods is $0.75. The amount of interest revenue that should be included in West Park's income statement for the year 2011 is:

a. $0.
b. $36,000.
c. $39,600.
d. $48,000.

**Explanation:** The note received in exchange for equipment is an arms' length transaction and the stated interest rate is unreasonable in relation to the market rate of interest. The fair value of the equipment is not available information. Therefore, the present value of the note is to be approximated by discounting all of the future cash receipts related to the note, and the discounting is done using the market rate of interest (borrower's incremental borrowing rate). The face amount of $480,000 is discounted back three periods to yield a present value balance at January 1, 2010 of $360,000 ($480,000 X .75 = $360,000). The effective interest method is used to determine the amount of interest to report each period.

Present Value Balance   X   Interest Rate Per   X   Time   =   Interest
at Beginning of Period       Period

$360,000 X 10% X 12/12 = $36,000 Interest for 2010

The interest for 2011 (the second year) would be computed as follows:

| | |
|---:|---|
| $360,000 | Present value, January 1, 2010 |
| + 36,000 | Interest for 2007 |
| 396,000 | Present value, December 31, 2010 |
| (0) | Payment |
| 396,000 | Present value (carrying value), January 1, 2011 |
| X 10% | Effective or yield rate of interest |
| $ 39,600 | Interest for 2011 (the second year) |

(Solution = c.)

**QUESTION**
10.   (L.O. 8) A company has a large amount of accounts receivable and a ready need for cash. The company may accelerate the receipt of cash from customers' accounts receivable thru:

| | Factoring | Assignment |
|---|---|---|
| a. | Yes | Yes |
| b. | Yes | No |
| c. | No | Yes |
| d. | No | No |

**Explanation:** The company can transfer accounts receivable to a third party for cash by the assignment or factoring (sale) of the accounts receivable.   (Solution = a.)

**QUESTION**
11.   (L.O. 9) The accounts receivable turnover ratio measures the:
   a.   number of times the average balance of accounts receivable is collected during the period.
   b.   percentage of accounts receivable turnover over to a collection agency during the period.
   c.   percentage of accounts receivable arising during certain seasons.
   d.   number of times the average balance of inventory is sold during the period.

**Approach and Explanation:** Write down the components of the **accounts receivable turnover ratio.** Think about why it is computed. The computation is as follows:

$$\text{Accounts Receivable Turnover Ratio} = \frac{\text{Net Sales}}{\text{Average trade receivables (net)}}$$

Because cash sales do not go through the Accounts Receivable account, only net credit sales belong in the numerator; however, very often that information is not available. The accounts receivable ratio measures the number of times, on average, the accounts receivable balance was collected during the period. This ratio is used to assess the liquidity of the receivables. This ratio can be divided into 365 days to obtain the **average days to collect accounts receivable.** (Solution = a.)

**QUESTION**
*12.   (L.O. 10) The term "outstanding checks" refers to:
   a.   checks that have been lost in the mail or for some other reason have been misplaced.
   b.   depositor checks which have been processed by the bank but have not yet been recorded by the depositor.
   c.   customer checks which have been returned by the bank because the customer's bank would not honor them.
   d.   depositor checks which have not yet cleared the banking system.

**Explanation:** There is a lag time between the date a check is issued and the date the check clears the banking system. During the time between these two dates, the checks are referred to as "outstanding checks." Checks written by the enterprise but not mailed until **after** the balance sheet date should not be included with outstanding checks. Rather, they should be added back to the cash balance and reported as accounts payable. (Solution = d.)

**QUESTION**
*13.   (L.O.10) The following information pertains to Cruiser Co. at December 31, 2010:

| | |
|---|---|
| Bank statement balance | $20,000 |
| Checkbook balance | 28,200 |
| Deposit in transit | 10,000 |
| Outstanding checks | 2,000 |
| Bank service charges for December | 200 |

In Cruiser's balance sheet at December 31, 2010, cash should be reported as:
a.    $18,000.
b.    $20,000.
c.    $28,000.
d.    $30,000.

**Approach and Explanation:** When a question relates to data used in a bank reconciliation, you should sketch out the format for a bank reconciliation, put in the information given, and solve for the unknown piece.

| | |
|---|---|
| Balance per bank statement | $ 20,000 |
| Deposit in transit | 10,000 |
| Outstanding checks | (2,000) |
| Correct cash balance | $ 28,000 |
| | |
| Balance per books | $ 28,200 |
| Bank service charges | (200) |
| Correct cash balance | $ 28,000 |

In this particular question, the completion of either the top half or the bottom half of the reconciliation using the bank-to-correct balance method would be enough to solve for the answer requested. (Solution = c.)

**QUESTION**
*14.   (L.O.10) The following data relate to the bank account of Springfield Cleaners:

| | |
|---|---|
| Cash balance, September 30, 2010 per bank | $ 10,000 |
| Cash balance, October 31, 2010 per bank | 21,500 |
| Checks paid during October by bank | 5,900 |
| Checks written during October per books | 6,800 |
| Cash balance, October 31, 2010 per books | 22,200 |
| Bank service charges for October, not recorded on books | 100 |
| Deposits per books for October | 19,000 |

The amount of deposits recorded by the bank in October is:
a.    $19,000.
b.    $17,500.
c.    $11,500.
d.    $5,700.

**Approach and Explanation:** Think about how deposits recorded by the bank affect the cash balance per bank and other items that cause that balance to change. Plug in the figures given and solve for the unknown.

| | |
|---|---|
| Balance per bank, September 30 | $ 10,000 |
| Deposits per bank during October | X |
| Bank credit memoranda | -0- |
| Checks paid by bank during October | (5,900) |
| Bank service charge for October and other bank debit memoranda | (100) |
| Balance per bank, October 31 | $ 21,500 |

Solving for X:
$10,000 + X - $5,900 - $100 = $21,500
X = $21,500 - $10,000 + $5,900 + $100
X = $17,500 (Solution = b.)

## QUESTION

*15.    (L.O.10) The following information pertains to Tommy-Jer Corporation at December 31, 2010:

| | |
|---|---|
| Balance per bank | $ 10,000 |
| Deposit in transit | 3,000 |
| Outstanding checks | 8,000 |
| Bank service charges for December | 200 |
| Bank erroneously charged Tommy-Jer's account for Sonny-Ber's check written for $700. As of Dec. 31, the bank had not corrected this error | 700 |

Tommy-Jer's cash balance per ledger (books) before adjustment at December 31, 2010 is:
a.    $14,100.
b.    $5,900.
c.    $5,500.
d.    $4,100.

**Approach and Explanation:** The balance per books (before adjustment) can easily be computed by putting the data into the format for a bank reconciliation. Either format (balance per bank to balance per books or balance per bank to correct balance) can be used. Each approach is illustrated below: (Solution = b.)

| | |
|---|---|
| Balance per bank statement | $ 10,000 |
| Deposit in transit | 3,000 |
| Outstanding checks | (8,000) |
| Bank service charges | 200 |
| Bank error in charge for check | 700 |
| Balance per ledger | $ 5,900 |
| | |
| Balance per bank statement | $ 10,000 |
| Deposit in transit | 3,000 |
| Outstanding checks | (8,000) |
| Bank error in charge for check | 700 |
| Correct cash balance | $ 5,700 |
| | |
| Balance per books (ledger) | $    X |
| Bank service charge | (200) |
| Correct cash balance | $ 5,700 |

X = $5,900